# MAKING E

Levelling Up is widely recognized failed as policy in the UK. 'Making Equal: New Visions for Opportunity and Growth' considers what lessons can be learnt and what might be done differently with cogent views from across the political spectrum. A century ago something similar happening in the UK, the 1920s were a time of failure, but by the 1930s the idea that Special Areas needed an Act of Parliament to help them was accepted. In these pages, we may be seeing history and consensus repeat.

—*Danny Dorling*, University of Oxford

This is a hugely impressive book – hooked onto the 125th anniversary of Ruskin College but whose writ encompasses Dickens' ghosts in A Christmas Carol – past, present, and future. Its editors, Graeme Atherton and Peter John, have attracted a galaxy of impressive contributors – academics, politicians, social scientists, journalists, researchers – and let them fly.

The mounds of statistics are the backdrop to an urgency to that – and Graeme Atherton's introduction has all the figures you might want, but along rising with eloquent anger – real people, real places, real heartbreaks, but also the determination to put things right.

As I am a historian, a tutor for The Open University for 20 years, and a further 22 years as a Blackpool MP (where Graeme grew up) I assure you this book is the genuine article. The five sections – Creating Opportunity from Birth, Higher Education – The Driver of Growth and Opportunity, Making Places Matter, Growth, the Economy and the Role of Business, Labour and Inequality – Past, Present, and Future – bring out in David Blunkett, Hilary Armstrong, John Bird and Rupa Huq some very personal narratives when the stats hit home.

What happened then matters now – echoes of Victorian philanthropists (Titus Salt and Robert Owen …) rub shoulders with Place matters – the epiphanies of Sure Start but also 12 years' gaps of life expectancy within (let alone) cities and towns.

This could not be more timely – as a Labour government grapples with devolution, hard choices, and the growing divide between public and private, in the post-Covid world in education. This book should be on the virtual shelves of those who have the power to get some of this right.

—**Gordon Marsden,** Honorary Doctor of The Open University, former Shadow Minister for Higher and Further Education and Skills, Co-Founder of Right to Learn

As the government's honeymoon has soured into widespread voter disillusion, it has offered us new 'missions', 'targets' and 'milestones'. What remains missing is a clear moral anchor, rooted in the Labour Party's history. This book, by contributors with deep practical experience of struggles against social injustice, helps to fill that lamentable void. It needs to be read by those with the power to reset public policy.

—*Paul Collier,* The Blavatnik School of Government, Oxford University

Ruskin College with its history of opening its doors to those who have been historically marginalised and offering them socially just pathways to empowerment and consciousness raising is reflected in this outstanding, timely, visionary and politically engaged collection.

The contributors bring a dynamic, multifaceted, radical and engaging lens for exploring, challenging and repositioning what it means to resist and remove the tough and often deep layers of inequality in society and education.

They offer critical in and out roads for humane and sustainable action and change, where people and their community are at the heart of levelling up; no matter what the circumstances of birth, dignity, hope and fairness are offered a space to flourish.

I will be dipping into this robust collection again and again. I highly recommend it for academics, educationalists, policymakers, students and anyone who cares about, challenging inequality and exploring real solutions for a shift towards a more just and joyous society.

—*Vicky Duckworth,* Professor of Further Education, Edge Hill University

# MAKING EQUAL

## New Visions for Opportunity and Growth

EDITED BY

### GRAEME ATHERTON

*Ruskin College and Ruskin Institute for Social Equity, UK*

AND

### PETER JOHN CBE

*University of West London and Ruskin College Oxford, UK*

United Kingdom – North America – Japan – India
Malaysia – China

Emerald Publishing Limited
Emerald Publishing, Floor 5, Northspring, 21-23 Wellington Street,
Leeds LS1 4DL.

First edition 2025

Editorial matter and selection © 2025 Graeme Atherton and Peter John.
Individual chapters © 2025 The authors.
Published under exclusive licence by Emerald Publishing Limited.

**Reprints and permissions service**
Contact: www.copyright.com

**British Library Cataloguing in Publication Data**
A catalogue record for this book is available from the British Library

ISBN: 978-1-83608-919-3 (Print)
ISBN: 978-1-83608-916-2 (Online)
ISBN: 978-1-83608-918-6 (Epub)

INVESTOR IN PEOPLE

# CONTENTS

### Section 3: Making Places Matter

### Section 4: Growth, the Economy, and the Role of Business

### Section 5: Labour and Inequality – Past, Present, and Future

# FOREWORD

## Peter John

Professor Peter John CBE, Vice-chancellor of the University of West London and Principal of Ruskin College Oxford

The chapters in this book are part of a series of colloquiums held at Ruskin College during the past year to celebrate its 125th anniversary. Established in 1899, the College's roots were firmly embedded in the workers' education movement; one that would be of use and benefit to those who had been cut off from the standard educational routes. As an opportunity and access institution (to use the modern parlance), it catered for those with an intellectual thirst and a desirous aspiration. It was also a lever for those who wished to gain entry to higher education for personal, social, and economic reasons. In addition, from its inception it had, and continues to have, close ties with the Trade Union movement. And as I am apt to say, it is the institution that Jude Fawley (he of Hardy's Jude the Obscure) would have studied at.

Throughout the decades Ruskin kept a strong focus on challenging inequality in all its forms; a concept that varies according to time and place as well as structure and magnitude. But as Thomas Piketty reminds us, at its core it is always 'ideological and political'. At Ruskin, this took centre stage as it challenged orthodoxies and came up with new and alternative solutions to this common problem; one that enabled its students and others to imagine new worlds and different types of society. As the book title indicates, many paths are possible when you are exploring new 'visions for opportunity and growth'.

Despite contending groups, political positions, and competing discourses, Ruskin College kept its principles unclouded and was always concerned to limit the deracination of its students. From the setting up of the Plebs League in 1908 to the present day, its staff and learners continue to stick to its values which remain driven by critique, possibility, and alternative progressive ideas which shape conceptions of social justice. And readers of this excellent volume will find these thoughts somewhere on every page. So, I will leave the last word to a legendary Ruskin tutor, Raphael Samuel, when writing about the death of Raymond Williams, the great cultural historian and critic, he said that we need a 'recovery of a lost wholeness ... a matter of age-old solidarities reasserting themselves, in conditions of difficulty and complexity'.

# 1

# INTRODUCTION: INEQUALITY AND BREAKING WITH THE NORM

## Graeme Atherton

*Ruskin College and Ruskin Institute for Social Equity, UK*

Recent years, especially after Brexit, have seen a resurgence in the debate around what constitutes Britain and British identity as those on the right have sought to establish new dividing lines in order to justify what they do. Language, culture, and history are all seen as part of what makes Britain a country different from others. However, there is something else: what was always a characteristic of Britain since the 19th century (Szreter, 2021) has now come to define the country again and that is inequality. The facts regarding inequality in the UK are depressingly familiar. In the UK, after 2021, the bottom 50% of the population owned less than 5% of wealth, the top 10% owned 57%, and the top 1% owned 23% (Chancel et al., 2022). Even under the last Labour government, income inequality did not decline. As a result, the UK is one of the most unequal countries in the OECD and Europe, and the second most unequal in the G7 (Francis-Devine, 2024). Inequality is costing the UK £106.2bn more a year compared with the average developed country in the OECD (The Equality Trust, 2023).

Inequality pervades everyday life in the UK. We are presented continually with images of relative affluence through the overwhelming power of television and social media. Food, for example, has gone from a functionary part of British life in the 1980s to the epitome of your lifestyle choice. But while, on the one hand, we spend £100bn a year on eating out in the UK (Restaurant, 2024), 5.1 million low-income households are cutting down on the size of meals or skipping them and 4 million are going hungry. Food also provides the best example of the normalisation of poverty in 21st century Britain. The last 10 years have seen an exponential rise in food banks with the number of parcels distributed by food banks growing from 0 in 2006–2007 to over 3.1 million in 2023–2024 (Trussell Trust, 2024). In early 2025 the Labour Party government announced free breakfast clubs in all schools. A welcome policy but also a shocking admission that millions of parents can't afford to feed their children in the morning and schools now should do it for them.

Efforts to reduce inequality have at best plateaued in recent years, with much of what government has done only exacerbating it. Those out-of-work households receiving benefits have lost on average £2,200 a year since 2010 (Sheffield, 2024). Since 2011–2012, there has been little growth in incomes in the bottom half of the income distribution, particularly for those in the bottom 10% (Francis-Devine, 2024).

Through the 2010s child poverty targets and the Equality Act's socio-economic goals were also scrapped, and social mobility strategies were likewise shelved with the Social Mobility Commission politicised and marginalised. This gradual retreat since the late 2000s from explicit attempts to address inequality is what has laid the ground for the changes in the benefit system which have pushed more people into poverty.

This normalisation of inequality and poverty in the UK is not the consequence of the Conservative and Conservative-led governments from 2010 to 2024 alone. Inequality has a long history in the UK. In 1670, around 82.7% of wealth was in the hands of the top 10% (Lindert, 1986). Little over 100 years ago in the first decade of the 20th century, Thomas Piketty (2020) found that the wealth of the top 10% of property holders peaked at a high of 94% while the bottom 50% held less than 1%. Things did start to improve slowly although not in a meaningful sense until after the Second World War. This is the period when so many of the 'costume dramas', which British people appear to be obsessed with, are set. *Downtown Abbey*, for example, once watched by nearly 10 million people every week, was first launched in 2012. Our fascination with historical dramas, which show life from the perspective of the wealthy and portray inequality as the norm, reinforces the view that in Britain then and now, this is how life was and is.

However, it must be noted that inequality has undergone significant change since the actual days of *Downtown Abbey*. For example, over 40% of people from the Bangladeshi ethnic group are now in the bottom fifth of the income distribution – more than double the percentage from white backgrounds (Department for Work & Pensions, 2024). The education system, the preserve of the elite in the early 20th century, still acts to maintain the status quo of inequality as much as it does to enable progress away from it. For example, the gap between those progressing to higher education who are in receipt of free school meals (FSM) and those who are not has got wider since 2014 (Department for Education, 2023). Geographical inequality, as prevalent as it was in the days of *Downtown Abbey*, has also taken on new and more nuanced dimensions. Where higher education participation is concerned, for instance, in 2023 fewer than 15% of learners from FSM backgrounds progress to higher education in Swindon while nearly 70% do in Westminster. And as has been well documented, where you live dictates how long you live. From 2020 to 2022, male life expectancy was highest in Hart at 83.7 years and lowest in Blackpool at 73.4 years (Office for National Statistics, 2024).

That Blackpool offers the shortest expected life for men in the UK is not a surprise. It appears near the top of a raft of indicators of poverty. But how this place has come to be perceived encapsulates how we have come to accept inequality and poverty in new ways. A seaside town that once was the watchword for fun and entertainment, Blackpool is now more associated with deprivation and depression. Whenever the London-based media wished to cover anything associated with the Conservative government's 'levelling up' and regional inequality agenda, they would send a reporter to Blackpool to stand in the wind in an empty shopping centre near the seafront. The facts nor the reality of Blackpool do not lie. It bears the brunt of the post-industrial, socio-economic changes that have left working class communities so impoverished. Despite this being a 'poverty postcard' image of the town, there are also areas of Blackpool where good housing and parts of the population are in stable employment. Nevertheless, Blackpool, like many towns in the north, Wales, Scotland and elsewhere, accepts inequality as part of its way of life as we have come to accept the decline of places like Blackpool as all too typical.

## WHY MAKING EQUAL?

The purpose of focussing above on the normalisation of inequality in the UK was to illustrate that inequality and the poverty that comes with it are deeply entrenched not just structurally but culturally in the UK. Reducing inequality will require more than a focus on policy frameworks, new regional initiatives, and quick fixes, and it will also take more time than one term of office of any government. There is some hope, however. Research by the Fairness Foundation (2024) suggested that 75% of people are worried about wealth and income inequalities. However, turning concern into action will be a huge task though especially when so many of the population have seen their relative living standards decline over the last decade. It is estimated by the Resolution Foundation that had wages continued to grow as they were before the financial crash of 2008, the average worker would be £11,000 more per year better off than they are now (BBC Panorama, 2023).

This book reflects the need for a multi-faceted, radical, long-term approach to reducing inequality. By bringing together a diverse range of voices from politics, academia, civil society, and the private sector, the aim is to contribute practical ideas that can confront the roots of inequality in the UK. Many of the aspects of inequality in the UK are addressed, and not surprisingly given Ruskin College's history, educational inequality is included. Place is also a major focus, reflecting in part the work of the Centre for

Inequality and Levelling Up based at the University of West London from 2021 to 2024 now superseded by the Ruskin Institute for Social Equity. Moreover, these chapters also capture the increasing connectivity of us all and how this can play a salient role in addressing the causes and consequences of inequality on a national and individual scale. And we must be mindful of the fact that this is a problem that goes beyond governments and the public sector. The role of business, the voluntary sector, various community groups, and others will be vital if the structural, cultural, ethnic, and regional deficits are to be addressed.

The book is not exhaustive. It was not conceived as an attempt to map out a coherent agenda for reducing inequality. Health, for example, is not covered, and schools and the nations of the UK also have specific issues that other contributions to reducing inequality should address. Building such an agenda might suggest that we need a Mark 2 version of the UK government's levelling up policy. Levelling up was designed to be a focussed approach to reducing inequality via the pursuit of 12 missions related to education, health, crime, wellbeing, etc. It was imperilled by the pandemic, the war in Ukraine, and the inflation that followed but also by a lack of government commitment towards its fundamental aims. It also became a slogan, and it was never really created to address the systemic nature of inequality which is now so deeply engrained in the British economy and society. It will therefore take more than warm words and political catch phrases to overcome what Danny Dorling calls the 'Shattered Nation'.

The book is divided into five different sections. The rest of this chapter will outline the contributions in each section.

## CREATING OPPORTUNITY FROM BIRTH

The book begins, naturally given Ruskin's history, with a section on education and where inequality begins. Philip Collins is an experienced journalist as well as an ex official in the Labour governments of the 1990s and 2000s. His chapter to open the book looks at the evidence regarding the importance of early years' education.

Reflecting on this evidence and the success of the Sure Start initiative delivered by the last Labour government, Collins argues that:

> *government that mixed a concern for justice with a respect for the evidence would, without question, begin the process of shifting its spending from remedial work in the teenage years to the early years of life, when it still has a chance of making a difference.*

Lord David Blunkett was Secretary of State for Education for four years between 1997 and 2001 and was the Minister when the first Sure Start programmes were launched in 1999. Drawing on his years of experience in the politics of education, Lord Blunkett argues passionately for lifelong learning as well as a return for Sure Start, the introduction of Individual Learning Accounts, and citizenship education. He emphasises in his chapter, the pivotal role that education plays across all aspects of economy and society.

While education may play a pivotal role how it can best do this is tackled by following chapter from James Robson. He laments the instability in post-16 education policy in England over the last decade, the product of what he describes as a *carousel of Secretaries of State for Education and Junior Minister*. Robson outlines three foundational principles which need to be adhered to in order for post-16 education and training to work more effectively. These principles are: adopting a systems-based approach, embracing multiple purposes for education and training, and reconceptualising the role of employers. Robson argues that the policy changes in the direction of a smarter and more co-ordinated post-16 system in England depend on a change in political philosophy and points to how things are changing in Scotland and Wales as evidence of what is possible in this area.

This idea of a change in philosophy is picked up by Professor Jonathan Michie, President of Kellogg College, Oxford, in his chapter on lifelong learning. Michie points to the role that adult education and lifelong learning have and can play in enabling us to face major societal challenges. He describes how after the First World War, the Ministry of Reconstruction set up by Prime Minister Lloyd George 'created a Committee on Adult Education whose final report in 1919 argued that central to such reconstruction would be adult education, provided to all citizens, as a "permanent national necessity"'. Michie goes on to argue that adult learning is as crucial now as it was over 100 years ago but policymakers need to understand that its benefits extend beyond not just the economy but to the society as well.

The final contribution in this section comes from the next member of the House of Lords to contribute to the book. Lord John Bird was the founder of the *Big Issue* magazine. A serial social entrepreneur he has overseen the growth of the *Big Issue* into a leading social enterprise. Reflecting on his own experiences and those who the *Big Issue* serves, Lord Bird argues that creating opportunity for all can only be achieved if we focus specifically on preventing poverty rather than spending billions on managing its consequences. Such focus requires a new Ministry of Poverty Prevention.

## HIGHER EDUCATION – THE DRIVER OF GROWTH AND OPPORTUNITY

The last decade has seen a gradual ebbing away of support for the idea that higher education can drive opportunity from government. This ebbing away gathered pace from 2020 to 2024. In 2020, the then Minister for Higher Education stated that work to widen access to higher education being undertaken since the early 2000s was nothing more than an attempt to dupe working class young people. The early days of Labour government since their election in July 2024 have seen a different tone with the minister with responsibility for higher education stating that widening access will be her 'number one priority'. However, higher education still faces major challenges in terms of re-establishing itself as one of the major routes for reducing inequality available.

Steve Coulter's chapter meets this challenge head on arguing powerfully that the higher education expansion of recent decades has been a success and that we need to extend participation further over coming decades to enable higher economic growth. But in order to drive this expansion, Coulter argues that a more diverse, flexible system is required but also one that is more co-ordinated as James Robson also supports. For example, Coulter argues that 'every town or city with a population over 80,000 people should have its own university'. Recognising the interaction between higher education, inequality, economy, and place this chapter connects both with that of Mitchell et al. to come and the following section of the book devoted to place.

Digging further into how higher education can be a key player in opportunity and growth, Hilary Leevers's chapter looks at the unintended consequences that can ensue from adhering to a purely demand-driven higher education system. Leevers, the Chief Executive Officer of EngineeringUK, uses her chapter to describe how engineering stands as the test case of the problems where a demand-led system is failing to meet the needs of the economy. She describes a situation where only 6.1% of undergraduate entrants in the UK were studying engineering and technology in 2023 although engineering accounts for a quarter of job adverts in the UK, 40% of which ask for degrees.

Leevers is pointing to the importance of the outcomes of the higher education system. Professor Peter John, Vice Chancellor of the University of West London and the Principal of Ruskin College, takes this idea of equality of outcome as the theme for his chapter. Utilising the concept of opportunity hoarding, he meticulously unpicks the arguments used to justify educational inequality in the UK today, and how those who can navigate the system relentlessly draw from this river of strength to maintain their power and pre-eminence. Again, the limitations of change in one part of society if inequality is to be truly tackled are exposed. Education can only go so far when the inequalities that engulf it remain unchanged.

The last chapter in this section acts as an important bridge from the previous one, and to the next section looking at place. This chapter by Professor Kathryn Mitchell, Vice Chancellor of the University of Derby and colleagues describes how a university can play an active role in addressing place-based inequality. Through a range of initiatives supporting skills development at pre-degree level, working with local businesses and leading on social mobility-related activities through the region, the chapter provides an insight into what can be done at local level by collaborative, cross-sector partnership working.

## MAKING PLACES MATTER

The role of place where inequality is concerned has come to the fore since the introduction of the 'levelling up' policy agenda by the Conservative government in 2019. Regional inequality, however, has blighted the UK for centuries and a procession of attempts has been made to address such inequalities in the post-war era. Specific dedicated funding stretched back as early as 1945. Over the period of 1961 to 2020, on average, £3.5bn per year have been invested by the central government (at 2020 real prices) in regeneration projects at a breakneck speed (Martin & Tyler, 2022). From 1978 to 2017, there have been 52 different funds to boost local and regional growth – roughly one every eight months (Martin et al., 2022). How much has been learnt from this activity where addressing place-based inequality is concerned though is debatable.

The chapter by Matt Leach, Chief Executive Officer of Local Trust takes the focus under the levelling up policy approach on physical regeneration to argue that it's the social infrastructure of neighbourhoods which should be where resources are concentrated. He advocates a return to the concentration on neighbourhoods which characterised much of the investment before the early 2010s described above. However, for Leach, it is not just a matter of the where money flows to or how it is to be spent, but giving power to those communities facing the greatest challenges to shape how these resources are utilised.

This transfer of power, however, would need to be nested within strong collaborative partnerships between the public sector, private sector, and the community. In his chapter, Ian Taylor outlines the challenges associated with effective collaboration and the need to invest resources as well as learn from good practice in forming effective relationships that can impact place-based inequality. He draws on examples of work led by Business in the Community in the UK as well as pointing to lessons from Germany, the USA, France, Canada, Australia, and Spain to identify what works in partnership building.

The merits of learning from international experience are taken up in the next chapter by Abigail Taylor from the University of Birmingham. She draws on her own work with the Industrial Strategy Council and the Chartered Institute of Public Finance and

Accountancy to outline a number of factors associated with successful approaches used in promoting regional equality and driving economic growth. These factors include long-term investment, making places attractive to live in, engaging universities as drivers of innovation as well building robust, efficient transport, and digital infrastructure systems. Taylor also looks at how transferable some of these indicators of success are to the English context which is an important part of this chapter. It is tempting to look at other countries to see what success they may have and then assume everything is transferable across international boundaries but there must always be care taken here with such assumptions.

## GROWTH, THE ECONOMY, AND THE ROLE OF BUSINESS

The last two chapters of the preceding section offer a good bridge into this one. Ian Taylor's and Abigail Taylor's chapters both discuss the fundamental role of the economic and business context in reducing inequality. This theme is taken up by the chapters that follow here. This is a crucial section. As is discussed further in the conclusions, the last 40 years have seen too much of a reliance on education as the means of addressing inequality. As a book inspired by the history of Ruskin College, education must be axiomatic to the inequality struggle but so must fundamentally changing how the economy works. The normalisation of inequality described at the start of this chapter has gone hand in hand with the infiltration of the market into all aspects of our lives since the 1970s and the shift to a more neo-liberal economic orthodoxy. These ideas have to be challenged if any significant progress is to be made.

Nigel Wilcock's excellent chapter begins by reminding us of the extent of inequality in the UK today before summing up the need for system change precisely when he states that:

> the media often characterises the choices faced by the Government in delivering public services as the tax and spend debate. This has oversimplified the position and suggests that the pull of a lever here or the push of a button there might resolve some of these deep-set challenges.

Wilcock goes on to describe a raft of potential changes to the taxation and welfare systems that could increase redistributive capacity and reduce inequality. They include greater wealth-based taxation, strengthening inheritance tax, and specific taxation related to digital businesses.

Alternative models to the short-term shareholder capitalism that puts investor return above all else which predominates in the UK exist. One such model is co-operative ownership which Daniel Monaghan of the Co-Operative Party argues strongly for in his chapter. Monaghan marshals international evidence to illustrate how co-operatives can produce economic growth while also reducing inequality at both the level of the individual business and the wider economy.

The next chapter from Andy Boucher turns the lens intently on how firms do, or could, operate asking whether we should introduce specific regulatory measures to encourage better engagement from business with social mobility. He explores in detail what the aims of such work may be, what to consider when designing or implementing such regulation, and how it could work. Boucher's chapter provides another example in the book that recognises the need for a more pro-active approach to addressing inequality than what has been offered in recent years.

Across the economy, different sectors will contribute to both inequality and combatting it in different ways. Nimmi Patel is the Head of Skills, Talent & Diversity at techUK which is a membership organisation with over 1,000 technology-related companies as members. Her chapter looks at techUK's Local Digital Index which benchmarks local areas and regions in terms of their digital infrastructure. The index highlights significant differences in digital capabilities across the UK. Patel goes on to discuss a range of initiatives that technology companies have delivered in partnership with local authorities and others which have been a product of the intelligence gathered through the Local Digital Index work.

In the final chapter of this section, former Secretary of State for Education and founder of the Purpose Coalition, Justine Greening, draws on her experience working in government and now in civil society to pinpoint some of the recent shortcomings of government while analysing the key role played going forward by Labour's

Opportunity Mission. Greening argues, as contributors throughout the section have, that businesses must themselves take responsibility for social mobility. However, in order for this to happen government must create the right combination of incentives and policies that maximise their contribution.

## LABOUR AND INEQUALITY – PAST, PRESENT, AND FUTURE

The last section of the book concentrates on the relationship between the Labour Party and inequality. Looking at what we can learn from the past and the present is important here. Like any organisation, the Labour Party is a product of its history both going back to its formation and more recent events since the late 2010s and up to the early days of the Labour government elected in 2024.

Baroness Hilary Armstrong has served as part of three Labour governments. In her chapter, she traces the evolution of Labour's focus on inequality from time of the Beveridge report after the Second World War up to the present day. Baroness Armstrong frames the battle against inequality as a continuing struggle as changes in society and the economy mean how inequality manifests itself changes. She points to the progress that has been made but the continued difficulties that are faced by those on low incomes, calling for us all to draw on our experience and knowledge to act, and act swiftly.

As Baroness Armstrong did, Rupa Huq MP for Ealing draws on her personal experiences in politics to inform her chapter. Standing again and winning her seat she describes some of the issues that her constituents face in London, pointing to housing and the rise of generation rent as another dimension to inequality in the capital. Rupa also looks forensically at the riots of August 2024 following the deaths of a number of children in Southport. How these disturbances developed, the responses of other sections of the population and the government, and the environment created by some of those on the right where race is concerned are all explored in this chapter. This tumultuous time for the country with a seismic political change followed by the worst disorder for over a decade offers important potential insights for inequality and politics moving forward.

Appropriately enough, the chapter that closes out the contributions from authors, is a transcript of a lecture given at Ruskin College in May 2024 by acclaimed author and former MP for Dagenham and Rainham, Jon Cruddas. The chapter from Cruddas draws heavily from his most recent book on the history of the Labour Party but also looks at Ruskin's own past as part of the 'Oxford School' of labour relations studies of the 1960s. In his book, Cruddas describes what he sees as three strands of labour thinking. Closing the chapter, Cruddas suggests that it is time to revisit the study of labour relations, and concerted work from Labour to establish 'a compelling vision of modern justice'. The lack of such a vision risks, in Cruddas's view, a retreat away from challenges that require systemic reform such as inequality.

The final chapter of the book attempts to draw some common themes from this rich and diverse mix of ideas. It also tries to map out what needs to be done to take these ideas forward to make real changes to people's lives and how Ruskin College and others like it can contribute.

## REFERENCES

BBC Panorama. (2023, March 20). *Stalling wage growth since 2008 costs £11,000 a year, says think tank.* https://www.bbc.co.uk/news/business-64970708

Chancel, L., Piketty, T., Saez, E., & Zucman, G. (2022). *World inequality report 2022.* World Inequality Lab. https://wir2022.wid.world/

Department for Education. (2023). *Academic year 2021/22: Widening participation in higher education.* https://explore-education-statistics.service.gov.uk/find-statistics/widening-participation-in-higher-education/2021-22

Department for Work & Pensions. (2024). *Households below average income: An analysis of the UK income distribution: FYE 1995 to FYE 2023.*

https://www.gov.uk/government/statistics/households-below-average-income-for-financial-years-ending-1995-to-2023/households-below-average-income-an-analysis-of-the-uk-income-distribution-fye-1995-to-fye-2023

Fairness Foundation. (2024). *New polling shows concern about inequality extends beyond regional inequalities.* https://fairnessfoundation.com/unequal-kingdom

Francis-Devine, B. (2024). *Income inequality in the UK.* House of Commons Library. https://researchbriefings.files.parliament.uk/documents/CBP-7484/CBP-7484.pdf

Lindert, P. H. (1986). Unequal English wealth since 1670. *Journal of Political Economy, 94*(6), 1127–1162.

Martin, R., Gardiner, B., Pike, A., Sunley, P., & Tyler, P. (2022). *Levelling up left behind places: The scale and nature of the economic and policy challenge.* Routledge.

Martin, R., & Tyler, P. (2022, January 5). *Levelling up left behind places: Only a bold mission-orientated policy will succeed.* Bennett Institute for Public Policy. https://www.bennettinstitute.cam.ac.uk/blog/levelling-up-left-behind-places/

Office for National Statistics. (2024). *Life expectancy for local areas in England, Northern Ireland and Wales: Between 2001 to 2003 and 2020 to 2022.* https://www.ons.gov.uk/peoplepopulationandcommunity/healthandsocialcare/healthandlifeexpectancies/bulletins/lifeexpectancyforlocalareasoftheuk/between2001to2003and2020to2022

Piketty, T. (2020). *Capital and ideology.* Harvard University Press.

Restaurant. (2024, June 13). *Value of UK eating out market nears £100bn.* https://www.restaurantonline.co.uk/Article/2024/06/13/value-of-uk-eating-out-market-nears-100bn

Sheffield, H. (2024, June 13). Tory welfare reform cost working-age families thousands while pensioners benefited – report. *The Guardian.* https://www.theguardian.com/society/article/2024/jun/13/tory-welfare-reform-cost-working-age-families-thousands-while-pensioners-benefited-report

Szreter, S. (2021). *The history of inequality: The deep-acting ideological and institutional influences*. Institute for Fiscal Studies Deaton Review of Inequalities. Institute for Fiscal Studies. https://ifs.org.uk/inequality/wp-content/uploads/2021/11/IFS-Deaton-Review-The-history-of-inequality-1.pdf

The Equality Trust. (2023). *Cost of inequality 2023*. https://equalitytrust.org.uk/evidence-base/reports/equality-trust-releases-cost-inequality-report/

Trussell Trust. (2024). *End of year stats*. https://www.trussell.org.uk/news-and-research/latest-stats/end-of-year-stats

# Section 1

# CREATING OPPORTUNITY FROM BIRTH

# 2

# THE BIRTH OF INJUSTICE

## Philip Collins

*New Statesman, UK*

## INTRODUCTION: HOW LONG WE HAVE KNOWN

In 1963, Edward Boyle, Harold Macmillan's Education minister, commissioned the Central Advisory Council for Education to look into primary school-age education in England. They did not report until 1967, but Children and their Primary Schools (the Plowden report as it became better known) presented an insight that has been acknowledged but ignored ever since:

> *There is some evidence that the gap between measured intelligence of the children of manual workers and of middleclass parents begins to widen at a very early age and that the causes are both genetic and environmental. (Central Advisory Council for Education (England), 1967, p. 31)*

Plowden cited evidence from contemporary academics[1] which had shown a gap in educational attainment in preschool years and primary years, and commented that 'the polarisation continues ... at 11 the scores and achievement of children from the different classes are further apart than they were at eight. In England, the

---

[1]Such as Hindley (1962).

process persists in the secondary school' (Central Advisory Council for Education (England), 1967, p. 31).

We have known for six decades that inequalities between the social classes both originate and start to accelerate in childhood. Sadly, they still do, and it is time we did something about it because – and this is not always true in social policy – we understand the problem well and we have a good sense of what we should be doing if we were seriously intent on fixing it.

## WHAT WE KNOW ALREADY

After more than half a century of detailed investigation of the relationship between the intelligence scores of babies and their performances as adults across many dimensions, after endless inquiry into the balance of forces between the genetic and the environmental, after a long debate between the advocates of 'fluid' intelligence on the one hand and 'crystalised' intelligence[2] on the other, there is a great deal that we can say we know about the early origins of inequality.

The cost efficiency of early intervention in improving life chances is very well established, so much so that it has its own model – the Heckman Equation. With the help of a band of psychologists, economics and neuroscientists, Nobel laureate James Heckman found that intervention before the age of 3 generated returns of between 4 and 16:1. This creates the Heckman Curve, seen in Fig. 2.1, showing that the most effective and cost-effective way of tackling inequalities in life chances is to intervene as early as possible. As Heckman (2006) himself explained: 'The highest rate of return in early childhood development comes from investing as early as possible, from birth through age five, in disadvantaged families. Starting at age three or four is too little too late'.

By the late 1990s, the data were in. Policymakers were able to draw on a strong academic consensus about three vital questions. First, the evidence about the gap in attainment between social groups. Second, the moment when that gap first appeared

---

[2]See, for example, Hindley and Owen (1978).

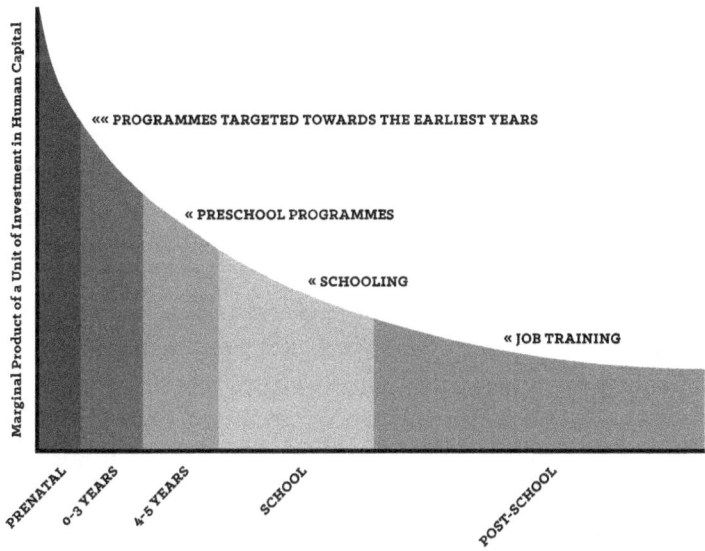

*Source*: Adapted from Heckman (2008).

**Fig. 2.1.  Marginal Products Per First Unit Invested Exclusively at the Given Stage of the Life Cycle.**

and third, the factors that helped to predict the first two problems. The work of Leon Feinstein at the Institute of Education, drawn from the 1970 cohort of births, showed that educational qualifications of 26-year-old adults could be predicted by their test scores from when they were just 22 months old. It was hardly a surprise, given that Plowden had said the same, that these scores were also strongly correlated with a child's socio-economic background. At 22 months, the cognitive attainment of children whose parents were educated to at least A-Level standard was already 14 per cent higher than the attainment of those whose parents had no qualifications at all (Feinstein, 2003).

The Deaton Review from the Institute for Fiscal Studies (IFS), published in July 2024, repeated this exercise for the later British cohort. Deaton reported that large inequalities in both cognitive and socio-emotional test scores had appeared among children born between 2000 and 2002 by the time they had reached the age of three. Children born to high-income households were 12 percentage points more likely to attain the top cognitive test scores than their poorer counterparts. Children from single parent families were 8 percentage points less likely to be top scorers and any child born to a mother whose highest qualification was a GCSE was 7 percentage points less likely.

Deaton's team at the IFS also echoed Plowden and Feinstein by illustrating that the disadvantage transfers through life. Their study of 17-year-olds in the millennium cohort revealed that a single standard deviation's increase in cognitive ability at the age of 3 was linked to a 12 percentage point increase in the chance of attaining 5 GCSEs at grades A* to C. It is possible, of course, that this persistent poor performance could be explained by the circumstances in which these children grow up – their poverty or their housing, for example. But when the IFS controlled for all relevant factors, the gap did not disappear. A single standard deviation's increase in cognitive ability at age 3 still improved a young person's chances of getting 5 GCSEs at A* to C by 8 percentage points (Cattan et al., 2022).

In fact, the evidence is by now clear enough that we can make some bold statements with some confidence. The child that has one more GCSE than its neighbour will, on average, enjoy a boost to lifetime earnings of £200,000 (Department for Education, 2021). Because the early origins of reduced life chances ramify all the way through a life, a child with low attainment at GCSE will have an increased likelihood of getting into trouble with the law and, ultimately, of ending up in prison (Ministry of Justice & Department for Education, 2022). We can say with confidence and with sorrow that adult social inequalities are formed in the nursery.

## THE THINGS WE KNOW WE CAN DO

A counsel of despair is by no means appropriate, though. Just as our knowledge of the problem has been a long time coming, so have the solutions. In the same era that we were working out the issue in the UK, there were policy experiments afoot in the USA that we can emulate. Five years before the Plowden report was published in the UK, researchers in Michigan were randomly assigning children to a high-quality preschool programme with the express hope that it would help their later educational performance. Their findings changed our understanding of how to improve life chances (Schweinhart, 2005). The High/Scope Perry Preschool Study placed 123 African American children, who were assessed to be at high risk of school failure, into two groups: one group accessed a preschool programme at the ages of 3 and 4 and one did not. The two groups were assessed on a range of measures regularly until they turned 40, generating unequivocal results related to the life-long positive impact of preschool intervention.

A decade later, around 120 infants in Carolina were randomly allocated to an early intervention education programme which would last from birth, until age 5. Researchers monitored the study group and control group's progress over time, assessing school performance and wider life chances until age 35. The Abecedarian Project, as it became known, found children participating in the programme completed 1.2 more years of college and were almost four times as likely to have graduated from college.

One of the early fruits in the policy of the growing base of evidence was the Head Start programme. Launched in 1965 as a summer catch-up programme for low-income children in the weeks before they began primary school, Head Start was expanded under the Act of 1981 which created a comprehensive early childhood education, health, nutrition and parent involvement service for low-income families. In 2020, an evaluation by the National Bureau of Economic Research found that children who participated in Head Start were 2.7 per cent more likely to finish high school, 8.5 per cent more likely to enrol in college and 39 per cent more likely to finish college than were their ineligible counterparts. Head Start decreased the likelihood of adult poverty by 23 per cent (Bailey et al., 2021).

## THE POSITION IN THE UK

The Starmer government will land in the UK more or less entirely barren. The Blair government's Sure Start programme, modelled on Head Start, is at least a model whose lessons are there to be taken up. Sure Start offered health, education, parenting classes and employment support to mothers from birth to five. More than 3,000 Sure Start centres were opened within a decade. At its peak in 2010, Sure Start received £1.8 billion a year (a third of overall early years spending; Cattan et al., 2021). In 2021, the IFS and the Nuffield Foundation published an analysis on the health impacts of Sure Start on children up to the age of 15. It found that the financial benefits from reducing hospitalisations offset almost a third of the cost of Sure Start provision (Cattan et al., 2021). In 2024, the same research team published *The Short- and Medium-term Impacts of Sure Start on Educational Outcomes*, which found that children who had access to a Sure Start centre between birth and 5 were still outperforming their peers at GCSE level (by 0.8 grades) (Carneiro et al., 2024). The effect was six times higher for children on free school meals.

It was a terrible mistake for the coalition government to dismantle Sure Start amid the vast cuts to local government between 2010 and 2015. Since 2010, 1,416 Sure Start centres in England have closed. A later incarnation of the Conservative government seemed to realise this. In 2020, Boris Johnson appointed Andrea Leadsom MP to lead the *Early Years Healthy Development Review*. Leadsom's (2021) report, entitled *The Best Start for Life: A Vision for the 1,001 Critical Days* led to the launch of Start for Life, a programme of joined up maternal health and young child support, and Family Hubs, a network of support centres for families with children up to age 19. Start for Life services would be housed in these Hubs.

It was a welcome admission of error but, alas, not a very effective one. Family Hubs opened in 2023 but only £300 million was allocated. At their peak, Sure Start was granted £2.1 billion (in today's prices), seven times as much in a single year than Family Hubs have been allocated for three years. Moreover, Family Hubs are not just providing services for the 0–5s, but for 0–19s. The budget is spread among a much larger cohort.

There is a lot of work to be done although there is at least some infrastructure on which to build. The Family Nurse Partnership (FNP), launched in 2007, provides intensive health-visiting support for first time, vulnerable mothers from early pregnancy until their babies are two years of age. FNPs were also modelled on a successful American programme (Early Intervention Foundation, 2024). Babies who have been through the FNP have been found to be less likely to be hospitalised, to have better health and improved cognitive skills in primary school (Molloy & Asmussen, 2021).

## THE URGENT NEED

A revival of Sure Start and an expansion of the FNPs are the place for the Starmer government to begin a radical shift in public spending towards the earlier years. The need now is urgent. Thirty per cent of British children live in relative poverty (Francis-Devine, 2024) and we have just lived through a pandemic which will have had a dreadful impact on the life chances of the youngest. Research published by the Nuffield Foundation in 2022 found that there were developmental delays among children who had missed out on early years care and education due to lockdowns (La Valle et al., 2022).

Fortunately, there is a manual of sorts at hand. The Early Intervention Foundation, since 2014, has published a guidebook which lists the most effective early intervention programmes that could be feasibly used in this country. The latest version has over 100 programmes from which a few clear principles can be adduced. The earlier the intervention the better which a new government should invest in pre-natal maternal health and dietary support to improve birth weight, help with breast feeding and help with positive attachment in the first weeks after birth. Intensive intervention, very heavily concentrated on those with the most to gain, is to be recommended. Then programmes should always be as comprehensive as possible. They should, for example, include language and cognitive development, alongside parental support.

There is never a panacea in public policy. Early years is as close to an ideal policy as you ever find but it is not an inoculation against the perils of circumstance. There is a large body of evidence attesting to the phenomenon of fade. Children from disadvantaged backgrounds need help that lasts. Bridge Phillipson, the Education Secretary, has just announced one such example. Universal entitlement to free breakfast in a disadvantaged primary school leads to two month's additional progress in learning outcomes. The effect is for all pupils. There is better concentration and less disruption in the classroom so even those who do not attend breakfast club experience this gain (Crawford et al., 2016).

It is only a small measure but it shows what can be done. A government that mixed a concern for justice with a respect for the evidence would, without question, begin the process of shifting its spending from remedial work in the teenage years to the early years of life, when it still has a chance of making a difference. By the time the state gets around to spending a lot on each individual, through schooling and further education and then the welfare system, it is too late. Of course, all this spending embodies important goods but if our principal objective were to equalise life chances as best we can, then there is no doubt about what we should do. The evidence is abundant and it is overwhelming. From Edward Boyle to Bridget Phillipson, Education ministers have known what they ought to do. It has never quite happened but if the Starmer government is looking for some radical credentials and for a mission to be proud of, surely this is what it should be.

## REFERENCES

Bailey, M. J., Sun, S., & Timpe, B. D. (2021). *Prep school for poor kids: The long-run impacts of Head Start on human capital and economic self-sufficiency* [NBER Working Paper No. 28268]. National Bureau of Economic Research. https://www.nber.org/papers/w28268

Cattan, S., Conti, G., Farquharson, C., Ginja, R., & Pecher, M. (2021). *The health impacts of Sure Start* [IFS Briefing Note BN332]. Institute for Fiscal Studies. https://ifs.org.uk/publications/health-impacts-sure-start

Cattan, S., Fitzsimons, E., Goodman, A., Phimister, A., Ploubidis, G. B., & Wertz, J. (2022). *Early childhood and inequalities*. Institute for Fiscal Studies Deaton Review of Inequalities. Institute for Fiscal Studies. https://www.nuffieldfoundation.org/wp-content/uploads/2022/06/Early-childhood-inequalities-IFS-Deaton-Review.pdf

Carneiro, P., Cattan, S., & Ridpath, N. (2024). *The short- and medium-term impacts of Sure Start on educational outcomes* [IFS Report R307]. Institute for Fiscal Studies. https://ifs.org.uk/publications/short-and-medium-term-impacts-sure-start-educational-outcomes

Central Advisory Council for Education (England). (1967). *Children and their primary schools: A report of the Central Advisory Council for Education (England), Vol. 1: Report*. https://education-uk.org/documents/plowden/plowden1967-1.html#03

Crawford, C., Farquharson, C., & Greaves, E. (2016). *Magic breakfast*. Education Endowment Fund. https://ifs.org.uk/publications/magic-breakfast

Department for Education. (2021, July 9). *Higher GCSE grades linked to lifetime earnings boost*. https://www.gov.uk/government/news/higher-gcse-grades-linked-to-lifetime-earnings-boost

Early Intervention Foundation. (2024). *Family nurse partnership (EIF guidebook)*. https://guidebook.eif.org.uk/programme/family-nurse-partnership

Feinstein, L. (2003). Inequality in the early cognitive development of British children in the 1970 cohort. *Economica, 70*(273), 73–97.

Francis-Devine, B. (2024). *Poverty in the UK: Statistics* [House of Commons Library Research Briefing SN07096]. UK Parliament. https://commonslibrary.parliament.uk/research-briefings/sn07096/

Heckman, J. J. (2006). Skill formation and the economics of investing in disadvantaged children. *Science, 312*(5782), 1900–1902.

Heckman, J. J. (2008). Schools, skills and synapses. *Economic Inquiry, 46*(3), 289–324 (Figure 18).

Hindley, C. B. (1962). Social class influences on the development of ability in the first five years. In A. G. Skard & T. Husen (Eds.), *Child education* (pp. 299–351). Munksgaard.

Hindley, C. B., & Owen, C. F. (1978). The extent of individual changes in I.Q. for ages between 6 months and 17 years, in a British longitudinal sample. *Journal of Child Psychology and Psychiatry, 19*(4), 329–350.

La Valle, I., Lewis, J., Crawford, C., Paull, G., Lloyd, E., Ott, E., Mann, G., Drayton, E., Cattoretti, G., Hall, A., & Wills, E. (2022). *Implications of COVID for early childhood education and care in England*. Centre for Evidence and Implementation. https://www.nuffieldfoundation. org/wp-content/uploads/2022/06/Implications-of-Covid-for-ECEC-in-England-June-2022-.pdf

Leadsom, A. (2021). *The best start for life: A vision for the 1,001 critical days* [Early Years Healthy Development Review Report]. Department of Health and Social Care. https://www.gov.uk/government/publications/the-best-start-for-life-a-vision-for-the-1001-critical-days

Ministry of Justice & Department for Education. (2022). *Education, children's social care and offending: Descriptive statistics*. https://assets. publishing.service.gov.uk/media/6227a9b58fa8f526dcf89e17/Education_children_s_social_care_and_offending_descriptive_stats_FINAL.pdf

Molloy, D., & Asmussen, K. (2021, February 18). *Worth the wait: New evaluation data shows positive impacts of family nurse partnership on school readiness and attainment*. Early Intervention Foundation. https://www.eif.org.uk/blog/worth-the-wait-new-evaluation-data-shows-positive-impacts-of-family-nurse-partnership-on-school-readiness-and-attainment

Schweinhart, L. J. (2005). *The HighScope Perry Preschool study through age 40: Summary, conclusions, and frequently asked questions*. HighScope Educational Research Foundation. https://image.highscope.org/wp-content/uploads/2018/11/16053615/perry-preschool-summary-40.pdf

# 3

# 'IT'S HUMAN CAPITAL, STUPID'

## David Blunkett

*Former Education and Employment Secretary,*
*Home Secretary and Work and Pensions Secretary, UK*

Readers will be familiar with the historic analysis of the socio-economic make-up of society by the great economist, J.K. Galbraith (1958). At the time he was formulating his thesis, and for some decades afterwards, whilst gross inequalities existed, they were not perceived by those worst affected as clearly as might have been expected, because the common experience of large swathes of the population separated them from the wealth and privilege of a tiny minority.

For Marxists, the mantra remained: it was workers versus bosses, or labour versus capital (Marx, 2007). Historically in Britain, palpable disparity of income and living space between the well-off and the majority did not lead to revolution. A combination of clever One Nation conservatism, deference and generally rising living standards were sufficient to avoid the reaction seen in other parts of the world – where the creaming-off of surplus, profit or rent led to a level of inequality between the very rich minority and the very poor masses that formed the breeding ground for genuine uprisings.

In countries which form Scandinavia there is a perception and, in many cases, a reality of a much more equal society than in many parts of the world, including wealthy nations like the USA. Books such as *The Spirit Level* by Richard Wilkinson and Kate Pickett (2009) formed a very persuasive backcloth, particularly for those on the centre and left, in terms of how more equal societies lead to greater distribution of wealth and, as a corollary, social cohesion and well-being.

A cursory look at authors portraying underlying societal challenges in countries across Scandinavia – such as Stieg Larsson and Jo Nesbø – tell, however, a different story. Perceived injustices, and unequal outcomes, remain fertile ground for the far right, just as much as in countries with flagrant displays of wealth and privilege.

There is a major challenge as to whether, in creating a more equal society, we should route the pathway to success in the development of opportunity for every individual, rather than concentrating on welfarism and top-down distribution.

This is not to say that redistribution is undesirable. Clearly, in imposing – as well as in collecting – taxes, the government, of whatever persuasion, is dependent on the yield – needed for investment not only in public services, but for national defence and to avoid upheaval caused by rapid economic, social and cultural change.

How much of the 'surplus' is taken by central and devolved government is a key battleground of democratic politics. Cash transfer – taking not only from the rich but also the comparatively well-off and redistributing it to the poor – is still strongly favoured on the moderate and far left of politics. The question often ducked is the 'legitimacy' and, therefore, consent of the people to this process, which was historically achieved by emphasising mutuality and solidarity, and therefore the reciprocity which springs from highlighting our interdependence.

## DISPARITIES IN PHYSICAL AND SOCIAL CAPITAL

It is important to recognise that societal injustice, the shared experience of deprivation, poor housing and indifferent schooling have a vastly greater impact than isolated incidents of disadvantage.

In other words, one's own community or neighbourhood, lack of aspiration and underinvestment in remedial action, leads to underachievement and potentially lifelong denial of success.

This 'critical mass' collectively experiencing a poor start in life is not an act of God. It emerges from historic generational disadvantage: not being able to afford to move house, to get and hold down a decent job or to breathe clean air. There is something much more fundamental about inequality than simply focussing on one's immediate income.

I'm talking here of massive disparity in wealth. As I shall demonstrate later in this chapter, there is one major asset which we can, as a society, make available to everyone through lifelong learning – starting at the time a child is born (or even with the mother, before birth), through to a point way beyond retirement when formal learning is no longer sought. Namely, education. However, before addressing the central challenge of the right to learn, opportunity throughout life and support through rapid change, I will reflect on how physical and social capital sit alongside human capital developed through learning.

The ownership of land and property, shareholding and, above all, passing down such assets from one generation to another is critical when examining intergenerational disadvantage, disparities in life chances and the resentment and alienation which comes from feeling 'abandoned'.

Put crudely, if a grandparent, uncle or aunt leaves you a house of even modest proportions in London and the south-east, it's the equivalent of winning the lottery. If you, your parents and grandparents grew up in rented accommodation, there is no such asset to pass down. Of course, social mobility allows change with new generations accumulating such capital assets, and thereby themselves being able to become the 'bank of mum and dad' and, in time, pass on resources to their family. The very wealthy, global elite have always been able to achieve this on a grand scale. But there are those of relatively modest means who find themselves in an advantageous position, sometimes because of Margaret Thatcher's 'right to buy' policies in relation to housing. She believed that democracy rested on ownership and the operation of the market.

This is why the flat rate Poll Tax, imposed on every adult, was a logical outcome from a philosophy that placed 'voting' as an entitlement arising from the ownership of property or contribution made financially, rather than from citizenship.

The incoming Labour government, in 1997, set in train research through the Department of Education and Employment, led by Gavin Kelly with Nick Pearce, to look at how it might be possible, in the 21st century, to provide a foothold, and therefore greater equality of opportunity, to those without prospects of asset distribution within the family.

The research was subsequently incorporated into a final Treasury policy paper and resulted in the development of the Child Trust Fund (HM Treasury, 2001). Suffice it to say here, that the idea was never fully debated publicly, little understood and sadly not embedded in the national psyche.

Had the amounts allocated from central government been greater, the programme linked with major ancillary programmes to encourage saving and spread as a 'collective' endeavour through churches, pubs and other community groups, there might have been a chance of gaining sufficient traction to protect the initiative from those with a very different ideology. In the end, the coalition government, to their absolute shame, stopped the Child Trust Fund in its tracks.

Consequently, only a small cohort of those reaching 18 found themselves entitled to a small nest egg. Too small to be significant, but an indication of what might be possible if the amounts allocated to the fund, the way it operated and linked with programmes such as the Savings Gateway (HM Treasury, 2001) (where, if you are on lower income and prepared to save a pound, the government would put in a pound to match), could have resulted in many thousands of pounds being available to youngsters – who otherwise had nothing else to draw down on as they reached adulthood. Given the amount of public money allocated, Treasury objections could have been overcome by confining the release of money for very specific purposes, so that cynics and those ideologically opposed could not have proffered the notion that youngsters would be taking themselves around the world or attempting to buy Ferraris – if only!

The research which led to the Child Trust Fund also demonstrated that an asset or stake in society correlated with voting, active participation in the community and a positive view of lifelong learning and child development.

Both physical and human capital contribute to the engagement of individuals in a positive sense, as they feel they have a stake in what is happening around them. Yet whilst the unequal distribution of capital wealth is, in the long term, deeply concerning, it is, after all, 'human capital' which will make the difference to individuals, communities and to the prosperity of the nation.

Unless there is recognition that wealth creation is about utilising the full potential of every single individual, then the emphasis is always related to the amorphous term 'business'. Businesses are, of course, dependent on the entrepreneurship, innovation and enterprise of individuals, and not solely the exploitation of existing natural resources or means of production.

## BRINGING BACK SURE START

As indicated earlier, there is one asset that accumulates success for every individual which remains immediately available to us. It is differential in its delivery and outcome; it requires not just investment but a change in mindset and collective experience. That asset is, of course, education. The very antithesis of the 'trickle down' economic philosophy is the empowerment, enrichment and therefore education and lifelong learning open to individuals. This begins from the moment a child is born.

Back in the 1990s, building upon the important work of Sir Claus Moser, the Paul Hamlyn Foundation, with the National Education Commission (1995), published *Learning to Succeed: The Way Ahead*, which is as relevant today as it was then: what we do with and to a child in those very early years is fundamental to their likely success in life.

Consequently, in the lead up to the 1997 general election, a group of individuals in the political, educational and child development arena started to put together a UK version of the initiative developed in Seattle, in the USA – described there as Head Start

(Seattle Public Schools, n.d.). This was the early Local Sure Start programmes.

Sure Start was not solely about childcare or, for that matter, the normal and important outcome measures of child development. It was so much more. A holistic approach to investing in and engaging the community in its widest sense. To develop, alongside nurturing a child from birth, self-belief, confidence and engagement with education in the parent or parents. It was about drawing down on the strength of community and not just a paternalistic approach to professionals coming in from outside. It was, above all, a long-term programme, with outcomes way beyond parliamentary terms or the attraction of votes. Just like overcoming the asset divide, Sure Start was about the future and a fundamental change in approach, not merely a sticking plaster.

Fundamental elements of Sure Start ranged from embedding each project within the community and joining up thinking and action at national level. As Secretary of State for Education and Employment, I was able to identify resources and work with the Treasury on the one hand, and – in partnership with my long-standing friend, the late Tessa Jowell (who was then Parliamentary Under Secretary for Health) – the Department of Health. This cross-departmental working and collaboration was a crucial factor in the early success of the programme.

Together with the development of the first ever national nursery education programme, linked separately to investment in childcare, the early years were beginning to get the attention which everyone paid lip service to, but rarely followed through.

The findings of the Institute for Fiscal Studies (IFS) in early 2024, reinforced, in my mind, just how criminal it was, again, that the coalition government colluded in the destruction of the Sure Start programme. The IFS (Carniero et al., 2024) found that children who lived within 2.5 kilometres of a Sure Start centre in the first five years of their lives scored an average 0.8 grades higher in their General Certificate of Secondary Education (GCSE) than those who did not; and for children from low-income families, the score was an average three grades higher than those in similar circumstances who did not have access to a Sure Start centre.

Of course, there were good and bad. There were some programmes, under the heading of Children Centres, which bore no resemblance to the original local Sure Start concept. But where Sure Start worked, it worked miracles. It doesn't matter what we call it – it can be refreshed and updated – but it is critical that something like the early Sure Start programmes should be, over time, reintroduced, focussing on those neighbourhoods and areas of the country so obviously and unnecessarily 'left out' in every measure of future success.

A report published in April 2024, *Children in Care in the North of England,* by Health Equity North (2024), revealed the staggering fact that whereas across the UK, one in every 140 children had sadly been taken into care, in Blackpool (and regrettably as bad in other parts of northern England), it was one in every 52. Whilst researchers and campaigners called for a massive increase in welfare benefits, they missed the point that programmes like Sure Start, which offered a holistic approach, were much more effective in diminishing both family poverty and dysfunctionality.

However, the initiative wasn't and shouldn't be a programme exclusively for the poor. As Richard Titmuss (1974) outlined 50 years ago, services which are only designed for the poor, will inevitably be poor services. As indicated above, drawing down on the strength of the wider community can entail programmes which are available to, and contributed to, by people who are not themselves, in any sense, disadvantaged. The issue in the most deprived parts of the country outside London is the density of multiple problems and the lack of geographic proximity to wealthier areas. Whilst it is a misnomer to talk about 'left behind towns' who are not, in any normal sense of the word, 'left behind', there is a challenge to ensure that social capital is developed so that the strength of community can be used effectively to lift the well-being of the whole area (Blears & Blunkett, 2019; Blunkett & Green, 1983; Putnam et al., 2003). There have been examples, over the years – one outstanding being Balsall Heath in the City of Birmingham (Atkinson, 2002, 2012).

Developing active citizenship requires that all schools should teach citizenship and democracy, and teach it well. Evidence from longitudinal studies, including from the National Foundation for Educational Research, commissioned by the Department for Education (2010) together with more recent research from Middlesex

University (Hyder et al., 2024), has demonstrated a marked improvement in the outcome measures for young people, at every stage of their education, when citizenship and an understanding of society and commonly held values are seen as an essential part of the curriculum. That is why a quality education system from early years onwards is one (but just one) way of ensuring that we overcome societal disadvantages.

The necessary investment in housing renewal, an industrial strategy which offers rewarding and meaningful employment, a transport system that makes opportunities accessible, and much more, also come into play. Joined up thinking and support for decentralised delivery of public services have historically been shown to work (Blunkett & Jackson, 1987). However, it is lifelong learning which will transform both the opportunity of adults and the contribution, in turn, they will make to nurture their own children.

## LEARNING THROUGHOUT LIFE

So often, when the Millennium Development Goals were being put in place through the UN, the mantra was heard, over and over again, 'we must educate the mothers, who will then educate the children'. What applied to Africa or Asia is just as important in the communities of the UK in the 21st century.

In facing a turbulent economic and social future, the notion that there are too many graduates who are not in what are called 'graduate jobs' – which is an ill-defined and extremely clumsy approach to what education is all about, is deeply depressing. Not least because it misses the point as to what education is for.

As someone who grew up in a city built on artisan skill – underpinned, until the 1980s, by large numbers of valued, if over-long, apprenticeships – I'm in favour of offering choice. I'm especially keen that people should play to their strengths, with the education process identifying where success is likely to be achieved, but not confining it to one route or outcome. Anyone who has had anything to do with education understands that we all mature at a different pace, we have strengths and weaknesses and, as Professor Howard Gardner (1983, 1999) spelt out many years ago, multiple 'intelligences', which he later refined to nine.

We learn not only at a different pace from others, but we also benefit from an understanding of pedagogy which approaches the individual as unique, rather than fitting the individual into a preconceived process, benefiting some, and discarding others.

You do not create a more equal society, however, by defrauding individuals into believing that you've offered them greater equality because you have invented a technical route as an alternative to 'academic A-levels', when in fact you make them jump through similar hoops to those taking an academic route, but narrow the perspective, thereby undermining their chance of coping with the fourth technological revolution.

In Parliament from 2019 to 2024, the Conservative government pressed ahead with what might be described as a 'scorched earth' approach to removing advanced qualifications which had formed the alternative to A-levels, but were perceived by some as blocking the transition to the newly introduced T levels. A philosophy which, at its core, demonstrated a will to make technical education as prestigious and valued as A-levels, but in reality, squeezing out the alternative vocational pathway described earlier. Although there have been eight changes to vocational training for 16 to 19-year-olds in 14 years, it was inevitable that a further review would have to be set in train to try and make sense of the rolling out of T levels and the foundation pathway to reaching them; and how tried and tested advanced qualifications, such as BTEC National Diploma, could be improved and would continue as an alternative.

That is why the incoming Labour government were wise to pause defunding of alternatives in order to take a realistic and honest approach to the way forward.

Yet as we rightly look to improving the qualifications landscape, there is one reason why lifelong learning is so critical to building a more equal society, experienced by us all. That is how we face the world of tomorrow.

A great deal is now spoken about artificial intelligence, robotics and the likely impact they will have on both the nature of work and, in the post-pandemic era, how individuals are able to cope with such rapid change.

I saw, in the 1980s, as Leader of the City of Sheffield, the way in which funding from the European steel and coal community was used in endeavouring to re-equip those losing their jobs for a reasonable alternative. However, the jobs they were training workers for were already overtaken by the technology of the moment. That is why any education system should not send young people (or, for that matter returners to learning) down narrow tramlines, but instead open up opportunities to take on new working methods, procedures and command of evolving technologies, rather than being victims of it.

This can only be achieved if there is a real and committed investment by the private sector as well as government; by the individual as well as devolved administrations. Not to just one or two second chances, but to return, whenever needed, to learn new skills within the workplace and beyond. Learning to adapt, respond, be flexible, develop critical thinking skills and contribute towards solutions rather than simply plug a hole, is the only way in which, economically and socially, we can flourish in the decades to come. That is why the curriculum review put in place by the incoming Labour government in July 2024 is important, and offers the opportunity to transform this part of our education system for decades ahead.

However, a collaborative approach from all those who have a stake in transforming learning through life is imperative. One idea would be to return to the original concept of Individual Learning Accounts (Comptroller and Auditor General, 2002). Not the distortion, engineered by the Treasury, which in 2001 led to vouchers which, in turn, led to massive exploitation of the public purse (Woodward, 2001). Instead, an approach where individuals, employers and government at every level can contribute, and resources can be drawn down at a time and in a place appropriate to being able to cope with change.

The development of a Learning Passport would allow individuals throughout their lives to have the continued learning they had undertaken accredited. Microcredits and the move towards modular learning are not only more flexible but less expensive for those who are either re-entering the learning process after many years; or, because of pressures of time, wish to embrace new hybrid systems and online learning opportunities (Blunkett et al., 2022). The delivery of education was affected directly by the pandemic of 2020 onwards and although inequalities in access to devices or to the Internet constitute a real barrier to some, the opportunities in the future are enormous. The developing iterations of ChatGPT, both in the learning process and in the workplace, require a rethink as to where, when and how, education is delivered. The very modest outline in the Act passed to introduce the Lifelong Learning Entitlement, whilst requiring a rethink, does have at least the basis of a way forward.

A more equal society of tomorrow, with equality of opportunity for all those willing to take it, is the polar opposite of sameness, dumbing down and putting people in their place – a place from which they can't escape. The simple truth is that everything else that faces this nation: net zero, sufficient housing for the future, dignified care where it's needed – none of this can be achieved without a skilled workforce and futuristic snapshot which will prepare us for the rollercoaster. Past transformations have left whole communities on the sidelines. We, as a nation, must do better.

## REFERENCES

Atkinson, N. (2002). *The renewal of urban neighbourhoods*. Centre for Local Economic Strategies. https://cles.org.uk/wp-content/uploads/2011/01/LW38-January02.pdf

Atkinson, N. (2012). *Nourishing social renewal*. Brewin Books.

Blears, H., & Blunkett, D. (2019). 5: The road to empowerment. In *Whose government is it?*. Bristol University Press.

Blunkett, D., Firth, J., Nargund, P., Rowan, K., & Sandby-Thomas, R. (2022). *Learning and skills for economic recovery, social cohesion and a more equal Britain*. The Labour Party. https://labour.org.uk/wp-content/uploads/2022/10/WR-16813_22-Labour-Skills-Council-report-Edit-19-10-22.pdf

Blunkett, D., & Green, G. (1983). *Building from the bottom: The Sheffield experience* (No. 491). Fabian Society.

Blunkett, D., & Jackson, K. (1987). *Democracy in crisis: The town halls respond.* The Hogarth Press Ltd.

Carniero, P., Cattan, S., & Ridpath, N. (2024). *The short- and medium-term impacts of Sure Start on educational outcomes.* Institute for Fiscal Studies. https://ifs.org.uk/sites/default/files/2024-04/SS_NPD_Report.pdf

Comptroller and Auditor General. (2002). *Individual learning accounts HC1235 Session 2001–2002.* National Audit Office.

Department for Education. (2010). *Citizenship education in England 2001–2010: Young people's practices and prospects for the future: The eighth and final report from the Citizenship Education Longitudinal Study (CELS).* https://assets.publishing.service.gov.uk/media/5a7b6c07e5274a319e77f2fc/DFE-RR059.pdf

Galbraith, J. K. (1958). *The affluent society.* Houghton Mifflin.

Gardner, H. (1983). *Frames of mind: The theory of multiple intelligences.* Basic Books.

Gardner, H. (1999). *Intelligence reframed: Multiple intelligences for the 21st century.* Basic Books.

Health Equity North. (2024). *Children in care in the North of England.* Health Equity North. https://www.healthequitynorth.co.uk/app/uploads/Children-in-Care-Report-2024-FINAL-2-1.pdf

HM Treasury. (2001, April). *Savings and assets for all: The modernisation of Britain's tax and benefits system* (Number Eight). https://revenuebenefits.org.uk/pdf/savings_and_assets_for_all.pdf

Hyder, F., Jerome, L., & Hilal, Y. (2024). *ACT research briefing 3: Pedagogy and citizenship education.* Association for Citizenship Teaching. https://www.teachingcitizenship.org.uk/wp-content/uploads/2024/04/ACT-Research-Briefing-3-Pedagogy-and-Citizenship-Education.pdf

National Education Commission. (1995). *Learning to succeed: The way ahead.* The Paul Hamlyn Foundation.

Marx, K. (2007). *Economic and philosophic manuscripts of 1844* (M. Milligan, Trans.). Dover Publications.

Putnam, R. D., Feldstein, L., & Cohen, D. J. (2003). *Better Together: Restoring the American Community.* Simon & Schuster.

Titmuss, R. (1974). *Social policy: An introduction.* Allen & Unwin.

Seattle Public Schools. (n.d.). *Head Start.* https://www.seattleschools.org/ departments/early-learning/preschool/head-start/

Wilkinson, R. G., & Pickett, K. (2009). *The spirit level: Why greater equality makes societies stronger.* Bloomsbury.

Woodward, W. (2001, October 15). Frauds scuttle adult learning scheme. *The Guardian.* https://www.theguardian.com/uk/2001/oct/25/ furthereducation.educationincrisis

# 4

## THE COORDINATION CONUNDRUM: THREE CORE POLICY PRINCIPLES FOR POST-16 EDUCATION AND TRAINING

James Robson

*University of Oxford, UK*

Having a resilient, agile, and effective post-16 education and training (E&T) sector is critical to economic growth, prosperity, social cohesion, and supporting the aspirations of individuals. There is a lot at stake. However, without appropriate policy frameworks and strategic coordination of the sector, there are significant economic risks and the potential to deepen and entrench social and geographic inequalities (Robson et al., 2024). Sadly, for the last two decades, post-16 E&T in the UK, and particularly in England, has been subjected to near constant policy churn. This has led to significant instability in Further Education (FE), Higher Education (HE), and adult education as well as structural incoherence, complex pathways, a 'qualifications jungle', a stretched and precariously employed E&T workforce, and a crisis in funding (Association of Colleges (AOC), 2020; Keep, 2015; Raffe, 2015; Robson, 2022).

Many of the policy initiatives, particularly in the last decade have been the product of the carousel of Secretaries of State for

Education and Junior Ministers, each attempting to make a mark on their new department and making change for change's sake (Robson et al., 2024). Policy memory has been short and little attempt has been made to learn from the past or from international contexts (Higham & Yeomans, 2007; Keep et al., 2022). At the same time, the recent Conservative government has further destabilised the sector by sucking E&T policy discourse into frivolous culture wars, attacking universities and students over low value, unevidenced 'Mickey Mouse degrees' (e.g. Gullis & Nici, 2023), while slashing FE and adult education budgets. The importance of post-16 E&T for the economy, society, and individuals alike is too great to be treated as a political pawn in this way and the fact that the sector is struggling is a sign of long-term catastrophic and shameful policy failure.

This raises the critical question of what should be done to provide a more stable and supportive policy framework that will enable the whole of the post-16 E&T system to deliver positive results effectively and efficiently for the economy, society, and individuals. Since devolution, approaches to E&T policy have been diverging significantly across the four nations of the UK, often shaped by different underpinning political philosophies (Robson et al., 2024). Although different approaches may hide tensions and inequalities inherent in them, these variations make the UK an ideal policy laboratory (Hodgson et al., 2019) to deepen our understanding of system-level coordination of E&T and provide the basis for a more strategic policy approach, based on existing best practice.

Therefore, in this chapter, I will draw on lessons learned from the different approaches to E&T across the UK in order to present three key foundational principles that must, in my opinion, underpin any effective policy approach to post-16 E&T. The focus is primarily on the policy opportunities for England as some of the devolved nations are already embedding these at the heart of their skills systems (particularly Scotland and the work by the Scottish Funding Council, SFC, and Wales establishing what is now known as Medr, the Welsh word for 'skills', to manage its tertiary education and research). The core argument behind the following principles is that only through a joined-up, holistic, tertiary, systems-based policy approach can we develop post-16 E&T that works for learners, employers, and the country in a way that will fundamentally lead to meaningful shared prosperity and real equity.

## PRINCIPLE 1: ADOPTING A SYSTEMS-BASED APPROACH

The debate around how E&T should be coordinated is long running and sits at the heart of all subsequent policy issues and decisions. However, this 'coordination conundrum' is rarely overtly discussed, or even articulated, because it is fundamentally rooted in the underpinning political philosophy of the government in power. How E&T is coordinated is usually rooted in core philosophic assumptions about the extent to which the state should play a role in the process of governance or whether it should be left to market models and logic.

For at least the last 15 years under the coalition and Conservative governments (and arguably in the reforms of New Labour), E&T policy in England has been firmly embedded in neoliberal logic, taking a market-based approach to coordination. This has foregrounded the concept of student choice and the idea of competition between institutions and, as a natural consequence, between HE and FE, as the mechanism for driving up quality of provision and aligning E&T with shifting labour market demands. The assumption being that students will choose the best courses that deliver the best labour market outcomes, measured in terms of salary returns. E&T providers will have to respond to consumer choice by improving provision and, most importantly, responding in an agile manner to labour market signals and skills gaps and shortages, ensuring their courses meet changing labour market demands. The assumption being that employers will reward individuals with the skills they require with higher salaries, thus shaping student choice. In other words, using Adam Smith's image, the invisible hand of the market is the coordinating force, with E&T being managed by principles of supply (E&T providers) and demand (students and employers) and competition between providers.

This was clearly articulated in 'Students at the Heart of the System' from the then Department for Business, Innovation & Skills (2011), which stated:

*We are committed to opening up the HE market, including to Further Education colleges and alternative providers, to meet the changing needs of employers, individuals, and their communities ... we want a diverse, competitive system that can offer different types of HE and FE so that students can choose freely between a wide range of providers.*

Implicit in this coordination model is the philosophical assumption that the role of the state in E&T should be largely limited simply to market regulation – ensuring market competition is maintained, protecting consumers, facilitating consumer choice with information, and avoiding market failure (e.g. through monopoly, oligopoly, or information asymmetry). In England, the Department for Education (DfE) articulated this very clearly in 2016 with the establishment of the Office for Students (OfS):

*A new Office for Students will put competition and choice at the heart of sector regulation ... by introducing more competition and informed choice into higher education, we will deliver better outcomes and value for students, employers and the taxpayers .... Competition between providers in any market incentivises them to raise their game, offering more innovation and higher quality products and services at lower costs. Higher education is no exception ... [marketisation] will allow us to improve the capacity and agility of the higher education sector, transforming its ability to respond to economic demands and the rapidly changing graduate employment landscape ....*
*(Department for Education (DfE), 2016, pp. 6–9)*

However, the doubling down on market logic as a mechanism for the coordination of E&T has categorically failed in a multitude of ways, even based on its own criteria for success. The approach taken in England has mutated away from a light touch, market-based model to one of the most centrally managed systems in the world (Morgan, 2020). However, the focus has been on central bureaucratic regulation rather than strategic coordination of a coherent system. As the government has become more and more frustrated with the fact that students don't seem to behave in the way economic modelling suggests they should and E&T providers struggle to respond to vague signals from the labour market, the DfE and regulatory bodies have become ever more interventionist, introducing more and more centralised regulatory policy in an attempt to control the players in an already broken market model.

However, regulation has been homogenised and tends to value what can be measured rather than measuring what should be valued. The fact that the OfS is not fit for purpose has been clearly stated in the damning report from the House of Lords (2023). At the same time, numerous other reports and research projects have clearly shown how damaging the reliance on competition in combination with dominant, but poorly framed regulation, has been for the sector (e.g. AoC, 2020; Raffe, 2015; Robson et al., 2024). Competition for students, and ultimately resources, has particularly stretched the under-resourced vocational side of the post-16 E&T system to breaking point, with FE colleges regularly reporting operational challenges and difficulties with staff recruitment and retention (AOC, 2020). It has also led to a homogenisation of all E&T provision, with FE colleges increasingly offering degree level qualifications and universities increasingly colonising the vocational space and offering sub-degree level qualifications (Hazelkorn, 2023; Relly & Robson, 2022; Shattock & Hunt, 2021).

This blurring of the boundaries between FE and HE and between universities is a form of isomorphism as, in such a strict regulatory space, organisations try and imitate the most successful providers to gain rewards. In technical terms, this can be seen as a shift from horizontal diversity, where different E&T pathways are maintained and celebrated, reflecting different social, individual, and economic needs, to vertical stratification, where regulatory mechanisms and market logic force organisations to compete in the same space and form hierarchies around prestige (Teichler, 2020). In practical terms, this has led to a narrowing of E&T pathways available for students, across FE and HE, which has restricted student choice. This sits at the heart of debates around parity of esteem between vocational and university-based E&T (Relly, 2021) and, critically, bakes inequality into the heart of the sector.

The result is that the current neoliberally oriented approach to the coordination of post-16 E&T in England is a fragmented series of quasi-markets, unable to take a strategic overview of FE, HE, and adult provision. Hierarchical homogenisation of provision dominates; narrow options and opportunities exist for students; and innovative approaches to skills formation in a way that might respond to changing economic needs are limited. However, it doesn't need to be this way. An alternative approach, as is being taken in Scotland by the SFC and in Wales by Medr is to adopt a systems-based approach. Rather than competition, the underpinning principle is complementarity and collaboration between different parts of the system. In normative terms, the different parts of a post-16 tertiary system should act together providing a diverse range of pathways and opportunities for students and adult learners, acknowledging that different people have different needs from E&T and that a diverse range of approaches to skills formation best serve the needs of employers and the economy.

A systems-based, holistic approach to tertiary education requires a more nuanced and tailored form of regulation, but importantly emphasises that the state has a broader role to play in the management of the system. Rather than light touch market regulation, the state should be more overtly involved in maintaining collaboration and complementarity between different parts of the system, assessing and supporting the system to respond to short- and long-term skills needs, and linking provision with wider public goods. While these are all ambitions in Scotland and Wales, some concerns have been raised that a country the size of England would struggle with this level of hands-on coordination. This points towards a devolved approach within a tertiary E&T system, rooted in trends towards regionalisation, linking the skills system directly to local social and economic needs.

Therefore, in normative terms, the first and most important key principle for managing post-16 E&T is to abandon market logic and take a systems-based approach. This means moving away from flawed thinking about competition as the core mechanism for coordination and instead taking a hands-on approach rooted in collaboration and complementarity between organisations and sectors.

## PRINCIPLE 2: EMBRACING MULTIPLE PURPOSES FOR E&T

Very closely linked with the underpinning political philosophy for coordination is a complex discussion about the purpose or purposes of post-16 E&T. As discussed above, FE, HE, and adult education arguably each has a slightly different set of purposes. However, recent policy approaches, particularly in England, have tended to reduce the purpose of all these different strands of post-16 E&T to a simple economic function: providing employers with skilled workers to meet their current and future skills requirements; and, by association, providing individuals with appropriate financial labour market returns.

These economic purposes of E&T are, in my view, fundamental. However, focussing solely on employer demands and labour market returns reduces the diverse range of other important functions the different parts of post-16 E&T perform. For individuals, these shouldn't simply be reduced to financial returns. There are broader issues related to functional skills, access, and progress; the development of life skills; the provision of transferable skills that enable individuals to navigate the labour market in the longer term and develop careers they find fulfilling; supporting wellbeing and human flourishing; enriching life through knowledge and a love of learning; social mobility; etc. (Trow, 2007). There are also broader public goods to consider. Economic growth and productivity are, of course, key. However, these extend well beyond meeting the short-term skills needs of employers and may include longer-term economic issues related to longer-term changes in the nature of work and a need for a just transition to a greener economy. There are also broader public goods, including citizenship formation, regional development, cultural development, etc.

The reality is that post-16 E&T has a complex array of purposes that cut across individual, social, and economic needs and relate to individual and public goods. They relate to short-term needs of the economy (in terms of skills gaps) and long-term needs of society (e.g. a just transition). Some of these will inevitably be in tension with each other. However, good policy should embrace this multiplicity and complexity and work with and celebrate multiple purposes effectively so they are enshrined in policy thinking and particularly regulatory frameworks. This brings us back to the critical relationship between systems thinking and diversity within a tertiary E&T system. Only an approach rooted in complementarity can allow different constellations of purposes in different parts of the system to flourish effectively.

## PRINCIPLE 3: RECONCEPTUALISING THE ROLE OF EMPLOYERS

All devolved nations of the UK have struggled with defining a coherent role for employers in E&T. However, in England particularly, employers have swallowed up so much airtime that policy discourse has shifted significantly in the last five years from putting students at the heart of the system to putting employers at the heart of the system (Department for Education (DfE), 2021). In part, this is a natural result of a marketised system that places two kinds of consumers (students and employers) in tension with each other. It is perhaps inevitable that the employers should dominate in a context that defines the core purpose of E&T primarily in economic terms. However, what this has meant in practice is that employers have increasingly become aloof customers of E&T, complaining about provision and skills gaps, while contributing little else to the process of E&T. As such their role has largely been reduced to supplying wish lists of skills that providers are expected to supply.

This distant role is manifested in the alarming reduction in employer investment in training their employees: the UK has seen a 28% drop in employer investment since 2005 (Drayton et al., 2023). The amount UK employers now invest in E&T for the existing workforce is less than half the EU average. Importantly, what money is invested is profoundly unequally distributed across the workforce, with people with degrees three times as likely to receive additional training in work than their 'less qualified' colleagues (Office for Budget Responsibility, 2023; Tahir, 2023). This has all meant that the UK, and England in particular, has, for the last decade at least, been sleepwalking into skills stagnation.

Some analyses of employer investment in E&T have naively suggested that the quality of initial skills formation, particularly in HE, and broader efficiencies in E&T have reduced the need for subsequent training of the workforce (Chartered Institute of Personnel and Development, 2019). However, given how much other countries invest in ongoing training, it seems very unlikely that the UK has hit on some magic formula in initial skills formation. The more likely scenario is that employers have shifted to low skills business models, a move closely linked with the concerns around poor productivity in recent years. Fear of other companies poaching staff a company has invested in has spiralled into a culture of low investment.

However, at its core, the most impactful reason for poor employer investment in the ongoing training of their workers is that policy frameworks disincentivise it. This is fundamentally linked with the broader positioning of employers within the whole of the E&T system as passive stakeholders, theoretically supplied with a constant stream of skilled workers to meet their demands. It's far easier to demand new skills from the initial skills formation part of the skills system than invest in subsequent ongoing training and risk competitors poaching staff.

Clearly, a new compact between employers and E&T system is required. This is something that SFC has been working towards (Scottish Funding Council, 2022), but all of the devolved countries of the UK need to rethink the way in which employers are engaged in the E&T system. Currently, policy discourse, that emphasises employers as customers of E&T, has become obsessed with the *rights* of employers, largely in terms of E&T responding effectively to their skills demands. However, a reorientation is required to shift the role of employers from customer to stakeholder and to emphasise not just their *rights* but also their *responsibilities*.

As illustrated by countries like Germany, Singapore, and, increasingly, Scotland, it is clear that such responsibilities must include active engagement in E&T that moves beyond skills demands to involvement in the actual process of skills formation. Of course, providing information on skills needs is critical, but this should be undertaken in collaboration with E&T providers, many of which have significant insight into sector-level needs as well as an understanding of long-term skills required by individuals for successful careers, rather than short-term roles. However, responsibilities within E&T should also involve broadening out the process of standard setting, as well as providing meaningful opportunities for work-based learning, more active engagement delivery of E&T, and, of course, meaningful financial input.

## CONCLUSION

Thus, in this chapter, I have highlighted some of the ways in which E&T in the UK, and particularly England, has struggled to meet the needs of all stakeholders and presented three key fundamental principles that, in normative terms, should underpin a successful system that works towards meaningful shared prosperity and equity. Clearly, some kind of paradigm shift is required. This is the most challenging thing. There are too many path dependencies in play; there is too much of a neoliberal muscle memory and too few people at the heart of Whitehall who have experienced or even thought about anything other than markets and competition as the core mode of regulation and coordination. However, a complete realignment and reframing of the underpinning political philosophy that drives the way in which E&T are structured is required. There are some positive movements in this direction. The work of the SFC has placed systems thinking and complementarity at the heart of its coordination model. Similarly, the new Australian accord is taking a joined-up approach to E&T policy and Medr seems to be taking a systems-based tertiary approach. It is essential that the sorry experiment in market logic as a method of coordination is finally brought to a close and that E&T, which adopts systems-based thinking, embraces a multiplicity of purposes, and reconceptualises the role of employers, is rolled out effectively across the whole of the UK.

## REFERENCES

Association of Colleges (AOC). (2020). *The impact of competition in post-16 education and training.* https://feweek.co.uk/wp-content/uploads/2020/12/AoC-report-sufficiency-efficiency-and-effectiveness-FINAL-publication-v2.pdf

Chartered Institute of Personnel and Development. (2019). *Addressing employer underinvestment in training*. https://www.cipd.org/globalassets/media/comms/news/addressing-employer-underinvestment-in-training_tcm18-61265.pdf

Department for Business, Innovation & Skills. (2011). *Students at the heart of the system*. https://assets.publishing.service.gov.uk/media/5a79900ce5274a684690a79c/11-944-higher-education-students-at-heart-of-system.pdf

Department for Education (DfE). (2016). *Educational excellence everywhere*. https://www.gov.uk/government/publications/educational-excellence-everywhere

Department for Education (DfE). (2021). *Skills for Jobs: Lifelong learning for opportunity growth*. https://www.gov.uk/government/publications/skills-for-jobs-lifelong-learning-for-opportunity-and-growth

Drayton, E., Farquharson, C., Ogden, K., Sibeta, L., Tahir, I., & Waltmann, B. (2023). *Annual report on education spending in England: 2023*. Institute for Fiscal Studies. https://ifs.org.uk/sites/default/files/2023-12/IFS-Annual-report-on-education-spending-in-England-2023-new.pdf

Gullis, J., & Nici, L. (2023). *The new conservative plan to upskill Britain*. The New Conservatives. https://www.thenewconservatives.co.uk/wp-content/uploads/2023/09/upskill-report-2023-v4_web.pdf

Hazelkorn, E. (2023). *Is it time to rethink our model of post-secondary education? Progressing a tertiary education eco-system* [Working Paper]. Centre for Global Higher Education. https://www.researchcghe.org/wp-content/uploads/migrate/working-paper-89july-2023.pdf

Higham, J., & Yeomans, D. (2007). Policy memory and policy amnesia in 14–19 education: Learning from the past?. In D. Raffe & K. Spours (Eds.), *Policy making and policy learning in 14–19 education* (Bedford Way Papers, pp. 33–60).

Hodgson, A., Spours, K., Gallacher, J., Irwin, T., & James, D. (2019). FE and skills – Is the 'UK laboratory' open for expansive policy learning?. *Journal of Education and Work, 32*(3), 277–291.

House of Lords. (2023). *Must do better: The Office for Students and the looming crisis facing HE* [2nd Report of Session 2022-23]. Industry and Regulators Committee. https://committees.parliament.uk/publications/41379/documents/203593/default/

Keep, E. (2015). Thinking about where to go and what next to do in the reform of vocational qualifications. *Journal of Education and Work*, 28(2), 117–125.

Keep, E., Richmond, T., & Silver, R. (2022). *Honourable histories, from the local management of colleges via incorporation to the present day: 30 years of reform in further education 1991–2021*. Further Education Trust for Leadership. https://fetl.org.uk/wp-content/uploads/2021/01/Honourable-Histories.pdf

Morgan, C. (2020). *No Strings Attached – How community-led devolution would transform England's skills system*. Further Education Trust for Leadership. https://fetl.org.uk/publications/no-strings-attached-how-community-led-devolution-would-transform-englands-skills-sector/

Office for Budget Responsibility. (2023). *Economic and fiscal outlook – November 2023*. https://obr.uk/efo/economic-and-fiscal-outlook-november-2023/

Raffe, D. (2015). First count to five: Some principles for the reform of vocational qualifications in England. *Journal of Education and Work*, 28(2), 147–164.

Relly, S. J. (2021). The political rhetoric of parity of esteem. *Oxford Review of Education*, 47(4), 513–528.

Relly, S. J., & Robson, J. (2022). Unpacking the tensions between local and national skills policy: Employers, colleges and local enterprise partnerships as collaborative anchors. *London Review of Education*, 20(1), 46.

Robson, J. (2022). Stigma and spoiled identities: Rescripting career norms for precariously employed academic and research staff. *British Journal of Sociology of Education*, 44(1), 183–198.

Robson, J., Sibieta, L., Khandekar, S., Neagu, M., Robinson, D., & Relly, S. J. (2024). *Comparing policies, participation and inequalities across UK post-16 education and training landscapes*. Nuffield Foundation.

https://skope.ox.ac.uk/wp-content/uploads/2024/02/UK-Nations-post-16-Report-FINAL.pdf

Scottish Funding Council. (2022). *Scottish Further and Higher Education Funding Council framework document.* https://www.sfc.ac.uk/wp-content/uploads/uploadedFiles/SFC_Framework_Document_September_2022.pdf

Shattock, M., & Hunt, S. (2021). *Intersectional relationships within HE: The FE/HE interface in the UK* [Working Paper Series Paper No. 70]. Centre for Global Higher Education. https://www.researchcghe.org/publication/intersectoral-relationships-within-higher-education-the-fehe-interface-in-the-uk/

Tahir, I. (2023). Investment in training and skills. In C. Emmerson, P. Johnson, & B. Zaranko (Eds.), *The IFS green budget: October 2023.* https://ifs.org.uk/publications/investment-training-and-skills (pp. 1–43). IFS.

Teichler, U. (2020). Higher education in economically advanced countries: Changes within recent decades. *Higher Education Governance & Policy*, *1*(1), 1–17.

Trow, M. (2007). Reflections on the transition from elite to mass to universal access: Forms and phases of higher education in modern societies since WWII. In J. J. F. Forest & P. G. Altback (Eds.), *International handbook of higher education* (pp. 243–280). Springer.

# 5

# INEQUALITY AND LIFELONG LEARNING

## Jonathan Michie

*Kellogg College, University of Oxford, UK*

## INTRODUCTION

Britain suffers from inequality of income, wealth, and geography. The inequality in income and wealth increased during the Thatcher years of the 1980s, and still hasn't been reversed, despite 13 years of Labour governments from 1997 to 2010. Since that time, wealth has grown more than income (Bell, 2024), exacerbating the problem for the majority of the population who rely on income rather than wealth for their standard of living.

Inequalities of geography have been getting worse in Britain inexorably since the active regional policies of Labour governments of the 1960s and 1970s were run down over time. The Johnson government was elected in 2019 with the promise of 'levelling up', but the funding made available was largely for relatively short-term projects that had to be bid for, rather than being the sort of long-term regional policies that are required. Consequently, the promise was not fulfilled. Regional inequalities remain as bad as when that government was elected.

Tackling these inequalities requires the full range of measures from central and local governments, and others. An important part of that mix is education, including adult education and lifelong learning. It is thus particularly relevant that the book in which this chapter appears is being published to mark the 125th anniversary of the founding of Ruskin College, which was created to challenge and overcome the class inequality of opportunity for degree-level study at Oxford. Ruskin went on to become the College of and for the trade union movement, thereby contributing to the wider efforts to tackle inequalities of income and power in society. The University of West London is to be congratulated on stepping in to secure the future of Ruskin College, and Graeme Atherton for his leadership on behalf of the University of West London to make this a reality, restoring Ruskin College to be a thought leader in the field.

## INEQUALITY

There is a vast literature on inequalities of income, wealth, geography, and power, and a long history of attempts to tackle such inequalities, of opportunity and outcome, some more successful than others. These are global issues, in every sense. Internationally there are inequalities between nations as well as within them. Indeed, one must be careful with descriptions of global inequalities rising or falling, to be clear what is being referred to. Reference is sometimes made to reductions in global inequality, when what is being referred to is largely the growth of China, during which inequality within most countries actually increased.

The global context is relevant, as one of the causes of inequality within most countries has been the 'capitalism unleashed' era,[1] launched by the Thatcher and Reagan administrations, with the abolition of exchange controls and the promotion of privatisation, deregulation, demutualisation, and financialisation, along with tax cuts for business and the rich. This created a free-market form of

---

[1]'Capitalism Unleashed' was the phrase coined by the late Oxford economist Andrew Glyn to describe the post-1980s era of free market globalisation – see Glyn (2007).

globalisation. As I argued in my book on globalisation (Michie, 2017), this is not the only form of globalisation. To criticise the economic policies of that era is not to criticise globalisation, but rather the particular form of free-market globalisation, which led among other things to the 2007–2008 international financial crisis, and the subsequent global recession of 2009 – the first time since the 1930s that the world's combined output actually fell.

Along with the financial crisis, and the crisis of inequality, we've been hit by the Covid-19 pandemic; the risk of future pandemics persists. And the climate crisis represents an existential threat. Perhaps not surprising, then, that we also face a mental health and wellbeing crisis, particularly amongst the young.

It is sometimes said that the scale of these combined crises is unprecedented. If there was a precedent, it might be the First World War. At that time, the British government of Lloyd George created a Ministry of Reconstruction to advise on how the country, its economy, and society, might recover and be reconstructed following such devastation. Probably the most impactful thing the Ministry did was to create a Committee on Adult Education whose final report in 1919 argued that central to such reconstruction would be adult education, provided to all citizens, as a 'permanent national necessity' (Ministry of Reconstruction Adult Education Committee, 1919).

## LIFELONG LEARNING

As the centenary of that November 1919 Report approached, an 'Adult Education 100 Campaign' was launched to use the centenary to reinforce the 1919 Report's message, that adult education and lifelong learning needed once again to be pursued as a 'permanent national necessity'. One thing the Adult Education 100 campaign did was to create the Centenary Commission on Adult Education, which published its report in November 2019, 100 years on from the 1919 Report.[2]

---

[2]Full disclosure: I am a member of the Adult Education 100 Campaign steering group, and was Co-Secretary (along with Professor John Holford) of the Centenary Commission.

The Centenary Commission on Adult Education (2019) concluded that adult education and lifelong learning are indeed more
important than ever, not just for economic reasons, with the rise
of Artificial Intelligence and all the other new technologies that
will require new skills to be learned, but also to overcome social
inequalities, to create resilient regions, promote social cohesion,
strengthen our democratic institutions and the degree and nature
of civic engagement and participation, and for individual intellectual enrichment and wellbeing.

Thus, benefits from education and learning extend well beyond
just the world of work. Ironically, though, even when we consider
the benefits from education and learning *for* the world of work,
governments all too often take too narrow a view, focussing on
skills for today rather than on capabilities for tomorrow.

Firstly, there is a tendency to think of 'work skills' as meaning
the 'STEM' subjects of science, technology, engineering, and mathematics. But even where this does describe the workplace skills,
there are other capabilities required, such as teamwork, critical
thinking, and imagination. A broader education is needed to provide these capabilities.

Secondly, increasingly we require interdisciplinary and cross-
disciplinary working. As the then President of the British Association for the Advancement of Science put it back in 1994: 'There is
a growing realisation that much of social science relies heavily on
the backing of natural science, and much of natural science only
makes sense in the context of social science' (McLaren, 1994). This
requires study and learning across the whole range of disciplinary
subjects.

And thirdly, some employers pay for their employees to study
with no restrictions on subjects or topics, as an employment benefit. While many in government might regard such study as 'useless'
for the productivity agenda, there is evidence that such support for
employees will enhance employee motivation and loyalty, reducing turnover and thereby actually enhancing productivity after all,
and indeed innovation. There is a strong body of evidence[3] that

---

[3]On which, see, for example, Michie and Sheehan (2003).

'high commitment work systems', involving progressive management practices that encourage participation and engagement, will boost motivation and commitment, leading to enhanced productivity, innovation, and organisational outcomes. The provision of education and training can thus contribute to enhanced productivity, innovation, and organisational outcomes through this route, in addition to any direct outcomes via enhanced skills and capabilities.

## MANIFESTOS FOR LIFELONG LEARNING

The case for bringing about not just a skills revolution, but a wider revolution in adult education and lifelong learning, has been made in two important 'manifestos for lifelong learning' which set out what the Labour government elected in July 2024 could do to begin the process of national renewal, utilising the benefits of adult education and lifelong learning, in much the way that the Ministry of Reconstruction urged, via its Adult Education Committee in 1919.

*Future Priorities for Lifelong Learning, Skills and Tertiary Education* was published by Right2Learn and supported by a range of organisations, including the Universities Association for Lifelong Learning. It argues that lifelong access to education is a central driver of the creation of a more equal, fair, and productive society and should be of the highest priority for any incoming government committed to increasing growth and opportunity (Right2Learn, 2024).

*A Permanent National Necessity – A Manifesto for Lifelong Learning* was drafted by an alliance of the Adult Education 100 Campaign, the National Educational Opportunities Network, and the Universities Association for Lifelong Learning. It highlights the key actions that an incoming government should take, to use adult education and lifelong learning to rebuild the economy and society from the series of crises being faced – from the continued threats of financial crisis and future pandemics, to the urgent and existential climate crisis (Holford & Michie, 2024).

This manifesto makes clear that while adult education and lifelong learning are necessary for economic renewal, they are also necessary for social cohesion, regional resilience, and individual wellbeing, as well as for the health of our democratic system, to enable and encourage informed and engaged participation.

Unfortunately, governments the world over, but perhaps particularly in the UK, tend to take a too short-term and narrow approach to adult education and lifelong learning. Firstly, they over-emphasis the world of work, and downplay and under-emphasise the rest of the world – involving society, communities, individual wellbeing, democracy, and civilisation itself. Secondly, even regarding the world of work, they take a misguided approach, thinking that teaching today's skills is sufficient when – as recognised by the Ministry of Reconstruction's Adult Education Committee in 1919 – what is needed are broader capabilities, creating and developing the *capacity* to learn, rather than simply having currently relevant skills. This links to the second error of government, which is to think that the world of work means 'STEM' subjects (science, technology, engineering, and mathematics), when this falls woefully short in two respects. Firstly, other skills and capabilities are important, such as imagination, critical thinking, teamwork, language, and so on. Secondly, interdisciplinary and cross-disciplinary working is becoming increasingly important, as issues such as climate change require the approaches of different disciplines to be brought together in a process of constructive engagement.[4]

It is to be hoped that these two manifestos for lifelong learning will prove an effective basis for a revolution in adult education and lifelong learning, creating the basis for an era of national renewal.

## CONCLUSION

The 1919 Report advocated the widespread provision of adult education to all, on a lifelong basis, for several reasons – including the importance of all being engaged in discussing the great issues of the day. This is more important than ever, and many such

---

[4]See Hale (2024) for a discussion of how importance the education of 'the population at large' is for tackling the climate crisis (pp. 95–96).

issues come to mind, but none more important than tackling the climate crisis. That challenge does require the active engagement of all citizens, locally and globally. It will depend on what people do at work – not just changing work practices to become more environmentally friendly, but also challenging where necessary the failure of companies and other organisations to be doing what they could and should. It will also depend on what people do at home, in their communities, and in society. This includes their participation in local, city, regional and national government elections and other activities, and their engagement with the whole range of civic activities, involving their local schools and colleges, clubs and societies, health centres and hospitals, and so forth. Hence the need for education to be lifewide as well as lifelong.

The university sector in Britain is facing a financial squeeze, with the undergraduate student fee having been cut in real terms almost every year since it was introduced. Universities do not have spare funds to be able to allocate to areas which might be desirable but for which there is no funding. The government needs to recognise that enabling universities to deliver a revolution in adult education and lifelong learning would help meet the whole range of the government's commitments, from social cohesion to tackling the climate crisis. Such a revolution in adult education and lifelong learning would also save huge sums of money through reductions in ill-health, both physical and mental, reductions in crime, and so forth, quite apart from improving organisational outcomes for companies and other organisations.

At the same time, there are opportunities for universities. Having lifelong learning at the centre of the university's strategy will create short courses and flexible learning opportunities. Many of these may pay for themselves. But even if they have to be subsidised – by the university if they are able, or by the government otherwise – they would be likely to lead to increased recruitment, both onto subsequent courses and in some cases to whole degrees (of which the courses may be constituent modules), thus improving the university's finances over the long term – and the government's finances, as tax revenues rise, and innovation and productivity are enhanced.

So, there are reasons why the current opportunities may be missed. Universities may decide that even though it may make sense over the long term they cannot currently afford to pay for the transition. And government may decide that there are no funds to be made available. To get stuck in this log-jam would be a tragic failure to overcome short-term constraints, thereby missing out on enjoying long-term benefits. We need the government to commit to supporting universities, provided they deliver on adult education and lifelong learning.

## REFERENCES

Bell, T. (2024). *Great Britain? How we get our future back*. The Bodley Head.

Glyn, A. (2007). *Capitalism unleased: Finance, globalisation, and welfare*. Oxford University Press.

Hale, T. (2024). *Long problems: Climate change and the challenge of governing across time*. Princeton University Press.

Holford, J., & Michie, J. (2024). A permanent national necessity – A manifesto for lifelong learning. *International Review of Applied Economics*, 38(4), 386–394.

McLaren, A. (1994, September 4). That's interesting, science is exciting: Anne McLaren, president of the British Association, invites young and old to come to Loughborough and join in the fun. *The Independent*. https://www.independent.co.uk/news/science/that-s-interesting-science-is-exciting-anne-mclaren-president-of-the-british-association-invites-young-and-old-to-come-to-loughborough-and-join-in-the-fun-1446896.html

Michie, J. (2017). *An advanced introduction to globalisation*. Edward Elgar.

Michie, J., & Sheehan, M. (2003). Labour market deregulation, 'flexibility' and innovation. *Cambridge Journal of Economics*, 27(1), 123–143.

Ministry of Reconstruction Adult Education Committee. (1919). *Final report*. Her Majesty's Stationery Office.

Right2Learn. (2024). *Future priorities for lifelong learning, skills and tertiary education.* https://www.educationopportunities.co.uk/news/future-priorities-for-lifelong-learning-skills-and-tertiary-education/

The Centenary Commission on Adult Education. (2019). *A permanent national necessity: Adult education and lifelong learning for 21st century Britain.* University of Nottingham. https://rdmc.nottingham.ac.uk/handle/internal/7890

# 6

# SOCIAL MOBILITY AND THE MINISTRY OF POVERTY

## John Bird

*The Big Issue, UK*

I have a bill going through the House of Lords calling for a Ministry of Poverty Prevention (MOPP). But what would an MOPP do that is not being done by various government departments today? Would it not be duplication, making government even more costly and top heavy?

MOPP would look at the state of government poverty support. What works and what does not work. It would audit all poverty spending. It would evaluate that spending and define how successful it was in achieving its intentions.

It would bring together examples of successful poverty busting and act as a database of successes. By advocating mainstreaming successful poverty busting solutions, we could move away from the rather jaundiced constant creation of costly initiatives. Hundreds of initiatives have been rolled out by various governments since the creation of the Welfare State, only for the mass majority to fall by the wayside.

There would be two principal roles for MOPP. Number one – help people escape poverty. Number two – end the inheritance of poverty. Turn off the tap and stop one generation passing on poverty to the next. All too often, the only thing a child of poor parents inherits is the social problems of their mother and father's poverty. This must end.

MOPP would direct resources towards early years. The few that escape the inheritance of poverty do so through education, skill enhancement, the arts, Trade Union activity; MOPP would fight for a full understanding of these escape routes and put the public purse in pursuit of their growth.

We live in a scattergun era where eight different government departments have a finger in the poverty pie, meaning that virtually all money they spend doesn't prevent or cure poverty, instead merely making those living in poverty slightly more comfortable. Our money gets swallowed up holding the hands of the poor. That cost is gargantuan – a growing burden on our schools, our justice system, and our health service, bogged down by the problems thrown up by poverty. It's the biggest single hit on the treasury, yet the government still maintains its separated and scattered responses to ending it.

When the Big Issue turned 10, I was asked by a reporter what were my plans for the next decade. Without a thought, I told him: 'For the last 10 years, I have been mending broken clocks. And for next 10, 20 years I'm going to try to prevent the clocks from breaking'. In other words, I decided to move my work further upstream, so that people did not fall into poverty and its most extreme consequence, homelessness. I was moving beyond the emergency, where we spend our time, resources, and energy, to concentrate on prevention.

Virtually the whole of Parliament is obsessed with emergency and relief, with prevention and cure hardly getting a look in. A leading politician once chastised me for being too obsessed with the idea of social mobility. It was yet another example of those in power accepting the existence of poverty as necessary, inevitable. You are poor, and therefore forever condemned in the category of poverty. An acceptance of the idea that you were in some ways part of another species to those not in poverty; 'King in his castle, beggar at his gates', enshrining of a class of people as poor.

This is not to deny that there are people in poverty who will find it virtually impossible to get out of it. Who have been so destroyed by poverty that they will always fall into poverty. We must continue to help those people, and improve the support we offer them, but we cannot make holding the poor's hand the only real policy that we practice. Virtually all the resources of the Department of Work and Pensions are spent on helping people survive their poverty.

The politician who looked down his nose at my 'obsession' with social mobility was not getting the irony of his own position – for he was socially mobile. And so were his cabinet, and all those who sat in Parliament, in both houses. All of society's ruling order is socially mobile. Yet because society sees the poor as poor, that is their status, they administer to them as the poor; hence they remain poor.

My own personal story revolted against this awarding of a social position to people in poverty. I recognised in my work that you had to help people in an emergency, even if the emergency lasted the whole of their lives. I realised you had to help people cope, even if it meant that they never escaped their poverty, but you helped them improve the quality of their lives. But if that was all you did – just kept people ticking over, providing for their crisis of poverty – you would always have poverty.

What government policy never did, and continues to not do, is revisit poverty afresh, and to see it as a challenge that can be eradicated over the generations. That if we invest in increasing social mobility, enshrine social mobility into our social constitution, we will reduce those thrust into poverty. Only social mobility can turn the tap off.

I was born to inherited poverty, and I did so with remarkable predictability. There was nothing in the landscape of my early life to lead me down a different path. I was born into slums just after the Second World War; my father was a labourer and my mother a barmaid before becoming a mother. The slum was a house shared with eight other families in London's Notting Hill. The very ugliness, the dirt, and the havoc of broken houses and destroyed spaces reduced one's perspective in life.

The other limitation, possibly the most condemning, was an inability to aspire beyond this wrecked and wretched state. Around the corner from our slum was a school. This school should have been a key to the future, an institution to raise one's aspirations beyond this meanness of the surroundings.

But my parents though took little or no interest in education. They could not see that this institution could lift me somewhere else, if used properly. They had been defeated by poverty and for the rest of their lives lived a poor, low paid life. So when, aged 5, I was taken to the school gate, there was no instructions to excel.

Poverty reduces one's ambitions and limits one's scope. I have called this the 'School Gate Syndrome'. Defeated by the pressures of the everyday and not having education themselves, it meant my parents were unable to see education as a potential escape route out of poverty. I was destined therefore to be a labourer in later life, living a low waged existence; and in fact, this was what happened to all my brothers.

The financial strain of soon having four, then five children led to the collapse of the family and a time in an orphanage. I sank like a stone in this temporary attempt at rescuing us from poverty. On leaving, I sank even further when we regrouped as a family. I did badly at school, started stealing and fighting and getting into trouble, truanting and running away from home.

Eventually, I was arrested and began a decade of wrongdoing interspersed with time in young offenders' institutions. This is where I got separated from my family, and with them the destiny of poverty that had been marked out of me as one of their class. With every arrest, I was taught something. Discipline and sport, order and structure, and eventually in a boys' prison aged 16, how to read and write properly.

A rough but life-changing education taught me valuable skills that helped me in the years that followed. I was allowed to turn my hand to painting and drawing, and when I left, I had an enormous portfolio. It led me to get a place at Chelsea School of Art and an education that upped my ability in the job market. Eventually, the social and creative literacy that I developed in the arts led me into middle-class life.

Social mobility was my saving grace. Social mobility meant I joined the class of people who owned their own homes, who went on foreign holidays, and ate better food. Eventually, I got there.

My own social mobility has driven me to do all I can to help people skill themselves away from a low wage economy. But here you run into what can only be called a 'class problem'. So is the acceptance of the class system, that if you are a member of the working class and you move into a higher wage bracket through social mobility, then you are seen as 'getting above yourself'. Betraying your class.

A few decades ago I sat in 'The Psychiatric Chair', across from Dr Anthony Clare, a legendary television psychiatrist with his own show on Channel 4. He had a very clever method to get you to spill the beans about your life. The first half of the hour-long interview would be warm and encouraging, supportive and reassuring. You fell for Dr Clare's charm. But the second half could be a nightmare. I watched other interviews and saw him bring one guest to tears, and another to pulling his hair out in rage. I wondered what he had in store for me. True to form, after the ad break, the mask came off.

*'John Bird, John Bird', he tinkled in a kindly sounding, softly spoken Irish accent, 'you were working class. Very working class. But John Bird now, now, you are middle class. Admit it. You're middle class John Bird. Admit it'.*

He hit spot on one of the biggest problems that screw the thinking around social mobility. If you escape, you're seen as a class traitor. 'Come on John', he pushed, 'Admit it; you're middle class'.

I could not help but smile, and sat for a few moments to gather my thoughts. Eventually, I responded: 'Of course I'm middle class. I was working class and through prison education I got the chance to get skills and abilities. Yes, I am middle class, and I got out of the working class as soon as I could'.

From there, my interview fizzled out. When the cameras stopped, the usually triumphant Dr Clare slunk away to his dressing room, mumbling to himself. But before he went, he admitted: 'You know, in all the time I have done this, I have never once got an Englishman to admit he is middle class'. With that, he shook my hand and left the studio.

The recent riots show there are many people in this country who are outside of society, left and angry and disappointed and broken by poverty. 'It's Expensive Keeping People Poor' is my new mantra. It drives me on to get people out of poverty through the sensible use of the public purse and to get as many people socially mobile as possible. A MOPP could also be called a Ministry of Social Mobility.

MOPP is my attempt at ending poverty once and for all. My attempt to bring together all the solutions and the problems into one ministry and end the joke of spreading poverty over eight government departments. My attempt to protect the public purse is because the budgets of our health, education, and justice systems are increasingly overwhelmed by poverty, meaning that no government ever gets around to liberating people through early intervention.

But who, I hear you cry, was that leading politician, who once chastised me for my obsession with social mobility? Who urged me to accept that we would always have poverty? It was in fact the then-leader of the Labour Party, Ed Miliband, who told me there would always be a class for the poor.

What hobbles social mobility is an acceptance of the continuation of this destructive class system. I have tried to stand against that, for social mobility is the only possible exit out of poverty – apart from, perhaps, winning the lottery. And winning lottery tickets are few and far between.

## Section 2

## HIGHER EDUCATION – THE DRIVER OF GROWTH AND OPPORTUNITY

# 7

# 'HIGHER EDUCATION EXPANSION AS A GROWTH STRATEGY'

## Steve Coulter

*London School of Economics, UK*

## INTRODUCTION

As well as lagging its peers economically, the UK is highly polarised in terms of inter-personal and regional equality (Bell et al., 2023). The expansion of higher education (HE) over the last 30 years has arguably contributed to this division, sparking criticism over its role in dividing society into graduates and non-graduates (Goodhart, 2020).

This attack ignores the critical role HE plays in providing the skills needed for the high-growth sectors of our economy. These are based on services and advanced manufacturing industries that are heavy recruiters of graduates, now and even more so in the future (Coulter et al., 2022b). Such critiques nevertheless point to the need to gear the next phase of HE expansion to delivering more extensive growth, achieving a better blending of academic and practical skills and knowledge, and putting the sector onto a more sustainable footing through changes to how degrees are delivered.

This chapter reiterates the economic value of HE, examines the nature of the future skills challenge for the economy and HE providers themselves posed by rapidly advancing technologies, and sets out a course of action for policymakers.

## HUMAN CAPITAL AND THE DRIVERS OF GROWTH

The UK's spatial disparities are stark and politically salient, attracting increasing attention from policymakers (Department for Levelling Up & Housing & Community, 2022). But the previous government's levelling up agenda gained little traction because of a lack of clear focus. A particular blind spot was the importance of skills and their role in delivering more extensive growth.

One thing we know is that, while human capital is only one of the six drivers of local growth listed in the Levelling Up White Paper, it is the skills of local people that largely explain the relative economic performance of place. Hence, there is no route to levelling up, or economic growth more broadly, that doesn't go through a radical skills agenda.

Equally, however, we also know that people will tend to move to where opportunity is – and the more highly skilled they are, the more mobile. Expanding skills provision in the abstract therefore won't help the areas currently struggling if more educated people simply move away for better opportunities (Stansbury et al., 2023). So how do we tackle spatial economic disparities through a high skills agenda?

The answer suggested here is that higher education institutions (HEIs) can help to square the circle on local growth as they can address both the supply and demand side of the skills equation: they deliver graduates, produce economically valuable research, and act as a focal point for employers, entrepreneurs, and researchers.

In short, they are anchor institutions, generating human capital and knowhow, and coordinating this with local opportunity through knowledge spill-overs (Moretti, 2013). They are therefore the key to levelling up locally and enabling the UK to match the world's leading innovation economies.

Yet, despite mounting economic problems of low growth and productivity, inadequate skills, and stubborn regional disparities, the Johnson, Truss, and Sunak Conservative governments were sceptical of the value of HE, with the freeze on tuition fees since 2016 implying a wish to squeeze student numbers. If continued, this neglect risks leaving the UK on the starting blocks in the global race to the top on skills and the creation of high productivity industries, which is the only way to sustain our public services and raise the standard of living.

The Labour government has so far kept its powder dry on HE, possibly over concerns about affordability under the current funding regime while it develops an alternative. But as well as the economic arguments it should not ignore the strong social justice case for HE expansion, given its role in levelling up the regions and increasing social mobility.

## ECONOMIC CONTEXT: WHY EARLIER HE EXPANSION WAS IMPORTANT, AND WHY WE NEED TO GO FURTHER AND WIDER

Graduate skills are pivotal to the success of the professional services industries which constitute our main comparative advantage, now and in the likely future. The expansion of HE over the last 40 years has tracked the UK economy's shift from manufacturing to services.

Vertically integrated manufacturing industries comprised the leading sectors of the UK economy up until the late 1970s, a structure requiring a relatively small number (less than 10% of school leavers) of HE graduates destined mainly for the upper echelons of business or the civil service. But city deregulation and the steep decline of manufacturing under Margaret Thatcher boosted employment in services industries, which sharply raised demand for graduates from the 1980s and 1990s.

The response of John Major's government was to grant university status to polytechnics and begin the long expansion of student numbers. New Labour took this further with its aspiration for a 50% participation rate and laid the foundations for a mass market in HE to raise enrolments and increase choice.

The sector must continue to grow and evolve as the economy shifts again toward knowledge-intensive industries. In a paper in

2022 for the Tony Blair Institute, we laid out the economic and skills case for expanding HE participation – defined as Level 4 and above qualifications, so not just degrees (Coulter et al., 2022b). Our argument was based on two sets of evidence.

First, was a growth-accounting analysis of our recent economic performance, which showed that the economy has become progressively more reliant on human capital over the last 25 years. The bulk of growth in human capital has been supplied by improvements to education, which accounted for almost all the improvements to human capital since the financial crisis, and a big chunk of overall growth.

We further estimated that raising participation in HE from the current 53% of school leavers to around 70% by 2040 would boost the size of the UK economy by almost 5% over the next generation compared to allowing educational attainment to stagnate.

The second was an analysis of official evidence of changing demand for different skills levels in the labour. The government-commissioned Employer Skills Surveys consistently shows existing skills shortages and skills gaps in sectors associated with high-skilled workers, a category typically associated with graduate level qualifications.

Furthermore, forecasts for the Working Futures analysis, based on Labour Force survey data, suggest that these shortages will get even worse in the future (Wilson et al., 2020). Meanwhile, Office for National Statistics's (2019) analysis of the vulnerability of jobs to automation according to how skilled they are clearly showed that jobs requiring HE and degrees are far less vulnerable to replacement by machines than jobs requiring lower levels of education.

## SKILLS, HE, AND THE IMPORTANCE OF PLACE

Nevertheless, while this demonstrates the importance of HE expansion in the aggregate, more attention is needed to the spatial distribution of both graduates and graduate labour markets. Skills policy in general (not just HE) has tended to focus on increasing the quantity of skills. More skills are a necessary but not sufficient condition for improving economic performance.

Policy also needs to address the local demand for skills as well as its supply (Keep, 2022).

Ignoring this has meant that the structure of HE that has evolved may have helped create a set of problems that will need tackling in the next phase of expansion.

First, was a lopsided economy. Increases in graduate numbers enabled the expansion of high productivity professional services firms which are mainly concentrated in London and the Southeast of England, as well as a few thriving ex-industrial cities like Manchester and Sheffield. The current distribution of graduates and non-graduates has therefore helped to sustain a fracture between successful, innovative urban and metropolitan areas, and much less developed exurban and ex-industrial cities. Further, HE expansion needs to happen in a way which reduces, rather than fuels, these divides (McNeil & Soskice, 2022).

Second is its inflexible structure. There is a rigidly academic focus to a lot of HE offerings, particularly in Russell Group universities, with an overly sharp distinction between academic and more vocational courses. The system also revolves too much around the delivery of one-off, three-year degrees begun at 18, delivered far from home at extra cost to the student, and with too little input from employers.

This will become increasingly anomalous in a reformed and expanded HE system recruiting more students from non-traditional academic backgrounds in HE cold spots, as well as reaching people already in the labour market looking to retrain.

## GRADUATE EDUCATION AND NEW TECHNOLOGY

Tackling these legacy problems is vital. But an equally important consideration is how technology will radically reshape the economy and labour market of the future, something the next phase of HE expansion must respond to. While raising demand generally for workers with graduate skills, the technological revolution poses specific challenges as well as possibilities for HE.

First, as an innovation follower rather than leader, the diffusion of new knowledge inside UK firms and across industries is critically important and heightens demand for employees with graduate skills (Blundell et al., 2022). However, the UK is weak in the intermediate skills (mid-level supervisory and applied-technical roles) that are particularly important for knowledge diffusion.

This suggests that, as well as increasing the supply of workers with the highest skills, graduate education might also become necessary in segments of the labour market currently dependant on intermediate skills to maximise firms' ability to absorb new technologies (Toner, 2011). HE can also play a role in knowledge diffusion between firms through executive and ongoing education (networking, sharing best practice, the creation of communities of practice, etc.).

Second, in a development that has been magnified by Covid-19 and the move towards flexible working, large firms are becoming less top-down and hierarchical. Work is increasingly organised at team level rather than directed from above by senior managers.

These developments have two further implications.

First, thriving in this work environment requires workers with very good high-order cognitive and non-cognitive skills (Coulter et al., 2022a). HEIs, along with schools, need to focus on instilling these alongside subject-specific knowledge, which will require changes to where and how many HE qualifications are taught.

A second effect is that there may be less need for these teams to be located in the same place, which has implications for the geographical distribution of graduate jobs. Large service firms originally congregated in London and a few other big cities to enjoy the network effects from co-location. But organisational changes and better information and communications technology (ICT) alter this calculation and may allow for thriving graduate job markets to be created in 'left behind' areas with lower living costs.

This would meet the aspirations of many graduates who would like to stay in and contribute to the areas where they have family ties (getting a 'London job' – in Burnley). But there is also a warning here: the UK potentially risks losing mobile white collar jobs to countries with lower costs and comparable skills unless we improve the skills of our own workers through more HE (Palmou et al., 2021).

In short, HE needs to expand and adapt to a changing labour market and economy driven by technology. But this can, and should, be done in a way that spreads and creates wealth and opportunity in 'left behind' areas of the country. Achieving this will not only be fairer and more politically sustainable, it will also make us more prosperous.

## WHAT IS TO BE DONE?

As already conceded, there are some problems and rigidities in the UK's HE system that need to be tackled. However, unlike schools, where the department for education (DfE) and Ofsted are powerful actors, government has fewer levers to influence HEIs. Where these levers exist, policymakers should maximise the use of the nudges available to influence how the sector grows and operates. New institutions may also need to be created.

The most important requirement is that HE expansion should not be conceived only at the macro level but as part of an explicit, place-based mission to spread growth and level up. Every town or city with a population over 80,000 people should have its own university. This means addressing the numerous HE 'cold spots' in areas like southwest England.

Where possible, new universities should be built by upgrading existing institutions with established roots in the community, especially Further Education (FE) colleges and technical institutes. The best of these could be merged with local universities as part of a 'hub and spoke' system. To enable institutions to exploit economies of scale in teaching, core instruction should be carried out in research-intensive inner-city hubs, allowing more specialisation in FE college spokes in surrounding towns, based on their existing strengths and local needs.

The system should also be much more diverse. More alternatives should be offered besides the traditional three-year bachelor's degree taught in a conventional university. This would match the diversity in other excellent HE systems, such as the Irish, US, and South Koreans' and mesh better with the needs of disadvantaged students and communities. Offerings available to students should include courses in two-year community colleges, technical universities (based on India's prestigious Institutes of Technology), and business and professional schools. Existing government policies on lifelong and modular learning should be developed and extended to support this (Soskice & McNeil, 2024).

A more favourable regulatory environment should be designed for new entrants into the HE provider market, thereby encouraging more diverse delivery models. New ventures, like the Dyson Institute and London Interdisciplinary School, have made it across the line but the threshold is far too high and may be stifling further innovations.

HEIs should build better links with employers. Many HEIs, particularly newer institutions like Coventry and London South Bank Universities already do this to great effect. But other HEIs, particularly Russell Group, should go much further. Ideally, most of the further expansion in graduate numbers should be in courses designed and delivered with and through employers.

Where appropriate, course content should be devised in conjunction with Local Skills Improvement Plans, or equivalent agencies, and perhaps overseen by regional government. Measures should also be taken to rapidly expand the number of degree apprenticeships available as these automatically bring employers and HEIs into close consultation with each other.

Local HEIs could also be given leading roles in local/regional enterprise partnerships – whether in the form of local enterprise partnerships (LEPs) or any future incarnations of such structures. This would bind HEIs more firmly into regional growth strategies and hold them more accountable for this. A good model for this is Massachusetts Institute of Technology (MIT), which has extremely good links with employers and coordinates local growth strategies in Massachusetts.

Finally, with tuition fees having been frozen and public money tight, more attention should be given to how to make degrees affordable for students from non-traditional backgrounds. A combination of more students living at home and the expansion of degree apprenticeships will help here.

But the new government should also commit to implementing the Lifelong Loan Entitlement (LLE) but resolve the major outstanding demand and supply-side issues around implementation. If executed properly, the LLE would extend student finance to a wider range of courses in such a way as to disrupt the current market and generate innovations away from the standardised three-year full-time undergraduate degree.

Ultimately, in a more competitive, knowledge-driven world, expanding HE is a necessity not a choice.

## REFERENCES

Bell, T., Clark, T., Fry, E., Kelly, G., & Thwaites, G. (2023). *Ending stagnation. A new economic strategy for Britain*. Resolution Foundation. https://economy2030.resolutionfoundation.org/reports/ending-stagnation/

Blundell, R., Green, D., & Jin, W. (2022). The UK as a technological follower: HE expansion and the college wage premium. *Review of Economic Studies, 89*(1), 142–180.

Coulter, S., Iosad, A., & Scales, J. (2022a). *Ending the big squeeze on skills: How to futureproof education in England*. Tony Blair Institute for Global Change. https://institute.global/insights/public-services/ending-big-squeeze-skills-how-futureproof-education-england

Coulter, S., Mulheirn, I., Scales, J., & Tsoukalis, C. (2022b). *We don't need no education? The case for expanding higher education*. Tony Blair Institute for Global Change. https://institute.global/insights/economic-prosperity/we-dont-need-no-education-case-expanding-higher-education

Department for Levelling Up, Housing and Community. (2022). *Levelling up the United Kingdom*. https://www.gov.uk/government/publications/levelling-up-the-united-kingdom

Goodhart, D. (2020). *Head hand heart: The struggle for dignity and status in the 21st century*. Penguin.

Keep, E. (2022). *What is the role of skills and the skills system in promoting productivity growth in areas of the country that are poorer performing economically?* Skills and Productivity Board. https://www.gov.uk/government/publications/how-can-skills-promote-productivity-in-poorer-performing-areas

McNeil, A., & Soskice, D. (2022). *Relational inequality in a (deeply) educationally polarised society: Feasible strategies in the longer term.* Institute for Fiscal Studies Deaton Review. https://ifs.org.uk/inequality/relational-inequality/

Moretti, E. (2013). *The new geography of jobs.* Mariner Books.

Office for National Statistics. (2019). *Occupations and the risk of automation.* https://www.ons.gov.uk/releases/occupationsandtheriskof automation

Palmou, C., Browne, J., Kakkad, J., & Britto, D. (2021). *Anywhere jobs and the future of work.* VoxEU, Centre for Economic Policy Research. https://cepr.org/voxeu/columns/anywhere-jobs-and-future-work

Soskice, D., & McNeil, A. (2024). Universities. In A. Bhattacharya & N. Lee (Eds.), *Labour economics: Thinking through labour's economic agenda* (pp. 32–36). Social Market Foundation. https://www.smf.co.uk/publications/labour-economic-agenda-essays/

Stansbury, A., Turner, D., & Balls, E. (2023). *Tackling the UK's regional economic inequality: Binding constraints and avenues for policy intervention* [M-RCBG Associate Working Paper Series No. 198]. Harvard Kennedy School. https://www.hks.harvard.edu/sites/default/files/centers/mrcbg/files/198_AWP_final.pdf

Toner, P. (2011). *Workforce skills and innovation: An overview of major themes in the literature* [OECD Education Working Papers No. 55]. Organisation for Economic Co-operation and Development. https://www.oecd-ilibrary.org/education/workforce-skills-and-innovation_5kgk6hpnhxzq-en

Wilson, R., Barnes, S. May-Gillings, M., Patel, S., & Bui, H. (2020). *Working futures 2017–2027: Long-run labour market and skills projections for the UK.* Department for Education. https://assets.publishing.service.gov.uk/media/5e39e13ae5274a08e61863b2/Working_Futures_Main_Report.pdf

# 8

# SHAPING HIGHER EDUCATION: DRIVING ECONOMIC PROSPERITY AND SUSTAINABILITY THROUGH ENGINEERING AND TECHNOLOGY

Hilary Leevers

*EngineeringUK, UK*

A demand driven education system is nice in principle, but how can we ensure that essential workforce needs are met? In this Chapter, I make the case that the government and Higher Education Institutions (HEIs) themselves have a responsibility to more actively shape uptake across courses to ensure that the nation has the graduates needed to address areas of great societal importance. The imperative to grow graduate numbers in engineering and technology is presented as a test case, inequalities in opportunity that have limited access are described, and actions are offered to improve the situation.

## A TEST CASE OF SOCIETAL IMPORTANCE

The approach of recent governments to workforce planning has had little connection to subject numbers across university courses.

The government will need to intervene if it is to ensure the education and training of critical workforces and it has already recognised the need to develop workforce and training plans in shortage sectors, such as engineering, technology and construction.

Here we look at the important example of uptake of engineering and technology courses. Uptake of these subjects simply cannot be left to the mercy of student choice and opportunity. Graduates in these areas are vital across areas of national need including combating and adapting to climate change, providing digital and energy security, delivering core infrastructure, and underpinning economic growth. Engineers and technologists design, create, improve and deliver solutions for societal challenges and opportunities, from decarbonising the energy system and enhancing digital connectivity to the adoption of AI and automation. Engineering is estimated to generate up to £646bn gross value added to the UK's economy annually, 32% of the country's economic output (Royal Academy of Engineering, 2023).

We know that businesses are already struggling to fill vacancies (Institute of Engineering and Technology, 2022). Research by Lightcast commissioned by EngineeringUK (2023b), identified over 6 million roles in engineering and technology, accounting for 19% of the UK workforce but a much higher 25% of job adverts. The further education system is set up to respond to workforce needs, but over 40% of those advertised roles asked for degree level qualifications.

The high pay seen in engineering and technology likely relates, at least in part, to unmet demand (alongside high skills). Median advertised salaries in the engineering footprint are 30% higher than average (£38,600 v £30,000; EngineeringUK, 2023b). Analyses of HESA data also revealed higher pay for engineers, with the most common salary 15 months after qualifying reported as between £25,000 to £30,000 compared to £20,000 to £25,000 for other areas (EngineeringUK, 2024a). Indeed, engineers out-numbered non-engineers in all higher salary ranges.

We should therefore be seriously worried to learn that we are not only already struggling with workforce shortages, but that the number of engineering and technology roles is forecast to grow in all UK regions faster than other occupational areas up until

2030 (EngineeringUK, 2023b). Much of this growth relates to the green economy, and last year, the Climate Change Committee (2023) estimated that up to 725,000 new roles would be needed for the transition to net zero. Other more specific estimates include 100,000 for on and offshore wind and 50,000 for heat pumps (EngineeringUK, 2024b). Filling these roles cannot be left to chance.

The workforce also lacks diversity with women particularly underrepresented, making up just 15.7% of the engineering and technology workforce, compared with 56% in the rest of the workforce. People from other demographic groups are also underrepresented in engineering and technology, but to a lesser extent: 12% are from UK minority ethnic groups compared with 16% in other occupations, and similar comparisons are 14% vs 18% for disabled people and 24% vs 26% for people from poorer socioeconomic backgrounds (EngineeringUK, 2024c).

These inequalities mean that many groups have limited access to impactful and rewarding career opportunities; a lack of diversity of thought and background will also limit the quality and relevance of engineering and technology solutions, at a time when increasing innovation and productivity is more critical than ever. This sits alongside the general business case that a diverse workforce leads to better financial outcomes. Companies with the greatest gender, ethnic and cultural diversity are now more likely than ever to outperform less diverse peers on profitability (Hunt et al., 2023).

Because of the scale of underrepresentation in engineering and technology, improving diversity and inclusion creates an opportunity. A quick calculation shows that if underrepresented groups were present in similar proportions as in the overall workforce, we'd have around 2 million more people working to solve and deliver against our engineering and technological challenges. This must surely give the impetus to invest in the actions needed.

## THE MISMATCH BETWEEN STUDENT PROFILE AND WORKFORCE NEEDS

If a demand-led system was working, we should see large intakes of engineering and technology students. Unfortunately, in 2020/21 only 6.1% of undergraduate entrants in the UK were studying engineering and technology (EngineeringUK, 2023a) – please recall that these areas account for a quarter of job adverts in the UK, 40% of which ask for degrees (EngineeringUK, 2023b). Furthermore, just 18.5% of engineering and technology undergraduate entrants were women, compared to 56.5% across all subjects (EngineeringUK, 2023a). Representation was higher on engineering and technology postgraduate courses (26-28% were women) but still much lower than across all subjects. Just 10.5% of engineering and technology first degree entrants had a known disability, compared to 15.1% for all subjects. Engineering and technology students were also less likely to come from areas with low HEI participation rates – only 11.2% of undergraduate entrants were from the areas with the lowest participation (quintile 1) compared to 13.5% for other subjects and 32.4% from the highest participation areas (quintile 5). Interestingly, engineering and technology degrees had a higher proportion of UK minority ethnic entrants than other subjects, particularly Asian students.

It is indisputable then, that there is a significant mismatch between the nation's need for more and more diverse engineering and technology graduates and the numbers and diversity of graduates coming through.

## WHY THE MARKET ISN'T WORKING AND WHAT CAN BE DONE

There are likely a myriad of factors that disconnect demand from supply when it comes to graduate numbers. Here I discuss three – entry requirements; careers information and student choice; and the capacity of HEIs - as well as considering the part that degree apprenticeships play. These issues are related to engineering and technology, as an area of grave workforce need, but these factors may play out in similar ways for different subjects.

### Entry Criteria

The low admission of women onto engineering and technology degrees is unsurprising given that many HEIs ask for maths and physics A levels. Only 22% of the 32,000 undergraduate students in 2020/21 who had studied maths and physics A levels were women, in contrast, 40% of the 88,000 students who took maths A level were women (EngineeringUK, 2023d).

While physics is a valuable subject, requiring it can have detrimental impacts on the opportunity for A level students to progress into HEIs, particularly affecting certain demographic groups and driven, in part, by teacher shortages. Shockingly, up to 400 secondary schools lack even one physics teacher, affecting teaching quality and the likelihood of students taking physics post-16, with 70% of A level physics students coming from just 30% of schools (Institute of Physics, 2023). There are at least 300 schools, typically in deprived areas, that progress no students to A level physics.

HEIs must be aware of the impact of requiring physics for entry to engineering and technology. A more equitable pathway opens up courses to a wider range of students by providing additional support, perhaps including Foundation courses and summer schools, for those that had not taken and particularly those that had not had the opportunity to take, physics post-16. Some new HEIs – such as the New Model Institute for Technology and Engineering and The Engineering and Design Initiative in London – have taken an innovative approach to recruitment, weighting students' motivation and potential to succeed, rather than focussing on entry criteria.

An additional insight from the 2021 HESA data is that engineering and technology graduates were more likely to obtain first class honours– 44.8% as compared to 35.0% across all subjects (EngineeringUK, 2023a). This suggests that there are many more students who would perform well in these subjects but are either not applying or being admitted. Furthermore, 48.6% of women graduating in engineering and technology in 2021 did so with first class honours, higher than the 41.9% of men who did so, and the 35.1% of women who achieved firsts across all subjects. This supports the argument for HEIs to invest more in their efforts to recruit more students and particularly female students onto engineering and technology courses.

## Careers Understanding

Young people who have acquired a good understanding of careers are more likely to aspire to jobs in areas of labour market need and buck gender stereotypes, indeed, girls with the highest careers scores are twice as likely to want to become engineers (Careers & Enterprise Company, 2024). This makes a powerful case for the government to invest more into the careers system as a soft touch intervention to increase young people's progression into areas of labour market need.

HEIs should also continue to invest in their outreach and widening participation efforts. Government could review their regulatory regimes, such as Access and Participation Plans and performance metrics, as useful tools to enhance diversity. HEIs will need to consider the interactions between subjects and demographic groups, for example, recognising that while more women go to university overall, there are subjects where they are seriously underrepresented and extra efforts should be made.

## Course Capacity

It's important to understand whether HEIs have the appetite and capability to expand places in engineering and technology, but it is hard to get information on this; not least because they are reluctant to share commercially sensitive information about course attractiveness and delivery costs. Also, the situation varies across specific engineering and technology disciplines within as well as across HEIs. Some HEIs have said that they are at capacity and would need to make significant investment and take on considerable risk to expand facilities, equipment and teaching resource, and in some cases, accommodation.

HEIs will be discouraged by the costliness of engineering courses, which home-domiciled student fees cannot cover, even with the small funding boost via the strategic priorities grant and some top-up funding. Given the intense financial pressures most HEIs are under, it is realistic to acknowledge that many of those that can, will be prioritising the higher fee income that comes with overseas students. It's therefore unsurprising that 21% of engineering and technology undergraduates in 2021 came from overseas (6% from the European Union) compared to 11% (6% EU) over all subjects (EngineeringUK, 2023a).

As the new government develops workforce and training plans it needs to better understand the capacity and limits of the current system and be prepared to intervene. Most obviously and most urgently the government must surely increase the level of funding for high cost strategically important subjects.

## Degree Apprenticeships

Degree apprenticeships provide a powerful mechanism for HEIs to respond to employer needs. These are a welcome and growing route, although evidence suggests that many businesses are using them for current employees, which may be useful for upskilling and retention, but doesn't really increase workforce numbers or diversity (EngineeringUK, 2023c). Investing in current employees may limit capacity for entry-level apprentices who would genuinely add to workforce numbers. There are also diversity concerns. Perhaps counter-intuitively, higher and degree apprenticeships (across all sectors) are less common among socio-economically disadvantaged individuals than a university degree (Cavaglia et al., 2022).

## A CALL TO ACTION

HEIs have a crucial role to play in delivering the workforce needed by our society, economy and the environment. It must surely follow that if workforce needs are not being met, as is clearly the case, things need to change. As the government determines the nation's future workforce needs, it must be prepared to set targets for different educational and training pathways, and shape educational choices and spending to meet them, looking across higher education, vocational and technical routes. We must better understand the costs and capacity of higher education in critical areas, and the extent to which students are not applying to those courses or are being turned away. Spending is tight, but fuller funding of strategically important subjects is a must.

Setting limits on courses with low workforce need, in order to boost capacity elsewhere, would be a controversial path. But there is an easier option, greater government investment in careers provision will help more students follow labour market need. HEIs should, and should be incentivised to, make bolder efforts on widening participation, considering need within individual subject areas, not just across the cohort. They could learn more from businesses that have transformed their intake, including through flexibility in their entry requirements, looking for applicants' potential and compensating for the inequity of opportunity applicants may have experienced.

As HEIs look at their values and priorities, many are strengthening their commitments to improve environmental outcomes including through updating course content. But there is no greater opportunity than to prioritise recruiting more and more diverse students onto engineering and technology courses, to create the workforce essential to improving environmental sustainability and adapting to and mitigating climate change.

## REFERENCES

Careers & Enterprise Company. (2024). *Careers education 2022/23: Now & next.* https://www.careersandenterprise.co.uk/our-evidence/ evidence-and-reports/careers-education-2022-23-now-next/

Cavaglia, C., Ventura, G., & McNally, S. (2022). *The recent evolution of apprenticeships: Apprenticeships pathways and participation since 2015.* Sutton Trust. https://www.suttontrust.com/our-research/ the-recent-evolution-of-apprenticeships/

Climate Change Committee. (2023). *2023 progress report to parliament.* https://www.theccc.org.uk/publication/2023-progress-report-to-parliament/

EngineeringUK. (2023a) *Engineering in higher education.* http:// www.engineeringuk.com/research-and-insights/our-research-reports/ engineering-in-higher-education-report/

EngineeringUK. (2023b). *Engineering skills needs – Now and into the future.* www.engineeringuk.com/futureskills

EngineeringUK. (2023c). *From A levels to engineering: exploring the gender gap in higher education*. http://www.engineeringuk.com/research-and-insights/our-research-reports/from-a-levels-to-engineering-exploring-the-gender-gap-in-higher-education/

EngineeringUK. (2023d). *Fit for the future: Growing and sustaining engineering and technology apprenticeships for young people*. http://www.engineeringuk.com/fitforthefuture

EngineeringUK. (2024a). *Graduate outcomes – Engineering and technology*. https://www.engineeringuk.com/graduateoutcomes

EngineeringUK. (2024b). *Net zero workforce*. https://www.engineeringuk.com/research-and-insights/our-research-reports/net-zero-workforce/

Hunt, V., Dixon-Fyle, S., Huber, C., Martínez Márquez, M. M., Prince, S., & Thomas, A. (2023). *Diversity matters even more: The case for holistic impact*. McKinsey & Company. https://www.mckinsey.com/featuredinsights/diversity-and-inclusion/diversity-matters-even-more-the-case-for-holistic-impact

Institute of Engineering and Technology. (2022). *Engineering kids' futures*. www.theiet.org/engineeringkidsfutures

Institute of Physics. (2023). *Written evidence for Education for 11–16 Year Olds Committee inquiry*. House of Lords. https://committees.parliament.uk/work/7268/education-for-1116-year-olds/publications/written-evidence/?SearchTerm=institute+of+physics&DateFrom=&DateTo=&SessionId=

Royal Academy of Engineering. (2023). *Engineering, economy and place*. www.raeng.org.uk/eep

# 9

# EQUAL OPPORTUNITIES, EQUAL OUTCOMES AND HIGHER EDUCATION: CHOICE OR CIRCUMSTANCE?

Peter John

*University of West London and Ruskin College Oxford, UK*

The desire for greater equality has been in Labour's DNA since its inception. However, despite its longevity and many connotations, the ways of achieving it have been hotly contested. A key aspect has been equality of opportunity which has remained relatively uncontroversial especially when compared to the left's *leitmotif* of greater distribution of wealth and power. Put simply, it is based on the idea that individuals should have a fair and equal chance to succeed and not suffer disadvantage or discrimination. Equality of outcome, on the other hand, is about having greater fairness and parity in terms of where people end up as much as where they begin (Phillips, 2004). And it is in higher education (HE) where this fairness principle should predominate.

In recent years, despite the achievements of widening access and expanding enrolments in HE (Altbach, 2009; Scott, 2017;

Walsh, 2010), greater social equity remains problematic (Dorling, 2023; Savage, 2015; Todd, 2022). This is mainly due to the fact, that HE imports the inequalities that affect society at large and embeds them even deeper (Reeves & Friedman, 2024). One significant factor relates to the persistence of social and cultural endowments which continue to be obstacles to fair outcomes and occupational success (Savage, 2015; Todd, 2022). In this chapter, I will show that to overcome these obstacles, 'opportunity hoarding' (Tilly, 1999, p. 151) and other social inhibitors will have to be recognised and acted upon. If not, as Drayton et al. (2023) and Cribb et al. (2023) argue, today's educational inequality will be tomorrow's income inequality.

## EQUALITY OF OPPORTUNITY AND EQUALITY OF OUTCOME

Those who advocate for the primacy of equal opportunities claim that distributive justice does not need to entail equality of outcome but only that individuals should have as fair an opportunity as possible to achieve a said outcome. This then translates into personal responsibility or choice which is often connected to the effort expended (Littler, 2018; Wooldridge, 2021; Young, 1958). In this more meritocratic conception, social justice can be achieved simply by the creation of the so-called 'level playing field' with less attention paid to circumstance or differing initial conditions.

There is no doubt that individual difference does play a significant role in educational and social development. However, as Phillips (2004, p. 14) emphasises we should be cautious about explaining away inequality of outcome in that process by reference to the complexities of singular or group choices at the opportunity stage (Pignataro, 2012; Roemer, 2002; Shane & Heckhausen, 2016). As Phillips (2004, p. 15) further points out, too often critics of outcomes-based equality 'conjure up a large cast of contrasting individuals around which to build their stories of equality, responsibility or choice'. This creates a discourse of difference that tends to limit the effect of initial conditions, accidents of birth or location, unequal wealth distribution and the long-term impact of intergenerational transmission. These persistent endowments, she argues, affect not only opportunity but also outcomes (Phillips, 2004, p. 17).

## OPPORTUNITY HOARDING: DEFINITION AND IMPACT

These endowments are often moulded by what has become known as 'opportunity hoarding' (Friedman & Macmillan, 2017; Tilly, 1999). This is based on the Weberian (1922, p. 638) idea of social closure when groups and members of groups bind together to hold and retain access to a particular resource: one that is limited, valuable and renewable (Tilly, 1999, pp. 151–152). Tilly goes on to argue that such a process, by its very nature, creates and sustains inequality by transplanting existing social relations across generations and is one of the main mechanisms that produces unequal outcomes and skewed opportunities (Tilly, 2000, p.784). This gaining of exclusive access to a scarce resource is especially prevalent among parents who want to perpetuate their privilege and as John Rawls (1971) points out, this can limit the choices of others by reducing their chances of securing a fair share of those opportunities. This unfairness entrenches inequality, distorts the functioning of democracy and derails social mobility.

Too often this 'maintained inequality' (Hamilton et al., 2018, p. 112) allows advantaged social groups to shape various educational contexts around their familial needs and personal or class interests. Lareau (2003) suggests that this opportunity hoarding creates a further competitive edge when social and cultural capital come into play (Bourdieu & Passeron, 1977). This not only has strong socio-economic and cultural roots but also deep geographical connections (Desmond & Turley, 2009). For instance, as Friedman and Macmillan (2017) point out, London is where this hoarding is at its fiercest where access to HE is cut off to the large number of internal migrants, and those indigenous to the capital. When added together this adds up to considerable competitive advantage for certain advantaged groups, limits the room at the top and allows those who hoard to cling on to their socio-economic status (Reeves & Friedman, 2024).

As Reeve (2017) highlights in *Dream Hoarders*, opportunity hoarding also creates a glass floor for each affluent child by virtue of his or her wealth and familial status which then becomes a glass ceiling for another. Throughout the book, Reeve explores the creation and perpetuation of opportunity hoarding, and what should be done to limit it. He argues that in many ways, changes in policy and social conscience may be the only ways to address the persistent problem. Research also indicates that people's well-being is closely connected to this hoarding, as is their socio-economic position and educational attainment (Li & Painter, 2016). Others further show that income and educational inequality impact health differences, erode civic engagement and shape political preferences across the life course (McNeil et al., 2023; Wilkinson & Pickett, 2009, 2018). In effect it eats away at the idea of the common good and as Womersley (2024) notes in a review of Dorling's new book on 'Inequality and Britain's Next Generation', Britain has tolerated inaction about inequality for so long that a shared responsibility for one another's well-being has eroded.

## HE: OPPORTUNITY AND DISPARITY

Universities, we are led to believe, can challenge this hoarding and disparity through the fairness principle, where competition for entry is even handed and unfettered. The system is therefore supposed to benefit the worst-off members of society as well as others through what John Rawls (1971) called 'the difference principle'. Furthermore, such a system should generate high levels of social mobility as entrance into higher-level occupations automatically follows. Put simply, individual talent and effort, rather than ascriptive traits or 'accidents of birth' (Mill, 1859; Rawls, 1971) should determine an individual's place in the educational, social and occupational hierarchy. However, this is not the case, because too often variables such as place of birth, aspiration, wealth, ethnicity, school context, family involvement, social background all 'structure and constrain participation in higher education' (Liu, 2011). As a result, what is often viewed as a neutral zone has become a contested area (Brennan & Naidoo, 2008).

This contestation has been most noticeable during the expansion of HE, which despite the efforts of the champions of widening participation, fairer access and improved equity of outcomes remains elusive. Much of this is tied to the status and ranking systems of the institutions combined with their inherent differentiated wealth and privilege. Consequentially, despite all being designated as universities, to paraphrase Orwell, 'some are more equal than others' and we have what Bourdieu and Wacquant (1992, p. 106, cited in Naidoo, 2004) call 'resemblance within a difference'. Much of this is due to the histories of the civic universities and their grip on the rankings (often defined by their research records if not their teaching quality). However, access is only part of the story.

Outreach programmes and incentivising entry combined with improved careers guidance and mentoring alongside organisations such as the National Educational Opportunities Network have helped to alleviate some of the unequal treatment. Nevertheless, students from the higher income groups still have a firm grasp on university entry. Recent research also shows that the main civic universities including Oxford and Cambridge continue to recruit between 75% and 80% of their graduates from either the elite or established middle classes (Friedman & Laurison, 2019; Savage, 2015). Alongside these social advantages, more privileged entrants have greater access to extra tutoring, insider knowledge, school connections, economic resource, and other trappings. This accrual of advantage or opportunity hoarding translates into better school and college examination results, which in turn influences access and entry points, and a better chance of admission and graduation. As Lee Elliot Major, professor of social mobility at Exeter University, commented on the A level results for 2024:

> *I'm concerned the A level results this year will show growing academic divide, fuelled by Covid learning losses, record-level school absences and rising child poverty. This will be demonstrated by stark achievement gaps between state and private school, regional disparities in achievements amid falling numbers of the poorest applying for university. (Dimsdale, 2024)*

So, what does this actually mean when entry, and the experience of university is so widely uneven? The reasons for this are complex (Breen & Johnson, 2005; Reay, 2017; Social Mobility Commission, 2019). However, the effects are stark when you realise that educational qualifications are still the key to unlocking entry into particular occupations and the unequal academic outcomes in HE tells us a great deal about levels of inequality and social justice in society as a whole (Friedman & Laurison, 2019, p. 36). They highlight the fact that despite almost 50% of the requisite population now attaining at least undergraduate qualifications, rewards are still allotted inequitably (Friedman & Laurison, 2019; Savage, 2015). Those from professional or managerial backgrounds, for instance, are still far more prevalent in the top jobs than their counterparts from lower income families and backgrounds despite credential parity. According to Friedman and Laurison (2019, p. 38), after graduation, only 27% of those from lower socio-economic groups land a top job, while 39% of those from a professional higher income background do.

How can this be accounted for? Is it because those from more professional or managerial backgrounds go to the more prestigious universities and do better when they get there? Or is it that they are intrinsically more able? Or is there a negative genetic cloud hanging over particular regions and families? As Boris Johnson, the shamed ex-prime minister, claimed, 'IQ test is surely relevant to a conversation about equality' (Wilkinson & Pickett, 2018, p. 151, 2009). On closer inspection, however, the evidence shows that even when those from lower status backgrounds (socially, economically and occupationally) attend the same universities and receive the same, if not better degrees, they are still far less likely to enter the high-status professions. As Friedman and Laurison (2019) point out:

> [...] while nearly two-thirds (64%) of privileged origin respondents who achieved first class degrees from Russell Group universities progress to a top job, less than half (45%) of those from working-class origins with the exact same achievement do so. (p. 38)

If success is therefore defined by something more than which university you enter and the level of degree you achieve, what is it? One explanation can be found in the fact that those from lower socio-economic backgrounds do not possess sufficient or the correct social and cultural capital so essential for entry into certain occupations. Entry to the Bar, for instance, involves mimicking the habits, language and processes of Oxbridge colleges (Mansfield, 2009). Others see the cultural and social capital deficit as a series of 'class acts' (Wilkinson & Pickett, 2018, p. 185) where styles, tastes, conduct, language, behaviour, dress, confidence and the access to the right social and employment networks all cohere to create intergenerational privilege. Much of this is deeply connected to the type of school attended with those from the more exclusive independent schools 52 times more likely to reach elite societal positions (Reeves & Friedman, 2024).

All of the above plus associated forms of 'lookism' (Liu, 2017) can result in misrecognition, where comportment is mistaken for competence as the recent array of failed Conservative Prime Ministers and various Ministers have highlighted. Our HE system therefore designates those with the right cultural and social capital as academically talented and reproduces and reinforces deeper inequalities under 'the cloak of academic neutrality' (Naidoo, 2004, p. 460). And as the reproduction theorists (Bourdieu, 1996; Bowles & Gintis, 2002) argue, the outcomes of HE are therefore merely an expression of already ingrained inequalities and unequal benefits, all reproduced in a similar form.

## UNEQUAL BENEFITS

As Wooldridge (2021) and Case and Deaton (2020) point out, these poorly distributed benefits of HE have widespread ramifications for the rest of society. In part because those who benefit do not acknowledge the greater structural inequalities at play and instead hold the view that those who do not reach higher levels have simply failed to grasp the opportunity or did not put in enough effort. Put simply they failed of their own accord and ipso facto my achievement is mine and mine alone. As the late Raphael

Samuel (then a lecturer at Ruskin College) commented even if students have been 'expensively educated at the ancient universities, they believe that they owe their position not to the advantages of birth or wealth but rather personal excellence' (cited in Aitkenhead, 2006). Michael Sandel (2020) continues in the same vein when he comments:

> *In an unequal society, those who land on top want to believe their success is morally justified. In a meritocratic society, this means the winners must believe they have earned their success through their talent and hard work.*
>
> *Besides being self-deluding, such thinking is also corrosive of civic sensibilities. For the more we think of ourselves as self-made and self-sufficient, the harder it is to learn gratitude and humility. And without these sentiments, it is hard to care for the common good.*

However, it must be said that the widening of opportunity after the ending of the binary divide in 1992 in the UK, did give more young people access to a university education. But what was not grasped fully at the time was the increasing inequality that would flow from the restructuring of the British economy (Dorling, 2023; Hutton, 2024; Wilkinson & Pickett, 2009) and its effect. Consequently, we have had greater participation in HE running parallel with ever greater inequality. Much of this is linked to the way in which the meritocracy has become intimately connected to the neo-liberalisation of the political economy with its emphasis on individualism, marketisation, consumerism (the student as consumer is now familiar in universities), the work ethic, aspiration and 'responsibilism' (Owens & de St Croix, 2020). In this social template, advancement can only come through taking further steps on the rung of an increasingly lengthy social mobility ladder. And if you fall off then it's your fault. For the advantaged, this neo-conservative bedrock wrapped up in aspirational language, has created the privatised, 'meritocratic me' – a giant social selfie.

Due to these and other factors, social mobility as defined by the Social Mobility Commission has stagnated since 2014. In terms of reward, those from working class backgrounds earn on average

24% less per year than those from professional or managerial backgrounds. Even when those few who break through the barrier they earn on average 17% less than their more privileged counterparts while gender, ethnicity and disability cause a double disadvantage if you hail from a lower socio-economic group (Social Mobility Commission, 2019). For instance, women from working class backgrounds are paid 35% less than men from more affluent backgrounds. All this combined with the effects on well-being, mental and physical health, highlights the ways in which economic and social inequalities cause long-term health and social problems, while simultaneously robbing people of their ambition and desires (Sutton Trust, 2019).

In this sense, the winners in the economic system are lionised while defaming the losers for their alleged lack of merit, quality and hard work. And over time the blame shifts to the socially and economically disadvantaged as the makers for their own demise (Piketty, 2020). The social order thus created is legitimised by the HE system (Bourdieu & Passeron, 1977) where talent and academic success are perpetuated for some while those who lack the 'concerted cultivation' (Lareau, 2003, p. 11) remain locked out.

## CONCLUSION

Given the systemic nature of the inequalities that continue to haunt Britain, the new government should at the very least try to ameliorate the hoarding and address the inequities by following both re-distributive and pre-distributive methods. Increasing the link between contribution and reward in terms of work and study would also improve not only standards of living but also self-respect and confidence. In addition, employers should utilise wider selection criteria while universities should employ contextual data to bring about fairer comparisons between schools, regions and localities, and thereby ensure that particular schools are not given unfair advantages due to their backgrounds, intake and familial soft power in the educational marketplace.

Furthermore, the new government should quickly realise that greater social advantage means your family is less likely to be disrupted during the educational process and examination period. In addition, it should be recognised that such students have less likelihood of dealing with family illness or chronic, long-term health problems that require constant care. Many have cramped living conditions, caring responsibilities, suffer from mental health problems and patriarchy. These are daily problems for students trying to achieve against the odds. Furthermore, addressing child poverty can have a major effect on educational outcomes through all the school phases and into HE and beyond. High quality pre-school provision can in the long-term lead to increased educational attainment, higher earnings, lower welfare dependency and lower crime (Havnes & Mogstad, 2010). Moreover, it decreases absence (Felfe & Lalive, 2018) and improves long-term economic growth (Dunt, 2023).

There should also be greater parity of qualifications between independent schools and their state counterparts. The use of International General Certificate of Secondary Education (IGCSEs) should be looked at and greater parity established. In addition, school context should be used when assessing entry to all universities. In addition, familial circumstances, home and social background should be an essential part of all data gathering for access, progression and outcomes. Treating all students the same is grossly unfair and unethical. In addition, as Reeves and Friedman (2024) argue, capping privately educated UK undergraduates at 10% of admissions, compared to the current 30% would tackle the disproportionate influence of particular independent schools. Furthermore, categorising certain occupations and attaching unfair rewards to some does little to reflect the relative social value of others, for instance, nursing, social care, early years and many others so vital to the public good.

Finally, the Labour government would do well to look at the Putney Debates of 1647 because what mattered to those arguing about the future of society after the Civil War, was democratic consent and 'who you were as a human being' (Champion, 2018). Such arguments are pertinent today especially when poverty and inequality are so ingrained. I will leave the last word to Jack Aizlewood (2020), an ex-teacher who wrote the following in a letter to *The Observer* on 26 April:

> *I have experienced the meritocratic messages from both sides of the fence (as a pupil and a zero-hours contracted*

*teacher in a working class area of Sheffield). These messages, which often continue to be sticks with which to beat young people, eventually led me to leave teaching as I felt morally unable to promote an idea of the good life to those for whom it was unattainable. For those without pre-existing professional connections or the intangible characteristic 'polish', the future has been little more than zero-hours contracts, an unsustainable housing market and 'low skilled' employment opportunities for a decade or more.*

## REFERENCES

Aitkenhead, D. (2006, July 8). It's all about me. *The Guardian.* https://www.theguardian.com/commentisfree/2006/jul/08/comment. deccaaitkenhead

Aizlewood, J. (2020, April 26). Letters: A society to inspire young people? If only. *The Observer.* https://www.theguardian.com/commentisfree/2020/apr/26/society-inspire-young-people-if-only-letters

Altbach, P. (2009). *Higher education: An emerging field of research and policy.* Routledge.

Bourdieu, P. (1996). Understanding. *Theory, Culture and Society, 13*(2), 903–925.

Bourdieu, P., & Passeron, J. C. (1977). Reproduction in education, society and culture. Sage.

Bourdieu, P., & Wacquant, L. J. D. (1992). *An introduction to reflexive sociology.* University of Chicago Press.

Bowles, S., & Gintis, H. (2002). The inheritance of inequality. *Journal of Economic Perspectives, 16*(3), 3–30.

Breen, R., & Johnson, J. O. (2005). Inequality of opportunity in comparative perspective: Recent research and educational attainment and social mobility. *Annual Review of Sociology, 31,* 223–243.

Brennan, J., & Naidoo, R. (2008). Higher education and the achievement of equity and social justice. *Higher Education, 56*(3), 287–302.

Case, A., & Deaton, A. (2020). *Deaths of despair and the future of capitalism*. Princeton University Press.

Champion, J. (2018). The Putney Debates. In M. Bragg & S. Tillotson (Eds.), *In our time: Celebrating twenty years of essential conversation*. Simon & Schuster.

Cribb, J., Joyce, R., & Wernham, T. (2023). Twenty questions of income inequality in Britain: The role of wages, household earnings, and redistribution. *Fiscal Studies, 44*(3), 1–24.

Desmond, M., & Turley, R. N. L. (2009). The geography of college opportunity: The case of education. *American Educational Research Journal, 56*(4), 311–334.

Dimsdale, C. (2024, August 15). *Students could lose first choice university spots in record clearing scramble*. https://inews.co.uk/news/students-lose-first-choice-university-clearing-scramble-3227225

Dorling, D. (2023). *Shattered nation: Inequality and the geography of a failing state*. Verso.

Drayton, E., Farquharson, C., Ogden, K., Sibieta, L., Tahir, I., & Waltmann, B. (2023). Annual report on education spending in England: 2023. *Institute of Fiscal Studies*. https://ifs.org.uk/publications/annual-report-education-spending-england-2023

Dunt, I. (2023). *How Westminster works … and why it doesn't*. Weidenfeld and Nicolson.

Felfe, C., & Lalive, R. (2018). Does childcare affect children's development? *Journal of Public Economics, 159*, 33–53.

Friedman, S., & Laurison, D. (2019). *The class ceiling: Why it pays to be privileged*. Polity Press.

Friedman, S., & Macmillan, L. (2017). Is London the engine room of social mobility? Migration, opportunity hoarding and regional migration in the UK. *National Institute Economic Review, 240*(1), 58–72.

Hamilton, L., Roksa, J., & Nielsen, K. (2018). Providing a "leg up"': Parental involvement and opportunity hoarding in college. *Sociology of Education, 91*(2), 111–131.

Havnes, T., & Mogstad, M. (2010). Is universal child care leveling the playing field? Evidence from non-linear difference-in-differences. *Institute for the study of labor discussion paper series* (No. 4978).

Hutton, W. (2024). *This Time No Mistakes: How to Remake Britain.* Apollo.

Lareau, A. (2003). *Unequal childhoods: Class, race, and family life.* University of California Press.

Li, L. C., & Painter, M. (2016). Shirkers of toilers: Local strategic action and education policy in a time of fiscal abundance. *Journal of Contemporary China, 25*(102), 851–866.

Littler, J. (2018). *Against meritocracy: Culture, power, and myths of social mobility.* Routledge.

Liu, A. (2011). Unravelling the myth of meritocracy within the context of higher education. *Higher Education, 62,* 383–397.

Liu, X. (2017). Discrimination and lookism. In K. Lippert-Rasmussen (Ed.), *The routledge handbook of the ethics of discrimination.* Routledge.

Mansfield, M. (2009). *Memoirs of a radical lawyer.* Bloomsbury.

McNeil, A., Lucca, D., & Lee, N. (2023). The long shadow of local decline: Birthplace and economic adversity and longterm individual outcomes in the UK. *Journal of Urban economics, 136,* 103571.

Mill, J. S. (1859). *On liberty.* Parker and Son.

Naidoo, R. (2004). Fields and institutional strategy: Bourdieu on the relationship between higher education, inequality and society. *British Journal of Sociology of Education, 25*(4), 457–471.

Owens, J., & de St Croix, T. (2020). Engines of social mobility? Navigating meritocratic discourse in an unequal society. *British Journal of Educational Studies, 68*(4), 403–424.

Phillips, A. (2004). Defending equality of outcome. *Journal of Political Philosophy, 12*(1), 1–19.

Pignataro, G. (2012). Equality of opportunity: Policy and measurement paradigms. *Journal of Economic Surveys, 26*(5), 800–834.

Piketty, T. (2020). *Capitalism and ideology*. Harvard University Press.

Rawls, J. (1971). *A theory of justice*. Belknap Press.

Reay, D. (2017). *The cruelty of social mobility: Individual success at the cost of failure*. Routledge.

Reeve, R. V. (2017). *Dream hoarders: Why the American middle class is leaving everyone else in the dust*. Brookings Institution Press.

Reeves, A., & Friedman, S. (2024). *Born to rule: The making and remaking of the British elite*. Harvard University Press.

Roemer, J. E. (2002). Equality of opportunity: A progress report. *Social Choice and Welfare, 19*, 455–471.

Sandel, M. (2020). *The tyranny of merit: What's become of the common good*. Penguin.

Savage, M. (2015). *Social class in the 21st century*. Pelican.

Scott, P. (2017). Private commodities and public goods: Markets and value in higher education. In P. John & J. Fanghanel (Eds.), *Dimensions of marketisation in higher education* (pp. 15–26). Routledge.

Shane, J., & Heckhausen, J. (2016). For better or worse: Young adults' opportunity beliefs, motivation and self-regulation during career entry. *International Journal of Behavioral Development, 40*(2), 107–116.

Social Mobility Commission. (2019). *Social mobility in Great Britain – State of the nation 2018 to 2019*. https://www.gov.uk/government/publications/social-mobility-in-great-britain-state-of-the-nation-2018-to-2019/social-mobility-in-great-britain-state-of-the-nation-2018-to-2019-2

Sutton Trust. (2019). *Elitist Britain 2019: The educational backgrounds of Britain's leading people*. https://www.suttontrust.com/our-research/elitist-britain-2019/

Tilly, C. (1999). *Durable inequality*. University of California Press.

Tilly, C. (2000). Spaces of contention. *Mobilization: An International Quarterly, 5*(2), 135–159.

Todd, S. (2022). *Snakes and Ladders: The great British social mobility myth*. Penguin.

Walsh, T. (2010). *Unlocking the gates: How and why leading universities are opening up access to their courses.* Princeton University Press.

Weber, M. (1922). *Economy and society: An outline of interpretive sociology.* University of California Press.

Wilkinson, R., & Picket, K. (2009). *The spirit level: Why equality is better for everyone.* Allen Lane.

Wilkinson, R., & Pickett, K. (2018). *The inner level: How more equal societies reduce stress, restore sanity and improve everyone's well-being.* Allen Lane.

Womersley, K. (2024, September 30). Seven children: Inequality and Britain's next generation by Danny Dorling review – Essential reading. *The Guardian.* https://www.theguardian.com/books/2024/sep/30/seven-children-inequality-and-britains-next-generation-by-danny-dorling-review-essential-reading

Wooldridge, A. (2021). *The aristocracy of talent: How meritocracy made the modern world.* Allen Lane.

Young, M. (1958). *The rise of the meritocracy.* Pelican.

# 10

# LEADING IN PLACE: THE VALUE OF A HOLISTIC APPROACH TO DRIVING SOCIAL MOBILITY AND REGIONAL DEVELOPMENT

Kathryn M. Mitchell, Larissa Allwork and Gaynor Davis

*University of Derby, UK*

## INTRODUCTION

Creating opportunity requires a structural framework which is not targeted at an individual but is harnessed by the alignment of social, economic and educational components to drive prosperity for a region (Social Mobility Commission, 2024). The interplay of these components is complex and the current inequality of opportunity and the differential in regional prosperity across England highlight the importance of understanding place.

Place-based interventions are widely accepted as crucial in understanding and improving public health outcomes (Marmot et al., 2020), but the landscape of the impact of widening access interventions for place within the UK Higher Education (HE) system is not so profound.

HE participation rates highlight discrepancies based upon place, with London showing participation rates in HE for students receiving free school meals at over 50% in comparison to the rest of England being under 30% (Department for Education, 2023). Therefore, it is fundamental for Higher Education Institutions (HEIs) to understand the barriers to engagement within their local communities in order to develop effective interventions to improve educational, social and economic outcomes for their region. At the University of Derby (UoD), we would argue that as an anchor institution, a more systematic approach to understanding and delivering place-based interventions is fundamental to realising the potential of individuals and their region. Potential can only be unlocked if local communities are integral to developing the opportunities and value can only be realised if these communities feel the benefits of an intervention.

## BACKGROUND

Derby is a city of contrasting social and economic fortunes. Despite average earnings being above the national average, more than one-third of households fall within the most deprived neighbourhoods in England. Whilst Derby is home to many highly skilled and specialist roles, especially in engineering, there is a substantial gap in the availability of entry-level graduate, management and skilled posts. There are also notable inequalities leading to childhood poverty and disadvantaged health outcomes (Department of Health & Social Care, 2023; Social Mobility Commission, 2023).

UoD believes in the transformational nature of education. As an anchor institution committed to improving and promoting social mobility, we strive to inspire and create HE opportunities for people across the city, region and beyond, regardless of their age, personal background or location. Delivery on this commitment to social mobility is seen through the provision of a range of high-quality, engaging, inclusive and industry focussed place-based initiatives.

## ENABLING STUDENT AND GRADUATE TALENT FOR SOCIALLY MOBILE FUTURES

UoD is committed to delivering research-informed teaching with a strong reputation for industry-relevant degree programmes. In 2021–2022, our student body consisted of 16,000 undergraduates and 5,000 postgraduates. For this cohort, UoD has maintained a strong performance in widening access and social mobility with:

- 49% of young, full-time, undergraduate entrants from neighbourhoods in England where young people are least likely to enter HE (compared to the England HE sector with an average of 28%).

- 36% of full-time undergraduate entrants were over the age of 21 (compared to the England HE sector with an average of 29%).

- 19% of full-time undergraduate entrants reported a disability (compared to the England HE sector with an average of 17%).

- 20% of full-time undergraduate entrants had previously been eligible for free school meals (compared to the England HE sector with an average of 18%).

Stimulating employer demand within the region for graduate talent has been key to the University's strategy to enable social mobility for our diverse student intake. Our Local Enterprise Partnership (Derby, Derbyshire, Nottingham, Nottinghamshire; D2N2, 2020) identified poor productivity amongst the region's firms as a key factor holding back the region's growth. As a result, the region's three universities collaborated to develop interventions to address this problem. The projects were funded by the European Structural and Investment Funds and were match funded by universities and employers. Of particular note, were the opportunities that these projects provided for students in terms of facilitating work experience and confidence needed for good progression outcomes.

The Driven project, led by UoD, is one example of such an intervention. Driven was delivered between July 2018 and December

2023 with a total budget of £3.6 million. Part-financed by the European Social Fund, 470 Small and Medium Enterprises (SMEs) were supported to participate, and 701 interns were employed. SMEs worked in partnership with the University to develop graduate roles and access the talent and skills of UoD students and graduates. Student and graduate participants benefitted from developing the following:

- Good digital skills and experience of using a wide range of technology.

- Capability of using their knowledge to solve real business issues and problems, because we build 'real world learning' into our courses.

- Being curious, passionate about learning and adaptable to change.

- Having the latest subject-specific knowledge.

As a result, students and graduates were supported to develop their own employability skills, and as importantly their confidence to enter the employment market. The impact of which is evidenced in the following student feedback:

> It was a life changing experience, as it was my first official tech and cybersecurity job. This led me to a career in cybersecurity. I believe it would have taken ... [me] ... longer or been harder for me to reach the level I have now in tech and security if it wasn't for my Driven internship! The internship was a total game changer for my career.

This holistic approach to industry support and engagement has delivered benefits for the region's businesses, its students and graduates. UoD further stepped up to ensure that Regional Growth Fund (RGF) monies could be secured for the benefit of the region's economic growth. Local authorities were not eligible to apply for phase 5 of RGF, so the University undertook the necessary due diligence to begin delivering the Invest to Grow programme in 2014. This programme provides finance to businesses in the East Midlands with the aim of creating new jobs. By July 2023, Invest to

Grow had directly enabled 2,521 jobs to be created or safeguarded. However, the scheme has delivered wider benefits aligned with the University's Civic agenda and maintained focus on social mobility. For example, specific activities were deployed to engage harder-to-reach small and micro businesses that would not typically work with universities, and these actions have benefitted all parties. This is evidenced by the following feedback from an Invest to Grow participant:

> 'The Invest to Grow grant has really opened doors for us, including the UoD itself. The University has helped us to identify further funding including to provide an internship for one of its students. We are also involved in the University's Productivity through Innovation and Innovate 4 Rail programmes.'

Being embedded in place, and by encouraging and targeting a diverse HE cohort beyond the traditional orientated school leavers, the University has built a reputation for alternative modes of study including apprenticeships from Level 2 to Level 7. These programmes are offered in areas synergistic with government priorities: business growth, industry innovation and public services, particularly around workforce challenges in nursing and policing.

Regional demand for new skills spearheaded the University to challenge traditional job recruitment practice, and in partnership with Rolls-Royce, one of the biggest employers for the D2N2 region, developed the Nuclear Skills Academy. This partnership has resulted in a range of Degree Apprenticeship programmes which drive economic growth, foster an entrepreneurial mindset and provide apprentices with practical workplace skills and industry-relevant knowledge. The combinations of salaried work with day release study time are not innovative, but the skills academy model puts the apprentice at the heart of delivery, assuring a strong student experience, embracing the academic, social and cultural benefits of HE alongside learning as you earn. This model of high-quality education and training can lead to a range of high wage, Industry 4.0 careers (Rolls-Royce, n.d.). The driver for this initiative was to provide new opportunities for the city and region and for the first cohort of 200 apprentices who began their studies at the Nuclear Skills Academy in 2022, 60% were local to the city, with 30% coming from the wider region. Placed in the context that Derbyshire and Nottinghamshire rank low (quintile 2) for socio-cultural advantage as a measure of social mobility (Social Mobility Commission, 2023), the fact that 90% of the Nuclear Skills Academy apprentices are local and benefit from this initiative of a full-time job and salary as they learn has significant implications for social mobility, particularly in Derby and Derbyshire. Importantly, the realisation by industry of their role in challenging the norms for recruitment practice and contributing to early interventions aligned to creating opportunity is fundamental in a place-based and structured approach to breaking down barriers and access to enable social mobility.

## BUILDING SOCIAL MOBILITY THROUGH IMPACTFUL RESEARCH AND INNOVATION

Research from the Institute of Education (IoE) at UoD advocates for social mobility through generating new knowledge and the understanding of educational needs and opportunities required for diverse communities: from teenagers in mainstream secondary schools, to the importance of making accessible work placement opportunities for young people with SENDs; to critically rethinking the Technical and Vocational Education and Training (TVET) offer and challenging race inequality in education. Contributing to a framework that directly seeks to shift positively and systematically the social mobility prospects of young people, the International Centre for Guidance Studies at UoD collaborated with the Gatsby Foundation to develop the Gatsby Benchmarks (2014) for career guidance, which has had a direct impact on national policy. Headline evaluative data exploring the impact of the Benchmarks almost 10 years on, with a view to mapping future trajectories, found that of 1,200 education and business stakeholders surveyed, 94% perceived the Gatsby Benchmarks to be a valuable framework for career guidance, whilst 88% of secondary school and college leaders concurred that the Benchmarks had a positive impact on their students (Gatsby, 2023).

As well as supporting government interventions, IoE researchers have also scrutinised and rigorously critiqued UK Department for Education Further Education (FE) and Technical Education policy in relation to social mobility, most notably the implementation of T-Level qualifications following the Sainsbury Panel Report (GOV. UK, 2016). Through interviews with students, employees, employers and teachers, researchers from the TVET team concluded that the main issue undermining the success of T-Levels is, 'the way that learning at work is organised' because:

> *[...] learning at work experiences is shaped by voluntarism and hence the societal differences among students. Because the current approach does not address these factors, learning at work has not become a means of providing greater access to job opportunities: it has instead become a driver of widening differences in educational access and life chances.* (Esmond, 2023)

As an integrated institution for HE and FE delivery, Esmond and team's findings are a call to pause, reflect and redouble our efforts to ensure that education actively mitigates against the reproduction of inequalities, creating an approach to social mobility that works for all.

## SOCIAL MOBILITY THROUGH WIDER PARTNERSHIP WORK ACROSS THE REGION

Derby City and Derbyshire are areas where pupil outcomes at the end of Key Stage 2 (KS2) and Key Stage 4 (KS4) are amongst the lowest in England with sustained underperformance at both primary and secondary levels. The Vice-Chancellor chaired the Derby Opportunity Area and leads the new Derby and Derbyshire Priority Education Investment Areas. Her experiences from both these government initiatives which were established to improve education and regional economic prosperity, further highlight the importance of a structural and integrated place-based approach to improving the opportunity and outcomes for the region. The coalition of anchor institutions within an infrastructure interlocking with local networks can unlock potential, but understanding place is central to any success (UPP Foundation, 2024).

The University plays a critical role in supporting the region in the raising of educational attainment through the Derbyshire & Nottinghamshire Collaborative Outreach Programme (DANCOP, 2022), as well as via the schools' engagement projects led by the University's Widening Participation team. Understanding place has led to a number of innovative collaborations including Derby Scholars with Oxford University (Bainham et al., 2022). Core to the approach is understanding the local needs which could drive raising educational attainment. Significant success has also been achieved through youth focussed creative participatory projects led by the Civic team, such as the UoD strand of the National Saturday Club and projects on Black Lives Matter and machine futures hosted in co-designed space for community dialogue, the Social Higher Education Depot (S.H.E.D., see Jones, 2022). Anchored in the University's Civic mission and rooted in a participatory approach, spaces like S.H.E.D. show the importance of sensitivity to place and direct community co-creation in addressing challenging topics and diversifying HE audiences (O'Farrell et al., 2022; UPP Foundation, 2024).

Within a widening participation context, outcomes from DANCOP interventions demonstrate both the effectiveness of targeted regional intervention to alleviate social inequality and the power of systematic data collection and evaluation to identify future areas of social mobility redress and focus. A partnership led by UoD, DANCOP is a collaboration of universities and colleges throughout Derbyshire and Nottinghamshire.

Funded by the Office for Students' Uni Connect Programme, DANCOP works with teachers, parents and carers to support learners through activities and advice to make informed choices about university and college as a future pathway to progression. Between 2016–2017 and 2019–2020, DANCOP received funding to work with Year 9–13 target learners who lived in 63 identified wards across Derbyshire and Nottinghamshire which had low-levels of HE participation (POLAR quintiles 1 and 2). The impact of these types of interventions has been significant. Nationally, progression to HE between 2017–2018 and 2020–2021 for young people living in POLAR quintiles 1 and 2 was 32%. For that same period, the rate of progression to HE increased by 11.2% to 43.2% for learners from the Derby wards who took part in DANCOP programmes. Significant for future social mobility interventions is post-activity analysis of DANCOP data tracking the effectiveness of its engagements. This has shown that for learners who live in DANCOP low HE participation target wards, a combination of campus visits and HE information, advice and guidance are the most impactful and beneficial ways of engaging learners with university and college pathways.

## CONCLUSION

This chapter provides an insight into the importance of place in tackling the inequality of opportunity experienced by many of our communities. The evidence presented highlights that an understanding of local/regional needs is a critical factor in unlocking the wasted potential across the UK. The evidence illuminates the impact of local and regional infrastructure in creating opportunity. Universities can and are critical in supporting social mobility and driving social and economic prosperity, but we would argue that they need to be part of an infrastructure not a deliverer of interventions for HE participation.

At the 2024 Universities UK conference, Skills Minister Jacqui Smith (2024) reiterated the importance that universities play in generating economic growth, offering life-long educational opportunities and acting as catalysts of social mobility. 'Universities have a broader role to play in shaping and enriching the society we live in and the culture that we enjoy, not just for each of us but for all of us', she stressed.

The UoD has proactively worked within this space for many years (UK Social Mobility Awards University of the Year 2020) and there is still more to be done. A critical issue for Derby, documented in our Access & Participation Plan (from 2024–2025 to 2027–2028), is a need to secure equality of opportunity for students of colour, students with a mental health condition, and students who were previously in receipt of free school meals. However, underpinned by our holistic place-based approach, industry engagement, our research expertise, our widening access programmes and our teaching excellence, we are well positioned as a regional anchor institution to accept the challenge of improving equality of opportunity. Indeed, many universities have this opportunity but without being embedded within the complexity and infrastructure of place, we would argue that this will not be realised.

## REFERENCES

Bainham, K., Baysan. K., & Gordon-Calvert, L. (2022, May 5). *BLOG: Derby Scholars high attainers programme.* National Educational Opportunities Network (NEON). https://www.educationopportunities. co.uk/neon-%20blog/blog-derby-scholars-high-attainers-programme/

D2N2. (2020). *The heart of the UK's green revolution.* https://d2n2lep. org/wp-content/uploads/2022/11/Recovery-Strategy-2020_V4_190121-compressed.pdf

Department for Education. (2023). *Academic year 21/22: Widening participation in education.* https://explore-education-statistics.service.gov. uk/find-statistics/widening-participation-in-higher-education

Department of Health & Social Care. (2023). *Fingertips: Public health profiles.* https://fingertips.phe.org.uk/

DANCOP. (2022). *BLOG: Meet the Data, Evaluation and Impact Team.* https://www.teamdancop.co.uk/blog/meet-the-data-evaluation-and-impact-team/

Esmond, B. (2023). *Policy brief: Rethinking further education for the 21ˢᵗ century's challenges.* University of Derby. https://www.derby.ac.uk/ policy-briefings/

Gatsby. (2014). *Good Career Guidance.* https://www.gatsby.org.uk/ education/focus-areas/good-career-guidance

Gatsby. (2023). *Good Career Guidance: The next ten years.* https://www. gatsby.org.uk/education/programmes/good-career-guidance-the-next-ten-years

GOV.UK. (2016). *Post-16 Skills Plan and independent report on technical education.* https://www.gov.uk/government/publications/ post-16-skills-plan-and-independent-report-on-technical-education

Jones, R. (2022). *Case studies: S.H.E.D*. National Centre for Academic and Cultural Exchange. https://ncace.ac.uk/wp-content/uploads/2023/03/Rhiannon-Jones-S.H.E.D.pdf

Marmot, M., Allen, J., Boyce, T., Goldblatt, P., & Morrison, J. (2020). *Health equity in England: The Marmot review 10 years on*. Institute of Health Equity. https://www.health.org.uk/publications/reports/the-marmot-review-10-years-on

O'Farrell, L., Hassan, S., & Hoole, C. (2022). The university as a Just anchor: universities, anchor networks and participatory research. *Studies in Higher Education*, 47(12), 2405–2416. https://doi.org/10.1080/03075079.2022.2072480

Rolls-Royce. (n.d.). *Apprentices and school leavers at Rolls-Royce*. https://careers.rolls-royce.com/united-kingdom/students-and-graduates/apprenticeships-and-school-leavers/#our-programmes-tabs

Smith, J. (2024). *Jacqui Smith's speech at the Universities UK conference*. Department for Education. https://www.gov.uk/government/speeches/jacqui-smiths-speech-at-the-universities-uk-conference

Social Mobility Commission. (2023). *Social mobility by area: Derbyshire and Nottinghamshire*. https://social-mobility.data.gov.uk/social_mobility_by_area/ITL2_regions/derbyshire_and_nottinghamshire

Social Mobility Commission. (2024). *State of the nation 2024: Local to national, mapping opportunities for all*. https://www.gov.uk/government/publications/state-of-the-nation-2024-local-to-national-mapping-opportunities-for-all

UPP Foundation. (2024). *The Kerslake Collection*. https://upp-foundation.org/kerslake-collection/

# Section 3

# MAKING PLACES MATTER

# 11

# A QUESTION OF SCALE: REFOCUSSING POLICY TOWARDS TACKLING NEIGHBOURHOOD LEVEL INEQUALITY

## Matt Leach

*Local Trust, UK*

## NEIGHBOURHOODS – A MISSING PIECE OF THE LEVELLING UP JIGSAW

With policy still under development, including through the work of the new Independent Commission on Neighbourhoods, the shape of the new Labour government's long-term approach to mission-led economic and social regeneration is still emerging. A key challenge will be to address gaps in the previous government's 'Levelling Up' agenda. Whilst the Levelling-Up White Paper set itself the challenge of 'unleashing opportunity, prosperity and pride' at all levels – including within, and not just between regions (Department for Levelling Up, Housing and Communities, 2021) – many of its accompanying initiatives were notable in their failure to adequately target resources at the places that needed it most. In practice, when not focussed on big ticket infrastructure projects, Levelling Up investment often focussed on the regeneration of city and town centres, with less of a focus on peripheral communities often suffering from the highest levels of economic and social deprivation.

A significant gap in the Levelling Up agenda was the extent to which it failed to appreciate the nature of disparities in outcomes and opportunities across England. Recent data show that regional imbalances are often underpinned by more spatially specific inequality, with disparities in outcome between neighbourhoods being particularly acute in the North of England (Institute for Public Policy Research, 2024). Rather than differences between regions and towns, neighbourhood-level inequality is at the root of many of the defining issues we face – from low growth, weak productivity to poor social outcomes – and is, also, often more deeply entrenched (Local Trust, 2019; Patias et al., 2021).

In other words, addressing peoples' concern about being neglected or 'left behind' cannot just be about turning around town centre high streets, it needs also to improve outcomes and cultivating pride in the places where they live – in their neighbourhoods.

Drawing on the Index of Multiple Deprivation and the Community Needs Index, which focusses on levels of social infrastructure, we can see that neighbourhoods that score within the lowest 10% on both indexes suffer from poorer socioeconomic outcomes across nearly every metric (OCSI, 2024). So far, this group of communities – often situated on the edges of towns and cities that have experienced industrial decline – have seen little by way of change over the past five years. If anything, a pandemic and soaring inflation have pushed them even further behind.

Data suggest they have failed to receive their fair share of Levelling Up funding, compounding an existing trend of having been under-resourced by 'core' government streams in the past (All-Party Parliamentary Group for 'Left Behind' Neighbourhoods (APPG), 2023). Other funds launched under the previous government aimed at addressing 'deep-seated geographical inequalities', most notably the UK Shared Prosperity Fund, have failed to reach them due to limited consideration of the social and civic dimensions of disadvantage (All-Party Parliamentary Group for 'Left Behind' Neighbourhoods (APPG), 2024).

Less geographically targeted funds aimed at neighbourhood-level change have not been accessible to them either. The Community

Ownership Fund, for example, has not reached the most deprived 30% of neighbourhoods due to an asset-centric approach that fails to provide the accompanying capacity-building support these communities need (Gregory, 2024). Lottery and other philanthropic funding follows a similar trend: between 1991 and 2023 severely disadvantaged neighbourhoods received fewer grants and a lower total amount per head from major grant funders – £499.71 compared to £1,329.80 for equally deprived neighbourhoods with a stronger base of social infrastructure (OCSI, 2023). With the launch in November 2024 of the new National Lottery Community Fund England Portfolio, which includes a clear commitment to addressing communities with low civic capacity, it will be interesting to see if they are able to turn these numbers around.

What is true to date is that, despite having some of the highest levels of need, severely disadvantaged neighbourhoods have not yet received the necessary funding and support to improve their outcomes and transform their areas. And whilst the major political parties have found a remarkable degree of consensus on the need to minimise inequalities as a means of unlocking growth, enabling social mobility and improving health, both are yet to disclose a clear strategy for on achieving this at a neighbourhood level. A new national strategy for neighbourhoods could fill a significant gap and level up policy and investment for those communities which have been neglected and ignored for far too long.

## NEIGHBOURHOODS AS A FOCUS OF INEQUALITY

As Labour develops its mission-led approach in government, it will be important that it addresses deep-seated disparities in many mission outcomes between the most and least advantaged neighbourhoods of the country.

Whilst we suffer from large geographic differences on multiple metrics, these disparities are often greater within regions, cities and towns than between them (Department for Levelling Up, Housing and Communities, 2021). Pockets of intense deprivation are often found adjacent to more affluent areas, with residents excluded from opportunities the neighbouring postcode might take for granted. Take, for example, the Big Local area of Littlemoor in Dorset where households earn £5,167 less annually after housing costs and have nearly triple the percentage of working-age Universal Credit claimants than adjoining wards (OCSI, 2023).

This is most visible in the plight of neighbourhoods which face the double disadvantage of high impoverishment combined with a lack of social infrastructure. Local Trust's work with OCSI has identified 225 of such neighbourhoods which suffer from several dimensions of acute deprivation, in many instances reinforcing one another, and resulting in some of the weakest outcomes nationwide (APPG, 2023).

In terms of economic deprivation, they have higher rates of poverty and financial vulnerability compared to similarly deprived areas which have existing social infrastructure – experiencing over four times the rise in fuel poverty between 2011 and 2020 than the England average. The local economy offers poor chances for residents to improve their circumstances, with higher rates of worklessness, a lower share in skilled employment and lower levels of economic activity than similarly deprived areas. Local people are also unlikely to access opportunities nearby – few have formal qualifications, especially at degree level. This under-qualification starts in childhood, and is linked to poorer educational attainment achieved by pupils from these areas at Key Stage 2 and GCSE (OCSI, 2023).

And then there are the social dimensions. A striking example is health: people from doubly disadvantaged neighbourhoods see a higher prevalence in 15 out of the most common 21 health conditions, including high blood pressure, obesity, stroke and COPD, when compared to areas that are similarly deprived but have an existing foundation of social infrastructure (OCSI, 2023) CLE. This has a knock-on effect on the volume of people out of work – twice as high in these neighbourhoods compared to similar areas.

The stark differences between 'doubly disadvantaged' neighbourhoods and those that have an existing base of social infrastructure highlight its importance as a foundation for socioeconomic development and levelling up outcomes over the long term – from the human capital accumulated through institutions like libraries and community centres to the direct benefits of educational and employment assistance programmes (Kelsey & Kenny, 2021).

Levelling up funding failed to target those areas which are both deprived and lack essential community provision – meaning investment and support have not gone to places with the greatest need. A plethora of other programmes and funding pots – whether on community renewal or ownership –have failed to account for differences in neighbourhood-level outcomes, or the reality that the communities requiring the most support and not already benefiting from a strong civic foundation have traditionally missed out. Going forward, the agenda needs to be refreshed to focus on addressing neighbourhood-level disparities, delivering for those communities which will otherwise fall further behind.

## DRAWING ON LEARNING FROM THE PAST

The neglect of neighbourhood as a critical part of approaches to tackling disparities in economic and social outcomes over the last 10–15 years is anomalous. Previously it was seen as a critical element of delivering improvements in areas blighted by poverty and disadvantage. During the 1990s and 2000s, both Conservative and then Labour governments invested in significant area regeneration projects, whose evaluations are largely positive and underline the potential of neighbourhood-level solutions (Crisp et al., 2023).

In the early 1990s, the Major government reworked regeneration policy to tackle geographic inequality. The City Challenge and Single Regeneration Budget (SRB) recognised that a post-industrial spatial policy had to be tailored and partnership-led. Entering office in 1997, New Labour took the next logical step: turning to deal directly with problems where they arise – in communities. The implementation of the National Strategy for Neighbourhood Renewal led the way for long-term, national, neighbourhood-focussed programmes, most notably the New Deal for Communities (NDC) and the Neighbourhood Renewal Fund.

Past and current programmes yield significant learning on what makes or breaks regeneration in the most deprived communities. As Labour develops its new agenda, it should not shy away from harnessing the key principles distilled from this evidence base to inform the process and delivery of mission-led regeneration going forward.

First, investment needs to be targeted at the appropriate scale. Of all previous initiatives, the most successful were those that took place in neighbourhoods. Evidence from the NDC, for example, shows that a 'tight spatial focus' improves outcomes not just in individual households but whole areas, reducing disparities between target communities and the rest of the country (Crisp et al., 2023; Fordham, 2010). Research drawing on these findings suggests, for greatest impact, levelling up should be targeted at communities of around 10,000 people (Tyler et al., 2019). This aligns, as much as possible, with boundaries local people understand and identify with, giving them a sense of agency and ownership (Tyler et al., 2019).

But other conditions must also be met. Too often, deprived neighbourhoods have been left disenfranchised by initiatives that parachute in consultants and organisations from outside the area and do not build community confidence or capacity. Analysis of the SRB and NDC underscores the importance of community leadership to reverse this trend and build capacity where it is most needed: projects funded by these programmes were most successful when communities were authentically involved and engaged with decision-making, although some required initial capacity-building to enable local people to take the reins (Onward, 2021).

The Big Local programme, delivered by Local Trust, is a more recent example of what works to regenerate deprived neighbourhoods with lasting effect. The most significant regeneration initiative since 2010, it provided 150 deprived communities with just over £1 million each to improve their areas. The starting point of Big Local is that the people who live in a locality know best what is needed to improve outcomes across the local area. This has proved true, with Big Local partnerships showing us what can be achieved when local people are trusted to build and restore civic assets and activity – from social clubs and pubs to parks and peer support groups – in the places where its loss has been most keenly felt.

Future approaches should draw on what's been learnt from Big Local, and aim to strengthen the local civic and social foundations of the most impoverished communities. This could be the gear shift some areas need: an independent evaluation of the programme shows that investing directly in strengthening the civic activity and mobilisation enables local people to take on more deep-seated issues over the long term – achieving positive outcomes that last way beyond the programme end-date (Crisp et al., 2023).

Learning from previous programmes suggests that a model strengthening the social and civic foundations of the most disadvantaged neighbourhoods, with local people trusted to lead on how to regenerate their areas, is most likely to generate improvements that are sustainable over the long term, and should be harnessed to support the development of a new policy approaches that leave no community behind and reduce disparities where they are most pronounced.

## HARNESSING THE POTENTIAL OF LOCAL PEOPLE

When communities are given the resources, support and autonomy to rebuild their civic and social foundations through, for example, developing and delivering initiatives like community hubs, cafes or walking clubs, the networks, relationships and connectedness that stem from them transform how communities feel about themselves and their ability to make change (Tyler et al., 2019).

In Scotland and Bushbury Hill, two disparate estates in northeast Wolverhampton, the Big Local partnership spent time building connections across the diverse community. So when local people heard about the planned closure of the community centre, they quickly developed a plan to take it over from Wolverhampton City Council. The Big Venture Centre is now fully self-sustaining and hosts a range of community activities, from cooking classes to employment support groups.

When neighbourhoods have rewoven their local social fabric, they often go on to make choices that enhance community economic development. Communities invest – when sufficient support, resources and autonomy are in place – to take on treasured neighbourhood assets, from boating lakes to pubs and community hubs, which function as footholds for local wealth generation, and provide a base for activities which boost employment and enterprise locally – for example, apprenticeship schemes, community-based skills academies and incubation hubs for new businesses (Centre for Local Economic Strategy, 2020). This has a marked impact on economic outcomes and quality of life locally. Labour market studies in the UK repeatedly show that people living in connected communities are four times more likely to find high quality employment and build sustainable livelihoods through local networks than through a Job Centre (Russell et al., 2022).

In Collyhurst, through in-depth consultation with the community, the Big Local partnership identified high unemployment and low pay as key issues for local people. They got to work developing a community economic development plan, using their funding to acquire derelict properties which were transformed into a local business incubation space. Businesses hosted employ locally and deliver community benefits, such as an organic food growing business and community café.

Community-led economic development does not only lift people in the most disadvantaged neighbourhoods out of poverty: improvements have significance beyond the immediate geographic area. A conservative calculation by Frontier Economics (2021) found that every £1 million invested in a deprived neighbourhood which lacks social infrastructure would generate approximately £1.2 million of fiscal benefits and £2 million of social and economic benefits over a 10-year period. As the lives of people in the most disadvantaged neighbourhoods improve, the whole country benefits from the transformation both regionally and nationally.

## A NEW AGENDA FOR NEIGHBOURHOOD-BASED REGENERATION

With a change of government, we now have a unique opportunity to refocus the agenda on repairing the social and economic fabric of our neighbourhoods, with particular emphasis on the most disadvantaged.

If the government programmes over the last decade have not recognised the scale of the challenges faced by 'doubly disadvantaged' neighbourhoods, and enabled insufficient collaboration with local people who know best what would benefit their community, there is now an opportunity to make a difference.

Policy needs to be re-imagined with a neighbourhood focus, delivering much-needed investment and support to the most disadvantaged communities in England. With evidence from previous regeneration programmes and more recent experience of the Big Local programme, we know that there are no shortcuts to achieving sustainable regeneration; it will require support and resourcing over the long term. We also know that people living in those neighbourhoods need to be in the driving seat – and that rebuilding social capital and the infrastructure that sustains it is the first step in enabling local people to be key players in improving outcomes and spreading opportunity from the bottom up.

## REFERENCES

All-Party Parliamentary Group for 'Left Behind' Neighbourhoods (APPG). (2023). *A neighbourhood strategy for national renewal: The final report of the APPG for 'left behind' neighbourhoods' inquiry into levelling up.* https://appg-leftbehindneighbourhoods.org.uk/publication/a-neighbourhood-strategy-for-national-renewal/

All-Party Parliamentary Group for 'Left Behind' Neighbourhoods (APPG). (2024). *Sharing in prosperity: Community renewal and the UK shared prosperity fund.* https://www.appg-leftbehindneighbourhoods.org.uk/publication/policy-short-sharing-prosperity/

Centre for Local Economic Strategy. (2020). *Building community wealth in neighbourhoods.* Local Trust. https://localtrust.org.uk/wp-content/uploads/2020/03/BuildingCommunityWealthLR.pdf

Crisp, R., Leather, D., McMullan, J., Pearson, S., & Wilson, I. (2023). *A return to neighbourhood regeneration? Reassessing the benefits of a national strategy for neighbourhood renewal.* Centre for Regional, Economic and Social Research. https://www.shu.ac.uk/centre-regional-economic-social-research/publications/a-return-to-neighbourhood-regeneration

Department for Levelling Up, Housing and Communities. (2021).
Levelling up the United Kingdom. https://www.gov.uk/government/
publications/levelling-up-the-united-kingdom

Fordham, G. (2010). *The New Deal for Communities programme:
Achieving a neighbourhood focus for regeneration*. Department for
Communities and Local Government. https://extra.shu.ac.uk/ndc/
downloads/general/Volume%20one%20-%20Achieving%20a
%20neighbourhood%20focus%20for%20regeneration.pdf

Frontier Economics. (2021). *The value of social infrastructure
investment*. Frontier Economics. https://www.frontier-economics.com/
uk/en/news-and-insights/news/news-article-i8602-impacts-of-
social-infrastructure-investment/

Gregory, D. (2024). *Unleashing community ownership: Report of the
Community Ownership Commission*. Co-operative Party. https://party.
coop/wp-content/blogs.dir/5/files/2024/01/20240104-community-
ownership-report-final-compress.pdf

Kelsey, T., & Kenny, M. (2021). *Townscapes: The value of social
infrastructure*. Bennett Institute of Public Policy. https://www.
bennettinstitute.cam.ac.uk/publications/social-infrastructure/

Local Trust. (2019). *Left behind? Understanding communities on the
edge*. https://localtrust.org.uk/insights/research/left-behind-understanding-
communities-on-the-edge/

OCSI. (2023). *'Left behind' areas – Revised data-set*.

OCSI. (2024). *Local insight*.

Onward. (2021). *Turnaround: Learning from 60 years of regeneration
policy*. https://www.ukonward.com/reports/turnaround-regeneration-
neighbourhood/

Patias, N., Rowe, F., & Arribas-Bel, D. (2021). Trajectories of neighbourhood
inequality in Britain: Unpacking inter-regional socioeconomic imbalances,
1971–2011. *The Geographical Journal, 188*(2), 149–308.

Tyler, P., Burgess, G., Muir, K., & Karampour, K. (2019). *Achieving
local economic change: What works?*. University of Cambridge. https://
localtrust.org.uk/wp-content/uploads/2019/10/Achieving-local-economic-
change_Oct_2019.pdf

# 12

# PULLING TOGETHER: A CROSS-SECTOR COLLABORATION APPROACH TO TACKLING INEQUALITY

Ian Taylor[a,b]

*aUniversity of the Arts London, UK*
*bThe Productivity Institute, University of Manchester, UK*

## THE CHALLENGE OF SPATIAL INEQUALITY

The UK has a longstanding problem with spatial inequality, exhibiting low regional productivity and prosperity levels. The poor social outcomes in some parts of the UK contrast starkly with more prosperous parts of the country. Phillip McCann (2020) has demonstrated that the UK is profoundly spatially unequal and 'almost certainly the most interregionally unequal large high-income country' in the world. Part of the problem is the low productivity of the country's 11 large second-tier cities which, despite producing a significant proportion of the UK's economic activity, underperform both the UK average and the performance of similar cities in comparator countries (Organisation for Economic Co-operation and Development, 2020). The places and regions that have fallen behind clearly need action to turn around.

Governments of different stripes have attempted to address the inequality problem, but it has proved to be persistent. Despite the Levelling Up agenda pursued by the 2019 Conservative government being very questionable in what it achieved, it undoubtedly addressed a real problem (Farquharson et al., 2024). The 2022 Levelling Up White Paper was significant in articulating the problem of inequality and its different aspects, making clear the scale of action required to meet the challenge. The Government has the responsibility for correcting the inequality seen in the UK's regions and left behind areas, but it is not one that must rely entirely on the actions of central government. Latent energy to address economic and social problems is replete across the country, with organisations that are passionate about their places. The UK Government can play a key role in activating this energy, directing it towards transformational change. Doing so will involve targeting its resources and convening power to draw together different sectors and actors in communities. Embracing genuine collaboration within and across sectors will be important, and the Government will need to lead a deeper appreciation of what-cross-sector collaboration involves. Businesses have the enthusiasm and the capacity to make an impact in struggling communities. Steered correctly and with due regard to pitfalls, Government can harness the dynamism of business for correcting spatial inequalities. Timing is ripe for innovative policy action given the need, the enthusiasm for responsible business and following the Labour Party's landslide election in the summer of 2024 that delivered a government with 63% of the seats in parliament. To further spur the collaborative approach that can see all sectors pulling together, the UK Government can point to and learn from international success stories of places that transformed post-industrial decline into the momentum of success.

## STRONGER COLLABORATION

Collaboration can be powerful, but it is difficult to achieve. If society is to benefit from the activation of the latent energy of actors in disadvantaged communities, then impactful collaboration, especially across sectors, is essential. Cross-sector collaboration is especially important for economic growth in the UK, where a strength in the generation of innovations does not translate into enhanced productivity and wider prosperity. Despite being a global leader in developing technologies, the UK does not seem able to diffuse these innovations to its wider economy. Greater working together by the public and private sectors has been identified as key to enhancing the capacity of the firms in the UK to absorb innovations and take advantage of the UK's capacity in this area (Van Ark & O'Mahony, 2023). Although such collaboration is difficult, it is eminently possible.

Many see the potential that can come from collaboration and there are undeniable benefits that come from successful collaboration, including economies of scale, economies of scope, representation and knowledge generation. Leaders from the public, private and third sectors acknowledge collaboration to be a vital approach to deal with the plethora of grand challenges facing us today, if also that it is a difficult thing to achieve satisfactorily. Even defining collaboration proves more difficult than one would assume. Though common and practical definitions do exist, it is possible to examine a collaboration to assess its characteristics using existing frameworks (Taylor & Ball, 2023).

Appropriate to the potential and complexity of collaboration, a lot has been written, both in academic and practitioner literature, offering valuable understanding on how to engage in collaboration. Cross-sector collaboration particularly calls for guidance as it involves tricky aspects of clashing cultures, norms and accountabilities. Recently, the Whitehall & Industry Group and the Blavatnik School of Government commissioned a study to distil a range of guidance, producing the *The Collaboration Playbook: A Leader's Guide to Cross-sector Collaboration* (Taylor & Ball, 2023). Reviewing the available literature, further refined through discussions with thought-leaders in the area, the playbook identifies five key themes that can help unlock impactful collaboration: trust, power, culture, leadership and learning. Trust, for example, is difficult to manage as it involves strong emotional and intuitive factors at play. Using guidance such as the *Collaboration Playbook* helps organisations at the place-based level to appreciate the difficulty of genuine collaboration and to embrace the challenge in order to realise what can be achieved. Government should champion such ambition.

## RESPONSIBLE BUSINESS

The prospects for governments stimulating collaboration through active businesses hold significant potential, as today we are faced with both opportunity as well as challenge. It is a common refrain that government capacity and finances are weak at a time when there are many calls for public sector action. In terms of timing, however, there is an opportunity presented by the current epoch of responsible business. Businesses are arguably more willing to accept social responsibility than ever before. Businesses acting responsibly to improve the social outcomes of the communities they are part of are far from new. However, it is only relatively recently that the drive behind responsible business has reached a crescendo. In fact, in 2025 there are indications that the tide may be ebbing, underscoring the need to seize the opportunity.

Although the economics of 'business knows best' has been in question since the financial crisis of 2008, it is since the end of the last decade that there has been a rhetorical breaking by business leaders of the adherence to the orthodoxy of Milton Friedman. Friedman's logic had been dominant since international competition drove the Anglo-American world to see the only purpose of business to be to make a profit for shareholders. Friedman (1970) was wary of the business executive who might spend the shareholders' money on their own, potentially aggrandising, concerns that did not focus on the business fundamentals, yet today socially responsible conduct seems more fundamental to business. Informed and socially conscious customers have combined with investors and shareholders who have a greater level of control over their ownership and consequently their ability to express a socially conscious preference (Taylor, 2023b). Management has responded and being more responsible has become a characteristic of a successful company. Having a measurable social purpose sends a signal of reliable management and a resilience to shocks, seen during the 2008–2009 financial crisis and the COVID-19 crisis (Johnstone-Louis et al., 2020). When, in 2019, 181 American business leaders signed a statement committing to lead their companies for the benefit of all stakeholders, rather than solely for shareholders, it was an appreciation of the circumstances that businesses now operate under (Business Roundtable, 2019).

Fully harnessing the rhetorical ambition to be more responsible and leaning into the trend will require care from governments. There are risks of damaging the efficiency and international competitiveness for businesses, as well as the risk of the capture of social policy by well-resourced companies with their own agenda (Taylor, 2023b). With due caution paid to the potential risks involved, there is an opportunity for governments to steer the energy behind responsible business into its key challenge of spatial inequality by incentivising place-based collaboration. Furthermore, the place-based nature of such an approach will place central governments in a position to mitigate any power imbalances between local stakeholders and businesses.

## PLACE-BASED PARTNERSHIPS

It is clear from those places that have mobilised the energy of organisations in deprived places with the assistance of charities, such as Business In The Community, that there is latent energy in places waiting to be activated (Taylor, 2022). Businesses have often seen their social responsibility to primarily reside in the communities in which they operate, where a shared value concept can benefit the business and their workforce (Porter & Kramer, 2011). Business and philanthropy combined in individuals, such as the 19th century's Sir Titus Salt, who went out of their way to better their communities and the conditions of their workforce (Collier & Kay, 2020). A contemporary manifestation of this shared value that has developed over recent decades in the UK is the place-based partnership. The model is a cross-sector collaboration for improving social outcomes in deprived towns and cities. Place-based partnerships involve active engagement from business partners and include other cross-sector partners such as local government, charities, educational institutions and even sports clubs. The partner organisations contribute resources, analyse the problems of the deprived place that has been targeted and engage the community on what actions the partners should be taking to achieve a vision of progress. Local government plays an indispensable role in these place-based partnerships, due to their service delivery function and democratic mandate, with other partners supporting them. Businesses not only have financial resources to offer, but skills and competencies that are valued by other sector partners (Taylor, 2022). Similarly, civil society, educational and other partners each bring unique strengths to the partnerships that complement those of the private sector partners.

The model of place-based collaboration for the regeneration of deprived places was the focus of a Taskforce inquiry, chaired by Lord Bassam of Brighton and involving the participation of experienced public figures such as the late Lord Bob Kerslake. Crucially, in seeking to examine the role for business in correcting spatial inequalities, the Taskforce membership included representation from major national UK businesses. The inquiry report heard organisations from across sectors attest to the need to create conditions that are more conducive to increasing business engagement in community work. By their nature, business partners are extremely well placed to assist local government and charities with programmes to enhance skills and employability. Together with supporting other programmes, such as on inward investment, education and improving health outcomes for communities, businesses can support action in policy elements that are very important aspects of the UK's spatial inequality and productivity challenge (Van Ark & O'Mahony, 2023). The place-based partnership model could be impactful if nurtured. Across the existing partnerships, there are examples of businesses activating other local businesses and involving their supply chains to multiply the number of businesses contributing their efforts to regeneration. Such a domino effect could thus result in a perpetuating scale of impact, if stimulated.

## GOVERNMENT ACTION

In order to stimulate cross-sector collaboration to regenerate deprived places, the UK Government can take long-term and immediate steps. Previous governments have clearly found it difficult to yield sufficient results in response to the problem of spatial inequality. To do so it seems likely that the UK Government will need to introduce substantial reforms, not just by increasing development spending substantially from its currently low base but also by building institutional capacity at an intermediate political and economic geography level to spur investment and productivity (McCann, 2021). Examples of what can be achieved with such reforms are available to be seen in peer countries that have been experiencing their own post-industrial decline. Eight cases of 'turnaround' cities in six countries have been examined in a piece coordinated by a team at the University of Oxford, looking at Germany, the USA, France, Canada, Australia and Spain (Frick et al., 2023). All of these examples had at their core a sense of cross-sector collaboration between the actors involved in the city, across the national, regional and city levels. Central government in these countries deployed instruments that brought actors together in the turnaround cities. Instruments used included infrastructure funding, special tax-incentivised development zoning and asset recycling bonuses. However, the international comparator case studies work revealed how collaboration was facilitated by the developed sub-national government structure in each of the cases. The absence of such intermediate governance structures in the UK underscores further the importance of taking action to facilitate collaboration in places, as a means of compensation.

Government action to empower partnerships between local government, civil society and business is important as there is a danger that centralised public policy is too slow to respond to ongoing innovations and disruptions that a competent cross-sector partnership at the local level can adapt to. Drawing on many international examples, Paul Collier (2024) has cautioned against an instinct to continue to try to manage from the centre in the face of 'radical uncertainty', arguing that places should instead be empowered to experiment utilising their local information. Devolution and investment are necessary, yet in addition to such seminal reforms central government can take more subtle action to unlock decentralised collaborative energy for regeneration.

Even in places with organisations that would like to dedicate time and resources to a collaborative effort, local authorities often lack the capacity to coordinate partnerships. In some instances, businesses and charities have stepped in, to generously dedicate coordinating staff to local partnerships but that cannot be expected

(Taylor, 2022). UK Government should coordinate with the existing partnerships to learn how the deployment of coordination, or 'connector', capacity can be dispersed across deprived places in the UK. Furthermore, modest tax incentive packages could be developed to help make the case for business and local authority involvement in partnerships. An example tax incentive model to encourage collaboration was outlined in the 2022 Place Taskforce report, where the extension of charitable tax status is extended to projects that are valuable to a regenerating communities (Taylor, 2022). This proposal is the only option to consider, but any such instrument would likely do as much in encouraging the contribution of community actors as it would provide in pure resources. Such an effect was seen in Tax Increment Financing schemes in the US success story of Pittsburgh, where modest financing had a disproportionately large impact on the scale of regeneration development there (Taylor, 2023a).

The major problem of spatial inequality in the UK has been persistent and will not be corrected quickly. Major reform is necessary, however, modest yet innovative actions by central government can begin to realise change quickly by stimulating genuine cross-sector collaboration in places. Leveraging instruments to incentivise and convene actors to work on regeneration projects can unleash latent energy in those deprived communities, especially from responsible businesses. As a consequence, institutional strengthening in places will assist with the necessary major reforms to come.

## REFERENCES

Business Roundtable. (2019, August 19). *Business Roundtable redefines the purpose of a corporation to promote 'an economy that serves all Americans.* https://www.businessroundtable.org/business-roundtable-redefines-the-purpose-of-a-corporation-to-promote-an-economy-that-serves-all-americans

Collier, P. (2024). *Left behind: A new economics for neglected places.* Allen Lane.

Collier, P., & Kay, J. (2020). *Greed is dead: Politics after individualism.* Allen Lane.

Farquharson, C., Milsom, L. H., Tahir, I., Upton, B., & Vyas, G. (2024). *IFS Report R323: How do the last five years measure up on levelling up?*. Institute for Fiscal Studies. https://ifs.org.uk/sites/default/files/2024-06/How-do-the-last-five-years-measure-on-levelling-up.pdf

Frick, S., Taylor, I., Prenzel, P., Penney, K., Collier, P., Goodstadt, V., Mayer, C., & McCann, P. (2023). *Lessons from successful 'turnaround' cities for the UK*. The Resolution Foundation. https://economy2030.resolutionfoundation.org/reports/lessons-from-successful-turnaround-cities-for-the-uk/

Friedman, M. (1970, September 13). A Friedman doctrine – The social responsibility of business is to increase its profits. *The New York Times Magazine*, 17. https://www.nytimes.com/1970/09/13/archives/a-friedman-doctrine-the-social-responsibility-of-business-is-to.html

Johnstone-Louis, M., Kustin, B., Mayer, C., Stroehle, J., & Wang, B. (2020). Business in times of crisis. *Oxford Review of Economic Policy*, 36(S1), S242–S255.

McCann, P. (2020). Perceptions of regional inequality and the geography of discontent: Insights from the UK. *Regional Studies*, 54(2), 256–267.

McCann, P. (2021). *Productivity insights paper no. 008: The fiscal implications of 'levelling up' and UK governance devolution*. The Productivity Institute. https://www.productivity.ac.uk/wp-content/uploads/2021/12/PIP008-Fiscal-Implications-FINAL-081221-1.pdf

Organisation for Economic Co-operation and Development. (2020). *Enhancing productivity in UK core cities: Connecting local and regional growth*. https://www.oecd-ilibrary.org/urban-rural-and-regional-development/enhancing-productivity-in-uk-core-cities_9ef55ff7-en

Porter, M. E., & Kramer, M. R. (2011, January–February). Creating shared value. *Harvard Business Review*. Retrieved, February 2011, from https://hbr.org/2011/01/the-big-idea-creating-shared-value

Taylor, I. (2022). *Partnerships in place: The business of levelling up*. Business in the Community. https://www.bitc.org.uk/wp-content/uploads/2022/05/Places-Taskforce-Report_May2022.pdf.

Taylor, I. (2023a). *Turnaround cities: Anglo-Saxon case studies insights from Pittsburgh, Newcastle and Windsor Ontario*. Blavatnik School of Government, University of Oxford. https://golab.bsg.ox.ac.uk/knowledge-bank/resource-library/turnaround-cities-anglo-saxon-case-studies/

Taylor, I. (2023b). Responsible government and responsible business: The challenge of harnessing CSR in a new epoch. *International Journal of Corporate Social Responsibility*, *8*, 7.

Taylor, I., & Ball, N. (2023). *The collaboration playbook: A leader's guide to cross-sector collaboration*. Whitehall & Industry Group & Blavatnik School of Government. https://www.wig.co.uk/campaigns/collaboration-playbook

Van Ark, B., & O'Mahony, M. (2023). The UK's productivity challenge: people, firms, and places. *Productivity Insights Paper No. 018, the Productivity Institute*. https://www.productivity.ac.uk/wp-content/uploads/2023/11/PIP018-The-UKs-productivity-challenge-FINAL-Nov-2023.pdf

# 13

# INVESTING IN REGIONAL EQUALITY: HOW ARE INTERNATIONAL SUCCESS FACTORS PLAYING OUT IN THE UK?

Abigail Taylor

*University of Birmingham, UK*

## INTRODUCTION

Whilst 'levelling up' is now out of the lexicon of the UK government, with the Department for Levelling Up, Housing and Communities returning to its former name of the Ministry of Housing, Communities and Local Government following the election of a Labour Government in summer 2024, economic inequality remains endemic within the UK. Addressing regional inequalities remains as important as ever. Despite the previous government's focus on levelling up, a 2024 report by the Institute for Fiscal Studies (Farquharson et al., 2024) argues that 'progress towards these levelling up missions has been glacial – and, on many metrics, gaps have widened since 2019 while the country as a whole has gone into reverse' (p. 2).

It is crucial that the new Labour Government takes steps to address social and economic inequalities across the UK. One tool for developing policies to address inequalities would be to learn from international examples of successful investment in regional equality. Existing work analysing international regions that have successfully levelled up is limited (Taylor, 2022). Nonetheless, learning from relevant international practice could be particularly valuable for the UK given it is one of the world's most geographically unequal developed countries (Davenport & Zaranko, 2020).

This chapter responds to this gap by drawing upon two studies which examine how international city-regions have successfully supported local economic growth and identify key success factors, and a further study which examined the transferability of these lessons to the English policy context. The chapter illustrates how local areas in England are developing innovative practices in line with international success factors identified. However, short-term competitive funding processes in England have meant that policy-makers have often struggled, compared to international counterparts, to invest for the long-term and conduct effective monitoring and evaluation.

## ADDRESSING REGIONAL INEQUALITIES: BACKGROUND TO CASE STUDIES

This chapter builds on findings from three reports published by the Industrial Strategy Council (ISC) and the Chartered Institute of Public Finance and Accountancy (CIPFA). The first report (Taylor et al., 2021) analysed experiences in four international case study areas: Estonia, San Antonio in the USA, Greater Lille in France and the Ruhr region in Germany. The case studies were selected in view of their success in 'levelling up' local economies and to provide insight into experiences in a range of differing governance contexts. The second report (Taylor et al., 2022) provided four case studies of how Fukuoka in Japan), Leipzig in Germany, Cleveland in the USA and Nantes have achieved progress in overcoming significant social and economic inequalities in recent decades. Both reports drew out governance, policy and funding factors which were important in driving change in the city-regions. A third report (Taylor et al., 2024) sought to understand the transferability of lessons from relevant international practice to the English context. Based upon case studies of four different areas in England – Dudley, Enfield, South Yorkshire and Tees Valley – the report explored whether the success factors are evident in England, whether they are working well and which barriers local authorities are facing in addressing inequalities.

Each of the three reports this chapter expands upon utilise a primarily qualitative approach. Across the reports, over 70 interviews were conducted with local, regional and national stakeholders including key policy experts, public sector officers, business representatives and academics. Semi-structured qualitative interviews were utilised to explore the depth, nuance and complexity of experiences in each city-region. Transcripts from interviews across the case study areas were analysed thematically to explore commonalities and differences in experiences.

## KEY FINDINGS

Both the ISC and CIPFA reports identified key components of successful approaches utilised to promote regional equality and drive economic growth. These are summarised in Table 13.1.

As indicated by the shades in Table 13.1, there is significant crossover between the components emphasised in the ISC and CIPFA reports. Five of the components identified in the ISC work are closely aligned with success factors in the CIPFA reports. The ISC work identified a further specific type of investment which can be valuable – investment in transport and digital infrastructure. Whilst not a success factor in the CIPFA study, this is nonetheless featured as important in driving change in some of the CIPFA case studies. The CIPFA work identified two further aspects – monitoring and evaluation and adapting national frameworks to address local needs – which support the other success factors.

The following section provides selected examples of these key components in action.

**Table 13.1.   Foundations for Levelling Up and Success Factors for Addressing Regional Inequalities.**

| ISC Foundations for Levelling Up | CIPFA Success Factors for Addressing Regional Inequalities |
|---|---|
| Scale and long-term investment | Investing for the long-term |
| | Adequate and responsive funding |
| Collaboration | Shared political will and partnerships |
| | Clear strategy and vision |
| Attractive place to live | Diversification |
| Skills and future sectors | Local knowledge |
| Universities and innovation | Key players |
| Transport and digital infrastructure | |
| | Monitoring and evaluation |
| | Adapting national frameworks to address local needs |

*Sources*: Adapted from Taylor et al. (2021, 2022).

## INTERNATIONAL SUCCESS FACTORS FOR ADDRESSING REGIONAL INEQUALITY

### Long-term Adequate and Responsive Funding

A commitment to scale and longevity was a vital component in the transformation of the city-regions studied. For example, policies to address regional inequalities in Germany totalled almost €2 trillion over the period from 1990 to 2014 (Taylor et al., 2022). The Ruhr region alone benefitted from €4 billion in European Union (EU) structural funding over the period 1989–2011. Regional government played an important role in investing urban development and addressing social and environmental issues. The state also contributed to environmental clean-up costs stemming from the region's history of steel and coal production (Schwarze-Rodrian, 2016). Essen (a city in the Ruhr region) becoming the 2017 European Green Capital in recognition of the city's creation of blue and green corridors, new rail links and improved green infrastructure, is emblematic of the success of the high levels of investment.

An important feature of the French and German public finance systems is the redistribution of funds across regions and cities to address regional and urban inequalities. Tax powers are designed to enable areas with low tax revenues to be compensated, reducing the entrenchment of inequalities. City-regions in France also benefit from various tax raising powers and incentives, as exemplified by Nantes Métropole (an administrative authority similar to an English Combined Authority). Nantes Métropole brings together 24 communes including the City of Nantes, and benefits from being able to apply tax breaks to support smaller firms and can levy a transport supplement in response to shifting public transport needs, so helping achieve inclusive growth goals.

## Shared Political Will and Partnerships

Most of the city-regions profiled benefitted from strong local and regional powers. Local institutions, often worked in partnership with regional and national governments to lead change. Positive relationships between central and local government, businesses and residents facilitated the identification of place-specific interventions and effective implementation. For example, growth of the Austin–San Antonio corridor was facilitated through close collaboration between the Chamber of Commerce, the Mayor, the City Council and universities.

The case studies point to the importance of informal collaboration in promoting discussion and developing shared solutions to economic issues. In 1993, the Comité Grand Lille was founded bringing together diverse representatives from financial institutions, local businesses, the Chamber of Commerce, social partners, local civil servants, artists and elected. Interviewees stressed how the network strengthened relationships between local actors and generated ideas for flagship projects including Lille's candidature for the 2004 Olympics and subsequent successful bid to become European City of Culture in 2004.

## Clear Strategy and Vision

Developing a clear strategy and vision for what the city should look and feel like for residents and workers and then working towards achieving that vision was another key reason for success. For example, Fukuoka, distinguished itself from other cities in Japan through the emphasis placed on becoming the start-up capital of Japan and an international destination for entrepreneurs. Start-up city Fukuoka was launched in 2012 and has since established a network of partner cities across the world to promote its start-up enterprises in new markets.

## Diversification

The case studies indicate that to attract young professionals and raise skills levels there is a need to move beyond a focus on economic and business growth by also investing in making places outstanding and renowned places to live and work in. Many of the city-regions studied invested in cultural and spatial development to change perceptions and attract new residents. Initiatives ranged from large-scale cultural events (e.g. European City of Culture) in Lille and Essen, to artistic trails in abandoned former industrial areas in Nantes, to citizen-centred development in Fukuoka.

## Local Knowledge

Local and regional policymakers and practitioners displayed an in-depth understanding of the strengths and weaknesses that drive their local economies and have built on these strengths to transition traditional sector into the 21st century. Nantes builds on traditional manufacturing strengths in shipbuilding to develop specialisms in high-end specialist cruise ship construction and aerospace.

Investing in skills and retraining was key to how areas building on past sector strengths to seize emerging opportunities. In San Antonio, the QUEST (Quality Employment through Skills Training) project responded to an acute skills mismatch following the move from a manufacturing-driven economy to service and technology-driven sectors by upskilling individuals to work in the advanced manufacturing, healthcare, IT and cybersecurity sectors.

## Key Players

Individuals, public and private organisations were key in enabling growth in the case study areas. Interviewees in Fukuoka, Nantes and Lille stressed the benefits brought by a charismatic mayor in setting a vision for the city-region and liaising with national and local government to achieve it.

Universities can be key actors in regional economic development through attracting national government and private-sector funding and improving the attractiveness of cities and regions for high-skilled workers. For example, over the period 1985–2014, the number of students in the Ruhr region increased by 78% and the number of universities rose to five, improving the attractiveness of the region for individuals and companies (Schwarze-Rodrian, 2016).

## Monitoring and Evaluation

Developing systems that enable policies and programmes to be regularly sense checked and updated in a timely way benefitted overall performance. The case studies indicate how flexibility and the ability to adapt to changing needs and circumstances are best integrated at the design stage and that successful places taking pragmatic decisions within an overall guiding vision.

## TRANSFERABILITY OF THESE SUCCESS FACTORS TO ENGLAND

This section considers how these success factors translate to the English context.

Analysis of experiences in Dudley, Enfield, South Yorkshire and Tees Valley found evidence of all of these success factors. For example,

- *Shared political will and partnerships* is illustrated by how institutions led by South Yorkshire Mayoral Combined Authority collaborated effectively to design the bid for an £80 million Advanced Manufacturing Investment Zone, coalescing around shared goals designed to spread benefits of the intervention across the region.

- *Diversification*: Building on historic strengths in manufacturing, partners in Dudley collaborated to develop expertise in very light rail.

- *Local knowledge*: evidencing strong local knowledge and drawing on local assets, local authorities have developed distinct identities in their local economic development plans.

- *Monitoring and evaluation*: Local London, a sub-regional partnership in Enfield, has developed a data warehouse to support evidence-based policy-making.

Nonetheless, compared to the international city-regions studied, implementing many of the success factors in England was more challenging, primarily due to more limited long-term funding and constrained staff capacity.

Local authorities are hindered in delivering visions they set out for economic development by shorter-term funding pots and greater change in policy across electoral cycles. Pressure to bid for everything going in a competitive funding model is stymieing a strategic approach to addressing regional inequalities in several cases. Whilst recent Devolution Deals provide Combined Authorities with long-term funding, they remain constrained in the powers they have and the duration of their funding. For example, even the new Trailblazer Devolution Deal in the West Midlands will only extend the ability of the West Midlands Combined Authority to retain business rates for 10 years.

Whilst local and regional stakeholders recognise the need to conduct effective monitoring and evaluation, limited staff capacity, high workloads and the rapid pace of day-to-day work can hinder the ability of local authorities to respond agilely to the launch of new government funding rounds and conduct effective monitoring and evaluation.

## CONCLUSION

International research offers insights into how inequalities can be reduced but demonstrates that there is no single solution. Instead, it points to the importance of places developing clear place-specific strategies drawing on local knowledge. To enable cities and regions in the UK to implement their visions, there is a clear need for government to display a sustained commitment to long-term funding and decentralised power and decision-making. Moving away from short-term funding pots is essential, with long-term flexible funding required. There is also a need for the central government to invest in (re)growing capacity of local institutions and structures, including monitoring and evaluation.

It is promising that at the time of writing in summer 2024, the Deputy Prime Minister has written to local authorities in regions without devolved power, inviting them to work with ministers to gain greater autonomy over services such as transport, housing and adult education and that the government has committed to publishing a new devolution framework as well as 'deepening powers of existing metro mayors and combined authorities'. The idea is for metro mayors to take on new statutory responsibilities for spatial planning, skills and employment support and to create 'local growth plans' (Breach, 2024). However, the government's plans for local government finance remain unclear. The resources and capacity need to be in place so that the rhetoric can be matched by action.

## ACKNOWLEDGEMENTS

The author gratefully acknowledges the contribution of Anna Romaniuk and Skye Sampson in co-writing the ISC report this chapter draws on. She also gratefully acknowledges Anne Green, Hannes Read, Jeffrey Matsu for their contributions in co-writing the 2024 report published in conjunction with CIPFA, and Anne Green, Liam O'Farrell, Hannes Read, Jeffrey Matsu, Gina Coe, Ben Brittain and George Bramley for their roles in co-writing the 2022 report published in conjunction with CIPFA. Particularly thanks are due to Professor Anne Green (University of Birmingham) for reviewing a draft of this chapter.

## REFERENCES

Breach, A. (2024). *Labour doesn't need to rush devolution*. Centre for Cities. https://www.centreforcities.org/blog/labour-doesnt-need-to-rush-devolution/

Davenport, A., & Zaranko, B. (2020). *Levelling-up: Where and how?* Institute for Fiscal Studies. https://ifs.org.uk/books/levelling-where-and-how

Farquharson, C., Heath Milson, L., Tahir, I., Upton, B., & Vyas, G. (2024). *IFS report R323: How do the last five years measure up on levelling up?*. Institute for Fiscal Studies. https://ifs.org.uk/publications/how-do-last-five-years-measure-levelling

Schwarze-Rodrian, M. (2016). Ruhr region case study. In D. K. Carter (Ed.), *Remaking postIndustrial cities. Lessons from North America and Europe* (pp. 187–209). Routledge.

Taylor, A. (2022). How can challenges in left behind places be addressed? Learning from Greater Lille, Nantes, the Ruhr region, San Antonio and Estonia. *Transactions of the Association of European Schools of Planning*, 6(1), 55–70. https://doi.org/10.24306/TrAESOP.2022.01.005

Taylor, A., Sampson, S., & Romaniuk, A. (2021). *What does it take to "level-up" places? Evidence from international experience.* Industrial Strategy Council. https://industrialstrategycouncil.org/what-does-it-take-level-places

Taylor, A., Green, A., Matsu, J., O'Farrell, L., Read, H., Coe, G., Brittain, B., & Bramley, G. (2022). *Investing in regional equality: Lessons from four cities*. Chartered Institute of Public Finance and Accountancy. https://www.cipfa.org/cipfa-thinks/insight/addressing-regional-inequalities

Taylor, A., Read, H., Green, A., & Matsu, J. (2024). *Investing in regional equality: Four English examples*. Chartered Institute of Public Finance and Accountancy. https://www.cipfa.org/cipfa-thinks/insight/addressing-regional-inequalities

# Section 4

# GROWTH, THE ECONOMY, AND THE ROLE OF BUSINESS

# 14

# WHY A FAILURE TO ADDRESS INEQUALITY FAILS US ALL*

## Nigel Wilcock

*Institute of Economic Development (IED), UK*

On 14 June 2017, Grenfell Tower was destroyed by fire, and tragically, 72 people lost their lives. The media and subsequent public enquiry have focussed on cladding, building systems and the amounts invested in building maintenance within social housing – and this in a postcode area where private housing can sell for more than £15m for an individual residence (UK House Price Index, n.d.). Although not linked, there is perhaps no better illustration of the inequality in British society.

Classical economics does not deal with inequality. Its theory suggests that markets adjust, find a new equilibrium and redistribute resources accordingly. However, classical economic theory does not consider economic actors' ability to hoard wealth or use their power to dominate a market. This ability is accelerating. The digital and global world has enabled a greater concentration of power and wealth across fewer organisations and individuals. At the same time, the dominant political orthodoxy of the West has been non-interventionist.

---

*The views and statements in this chapter reflect those of the author only, and not the Institute of Economic Development.

There is a clear economic case for change. Where wealth is spread more evenly, and less is locked away in unproductive assets, there is more to invest in society and the wider consumer economy would perform more strongly.

## UK, AN UNEQUAL COUNTRY

This should not only be an argument from the economic theory perspective, however, as inequalities at their greatest extremes directly impact individuals and society. In the UK, the life expectancy gap between the most and least deprived communities is almost a decade (Office for National Statistics, 2022). In addition, the most deprived communities in England have not shifted significantly over time, and the single most deprived community in England is Tendring in Essex, which has retained this position since first measured in 2010 (Ministry of Housing & Communities & Local Government, 2019).

There are a number of different measures of inequality. The Institute for Fiscal Studies has set out a number of these measures on a time series basis for the UK. Their analysis generally points to the greatest widening of inequality in the UK during the 1980s. For example, the gap between the 10% lowest income households and the 10% highest income households rose from 3.12x in 1979 to 4.44x in 1991 (Institute for Fiscal Studies, n.d.). On this measure, 1991 represented the highest gap over the 60 years of analysis (to 2022). Since 2000, the gap has remained roughly the same (2000 = 4.16x and 2022 = 3.97x).

A similar trend is seen when examining the income received by the highest 1% of earners in the UK. Since 2000, the share of income earned by the highest 1% of earners has remained broad-ly steady at around 8%, but in 1980, the highest 1% of earners secured 3% of earnings (Institute for Fiscal Studies, n.d.).

The picture is no different when the Gini coefficient is used as the measure. The Gini coefficient is a popular summary measure accounting for income across the distribution. A perfect equal-ity score would be a Gini of 0 (everyone has the same household income), and a perfect inequality score would be a Gini of 1 (one person has all the household income). The higher the Gini score, the more income inequality there is. Between 1979 and 1991, the Gini coefficient rose from 0.25 to 0.34. The score has since fluctuated around this level and was measured as 0.35 in 2022 (Institute for Fiscal Studies, n.d.).

The Organisation for Economic Co-operation & Development sets the Gini coefficient for each member state, and in 2021, the UK was ranked as the least equal country in Europe, except for Lithuania. Of the other larger Western democracies, only the USA is measured as less equal, with a Gini coefficient of 0.4 (Organisation for Economic Co-operation & Development, 2021).

Therefore, the conclusion can be reached that the UK has high levels of inequality by European standards. This change in the structure of society took place to the greatest extent during the 1980s. Since 2000, inequality has broadly stayed the same when measured in terms of income.

This finding is interesting when compared to perceptions within society. In September 2021, Ipsos Mori completed a report, 'Perceptions of Inequality in the UK', as part of the IFS Deaton Review. Among the report's many findings was the perception of the growth in inequality in the UK. The survey found that most people in the UK (53% of the study sample) thought that inequality was rising and that just 11% thought it was falling (Garrett & Day, 2021). The UK's inequality has not increased on most measures since 2000, yet most people believe it is worsening.

It is unclear why there is a discrepancy between reality and perception. It is possible that when real incomes have not been rising for workers in general, a greater awareness of inequalities has become apparent to those lower-income groups now facing difficulties due to the cost-of-living crisis. When all sections of society were feeling better off each year, less attention was given to those in the very highest income brackets.

## THE GROWING WEALTH GAP

It is also important to note that most inequality measures focus on income distribution, revealing only part of the story. In an economy with long-standing high disparities in income between different groups in society, the accumulation of wealth over that time period is likely to have widened dramatically. This wealth accumulation has been encouraged through tax incentives linked to saving (ISAs) or pensions.

This was illustrated most dramatically by Ben Tippet and Rafael Wildauer (2023) at the University of Greenwich, who calculated that in 2023, the 50 wealthiest families in the UK held more wealth than half of the UK population combined (33.5 million people). Outside the stratosphere of the top 50 wealthy families, Chancel (2022) estimated that in 2020, the top 10% of the UK's wealthiest individuals held 57% of the country's total wealth, while the lowest 10% held 4.7%. This gap has widened since the mid-1980s.

Wrapped up in this wealth accumulation is the ability of the most wealthy to access the highest-quality housing, schooling, nutrition, lifestyle and healthcare and to increasingly marginalise the least wealthy. Accumulating wealth creates an innate advantage for one section of society. At the same time, the state desperately attempts to create a level playing field for the remainder regarding housing, education and healthcare provision. In those areas of the highest deprivation, resolving the entrenched societal issues of poor housing, low levels or poor quality employment and poor health outcomes are becoming increasingly expensive.

The social contract based on providing high-quality universal services to all of the population is under threat. The needs and expectations of the least advantaged and the ageing population are growing. Still, the financial ability of the state to intervene has been limited by the financial crisis, from which investment has never recovered, and COVID-19 support, which has pushed public sector debt to its highest level since the 1960s (Public Sector Finance Delivery Team, 2024).

The difficulties are likely to continue as a result of demographic changes. In 2024, the working-age population makes up 64.3% of the population, but in 50 years, it will make up 61.4% (Office for National Statistics, 2024). The pension-age population will then rise to 23.7% from 18% in 2024. In 50 years, each pensioner will be supported by an average of 2.59 workers, compared to 3.58 currently.

The political narrative of the 2024 General Election has failed to surface these uncomfortable economic and fiscal truths. Continued income inequality in the UK will act as a compounding ratchet, creating ever-increasing wealth inequality. Life outcomes between groups in society will widen. The state will be increasingly impotent in its ability to equalise opportunity as its resources are stretched more widely.

## BALANCING GROWTH AND INEQUALITY

The media often characterises the choices faced by the government in delivering public services as the tax and spend debate. This has oversimplified the position and suggests that the pull of a lever here or the push of a button there might resolve some of these deep-set challenges. The reality is that some of the largest and most important businesses operating in the UK continue to grow rapidly but make virtually no contribution to corporation tax, the wealthiest in society frequently pay a lower overall rate of personal taxation by taking full advantage of legitimate tax incentives and securing earnings through capital gains which are taxed at a lower rate.

There is a strong argument that since the financial crisis, there has been a need to invest greater sums in public services and pay for this through higher levels of taxation. This did not take place, and this taxation foregone is locked away within the assets of the wealthiest sections of society. For public sector services to play catch up while also addressing the issues associated with deprivation and ageing would require very high levels of taxation. This is especially true when it is considered that the proportion of the population likely to be paying work-related taxation will fall.

At a national level, there is much talk about growth allowing the UK to avoid a debt trap and that to achieve this, productivity growth is required. Undoubtedly, the overall position of the UK economy would be strengthened if productivity were higher. It is a truism to say that in an economy at full employment, where capital created is reinvested, the only way to increase real wages is to increase output/worker. The productivity mantra, though important, also overlooks some elements of the debate. Firstly, the UK would increase its economic output if those not working could secure employment (even in low productivity employment). Secondly, productivity increases would not benefit real wages if the wealth created was not distributed equally. Without structural changes to both opportunities within society and the taxation system, increased productivity could lead to worsening inequality.

It follows that any work in the UK to improve productivity must be linked to approaches to address inequality, or the gaps between the least and most wealthy could widen.

At a local level, with few economic levers available, different approaches have been trialled to try to deliver more equitable outcomes for residents. Social enterprises, community ownership models and community wealth-building initiatives have delivered benefits, but in the face of globalisation and market forces, these initiatives, while interesting, cannot shift the dial in terms of the widest societal outcomes.

## CONCLUSIONS AND SUGGESTED POLICY MEASURES

Globalisation, digitalisation and shifts in the ability to accumulate and pass on wealth are creating new dynamics which will exacerbate inequality and increasingly divide society. At the same time, modest redistributive systems within national governments have not kept up with these changes. This is evident in all corners of the economy. Online retail has in-built tax advantages over bricks and mortar, the architecture of multi-national corporations has been cleverly designed to minimise local tax take, wealth generation is taxed at a lower level than earned income and legislative loopholes in the labour market are exploited to reduce the value and security of employment.

At the same time, the capital requirements of big tech are consolidating wealth and power in fewer hands. Corporations generate more income than some national economies, and capital owners and their C-suite employees are earning multiples of 100× the incomes of their lower-paid employees. Even at a more modest scale, in the middle classes, wealth can be consolidated and passed through the generations in terms of housing assets and pension savings like never before.

Large elements of society need the support of public services; recent under-investment and an ageing population are increasing the pressures on the public purse, all at a time when the taxation system has not kept up with the pace of change. We have a 19th-century domestic taxation system addressing a 21st-century globalised economy. So what can change?

- Growth is essential in the economy. Income and consumer-based (VAT) taxation dampens overall spending ability and restricts growth. Therefore, a taxation model that does not focus on income taxes or VAT increases is essential.

- There is a strong case for greater wealth-based taxation to re-secure the taxation foregone throughout a period when income taxation was too low to properly reflect the real cost of maintaining the UK's social infrastructure. This will need careful structuring since international examples have shown that securing the expected tax take is difficult. It could start with a more progressive approach to Council Tax and incorporate a longer tail of higher banded properties.

- Create new taxation mechanisms that ensure digital business-to-consumer organisations bear their share of the needs of the communities they serve. This is likely to lead to a specific online purchases levy placed on the business according to orders and a change to business rates that reflect revenues rather than property values, equalising the playing field between online and physical retail.

- Where software is purchased from overseas businesses and either downloaded or operated from the cloud but no/little corporation tax is generated for the UK, there is a need to consider a digital import levy. This is not intended as a protectionist measure but merely a method of generating the tax returns that would arise if the business had a corporation tax-paying UK entity.

- Strengthening inheritance tax to limit the funds and property that can be gifted or passed down through the generations using significantly stronger regulations and monitoring. A child's upbringing in a wealthier environment already bestows many in-built advantages within society without passing on ever-increasing and unequal levels of accumulated wealth, perpetuating the cycle of inequality.

- Use the taxation system to encourage limits on the multiples of income that the most senior staff within a company can earn relative to those paid the lowest. The requirement for transparency in reported earnings and activist shareholders has had a limited impact on achieving this.

- Enforce a real living wage and push this upwards while phasing out tax credits. The tax credit system, while well-meaning, has actually subsidised wages and allowed companies to attract staff while paying them too little. Many roles offered by low-wage employers would be unfilled if the tax credit system did not exist.

- Reverse or at least equalise the situation where income earned from working is taxed more than the income earned from retained (and unproductive) wealth. There appears to be little economic justification for such a system.

- Remove the limited liability protection from businesses that fall into administration without paying all their tax liabilities but have not met fair employment conditions.

- Place a requirement on large employers to provide a significant retraining dowry if large-scale redundancies are announced.

The policy areas set out a significant redistributive approach. Still, the intention is to ensure that across all areas of income generation and wealth creation, the carrot of rewarding achievement is balanced with a stick to ensure full participation in a refreshed social contract. Within the spirit of this approach, the public sector should never secure a benefit of more than half the endeavour undertaken by the individual or a business (assuming fair employment is always maintained). This would seem to undermine the need to encourage growth.

It is recognised that creating a redistributive taxation system fit for the 21st century requires reconsidering the welfare state's approach in light of societal changes.

A redistributive approach will also need to ensure that support is prioritised for the groups in society that want to make a positive contribution but face challenges in achieving this goal. In this area, more policy definition is required, but some initial policy areas to consider would include the following:

- Linking all out-of-work welfare payments to in-work taxation contributions in the past and tapering these welfare payments down over time to a universal standard and secure level with appropriate additional allowances for the profoundly disabled.

- Providing greater support to those with an in-work history with any out-of-work occupational health requirements at least partly funded by their previous employer.

- Providing every adult with a track record of employment with the ability to take out an interest-free training and living allowance loan to undertake a course from an approved provider in a skill relevant to the local economy's needs.

- Creating more established employer/education links with a dedicated employer liaison officer within all tertiary education establishments, very regular employer-led workshops with students throughout their tertiary education experience and setting out various opportunities and expectations within the work environment.

- Accelerating support for a cashless economy can help close down economic activities outside the mainstream economy, increase tax take and underline the integrity of the social security system for businesses expected to make a more positive contribution.

- Demonstrably linking any tax-take from wealth to the increased provision of public services which are universally accessible.

- Setting out a commitment to invest surplus revenue in the local provision of services for the young and their families, maintaining their support until school age and, in doing so, seek to replicate the success of Sure Start, which was one of the most important social welfare programmes of recent times. Continue this support through a dedicated social/community worker in all primary schools. Inequality can be addressed at an income and accumulated wealth level through the taxation system – but at a community level, equality can only be addressed one generation at a time.

Overall, a new social contract that recognises the circumstances of the 21st century is needed. A new social contract can celebrate the contribution of wealth creators, fair employers and the importance of ensuring that all businesses fully contribute to their role within the wider economy. The result of the shifts in the approach is that extra support can be provided (and, to some extent, restricted) to those who want to contribute but face challenges to engage fully.

The overall aim can be to reset an economic model with fairness and opportunity for those who genuinely endeavour to contribute.

## REFERENCES

Chancel, L. (2022). *World inequality report 2022.* World Inequality Lab. https://wir2022.wid.world/www-site/uploads/2021/12/WorldInequality Report2022_Full_Report.pdf

Garrett, C., & Day, H. (2021). *Perceptions of inequality in the UK: Quantitative survey for the IFS Deaton Review.* Ipsos Mori. https://ifs. org.uk/inequality/wp-content/uploads/2021/09/Summary-Ipsos-MORI-Public-Perceptions-of-Inequality-Key-findings-from-qualitative-research. pdf

Institute for Fiscal Studies. (n.d.). *Living standards, poverty and inequality in the UK.* https://ifs.org.uk/living-standards-poverty-and-inequality-uk

Ministry of Housing, Communities & Local Government. (2019). *English indices of deprivation 2019.* https://www.gov.uk/government/ statistics/english-indices-of-deprivation-2019

Office for National Statistics. (2022). *Health state life expectancies by national deprivation deciles, England: 2018 to 2020.* https://www. ons.gov.uk/peoplepopulationandcommunity/healthandsocialcare/ healthinequalities/bulletins/healthstatelifeexpectanciesbyindexofmultipled eprivationimd/2018to2020

Office for National Statistics. (2024). *Principal projection - UK summary: 2021-based interim edition of this dataset.* https://www. ons.gov.uk/peoplepopulationandcommunity/populationandmigration/ populationprojections/datasets/tablea11principalprojectionuksummary

Organisation for Economic Co-operation and Development. (2021). *Indicators: Income inequality*. https://www.oecd.org/en/data/indicators/income-inequality.html

Public Sector Finance Delivery Team. (2024, October 21). *Public sector finances, UK*. Office for National Statistics. https://www.ons.gov.uk/economy/governmentpublicsectorandtaxes/publicsectorfinance/bulletins/publicsectorfinances/september2024

Tippet, B., & Wildauer, R. (2023). *The good life at the top: analysing The Sunday Times Rich List 1989–2023*. The Centre for Political Economy, Governance, Finance and Accountability, University of Greenwich. https://gala.gre.ac.uk/id/eprint/42714/

UK House Price Index. (n.d.). UK Land Registry House Price Index. https://landregistry.data.gov.uk/app/ukhpi/?lang=en

# 15

# THE ROLE OF CO-OPERATIVE GROWTH IN REDUCING INEQUALITY IN BRITAIN

Daniel Monaghan

*Co-operative Party, UK*

## INTRODUCTION

Britain's inequality stands out among the world's most advanced nations. The scale of Britain's inequalities is present in all areas of society – between regions, races, gender, socio-economic incomes and more.

These inequalities have done significant damage to Britain as a nation and there are compelling moral, political and economic reasons why this inequality must be reversed.

The stagnation Britain currently finds itself in is to a significant extent driven by the rampant inequality across society. The Resolution Foundation's report *Ending Stagnation* identified Britain as trapped in a low growth, high inequality cycle which has led to stagnant or declining living standards (Bell et al., 2023). This evidence is supported by the International Monetary Fund (IMF), which found that high inequality reduces 'the pace and durability of growth' (Ostry et al., 2014).

The need for action is clear and there are many proposed solutions – increased redistribution, place-based funding and industrial strategies. All these policy interventions will have a role to play in reducing inequality – but one which is often overlooked is growing the co-operative and democratic economy. These business models enable the development of more inclusive local economies, which spread ownership to workers and members – giving them a greater stake in their workplace or service.

This chapter will lay out why the co-operative sector can be a crucial part of building a fairer, more prosperous Britain. The chapter will review the inherent benefits of the co-operative model and its impact on firms, employees, regions and nations. It will conclude by providing a plan for how to grow the sector and reduce inequality across the nation.

## THE CO-OPERATIVE MODEL

Britain was the birthplace of the co-operative model. In 1844, the Rochdale Pioneers formalised the co-operative principles and values which underpin the global movement to this day (Filson & Cole, 2015).

Since the Rochdale Pioneers, the British co-operative movement has had a significant role in economic development and raising living standards in communities across the country. In many sectors, co-operatives play a leading role in the delivery of services owned and controlled by their members. The Co-op Group is one of the UK's largest retailers, Nationwide Building Society one of the largest financial service groups, and Arla Foods UK the number one dairy company by revenue. These famous household names sit alongside a diverse array of over 7,500 co-operatives and mutuals – engaged in business activities from tech and renewable energy to arts and sports clubs (Co-operatives UK, 2023). Combined the co-operative, mutual and employee-owned sector generates £87.9 billion per annum for the UK economy.

The co-operative movement has expanded globally over the last 150 years to almost all countries across the world. Global membership now exceeds 1 billion, spreading benefits to people and communities across the globe (International Co-operative Alliance, n.d.). In many countries, the co-operative sector far exceeds the size and scale of the British co-operative movement. For example, in New Zealand, co-operatives make up 20% of national gross domestic product (GDP), while the figure is 18% in both France and The Netherlands (Dave Grace Associates, 2014). The combined turnover of the top 300 global co-operatives and mutuals was $2.41 trillion in 2023, which would make it the eighth largest economy in the world – below France and above Brazil (Business Council of Co-operatives and Mutuals (BCCM), 2024).

The co-operative model comes in diverse forms and has been adaptable to a variety of sectors. Co-operative ownership structure is always member owned and controlled. But who constitutes a member comes in a multitude of forms and can be adaptable to different sectors and settings. Throughout the economy, there are consumer co-operatives, worker co-operatives, producer co-operatives, community co-operatives and multi-stakeholder models. Each model aims to empower their members and ensure that they receive their fair share – whether that's a farmer in a producer co-op, a customer in a consumer co-op or an employee in a worker co-op. The adaptability of the co-operative model to meet the needs of a range of different types of membership means that it can be implemented across the economy – in every sector and industry.

## THE CO-OPERATIVE MODEL'S IMPACT

The democratic, membership-based model has provided the co-operative movement with numerous advantages which distinguish it from other forms of business ownership. The co-operative model can be advantageous to both the business, the workers and wider members – delivering above average outcomes on a range of key metrics.

The co-operative model's business resilience is renowned. Co-operatives and mutuals are twice as likely to survive the first five years of trading than other forms of business and were four times less likely to cease trading during COVID-19 (Co-operatives UK, 2019). Enhancing productivity is key to restoring growth and raising living standards – and is another strength of the co-operative model. In worker-owned co-operatives and businesses, productivity is 8–12% higher than other private businesses (Craig & Pencavel, 1995).

For employees, co-operatives are more likely to deliver a work environment which promotes wellbeing and job satisfaction. Co-operatives tend to have far lower levels of staff turnover and better retention of talent – by providing employees with a stake and voice at work (Lawrence et al., 2018). Absenteeism rates are lower, and staff report higher levels of job satisfaction and wellbeing than in other forms of business. These factors contribute to the higher levels of productivity witnessed in co-operative and mutual firms.

The co-operative model has proven effective in lowering inequality within firms. Evidence from French worker co-operatives over a decade reveal they compress wage differentials, leading to lower inequality within and between firms (Magne, 2014). This has been supported by further evidence from the Mondragon Corporation, where internal wage differences were compressed – leading to improved wages for lower-level workers when compared to equivalent workers in investor-owned firms (Titzler, 2016).

Research also shows that the size of the co-operative and mutual sector can make an impact on inequality at a national level. An academic paper from Illinois State University demonstrated a correlation between a nation's Gini coefficient and both the size of the co-operative economy's turnover as a share of GDP and overall co-operative membership (Titzler, 2016). Higher levels of both co-operative turnover and membership led to an overall lower Gini coefficient – indicating that a strategy for co-operative growth could be an innovative approach to reducing inequality.

## INTERNATIONAL EVIDENCE OF CO-OP IMPACT ON INEQUALITY

There are numerous standout regions and nations for co-operative development across the globe. Several advanced economies have far larger co-operative sectors in the UK – with many of them being highly diversified across different sectors.

Two of the most concentrated regions for co-operatives are Emilia Romagna in Italy and the Basque Country in Spain (Malleson, 2012). Both regions have utilised an extensive co-operative economy to stimulate economic development and create internationally competitive business sectors.

Located in central Italy, Emilia Romagna is a region known for its production of luxury vehicles, food and other agricultural products. The region has a long tradition of left-leaning governments – which have supported the emergence of a large co-operative movement following the Second World War (Lawrence et al., 2018). In Bologna, the capital of Emilia Romagna, two out of three residents are members of a co-operative with over 85% of social services delivered by social co-operatives. The clustering of co-operatives has helped to deliver a strong, resilient co-operative sector, in which co-operative federations help to facilitate local co-operatives to export and compete globally. The Emilia Romagna co-operative federations include Lega Co-op, Confcoop and Associazione – all of which have hundreds of co-operatives as members (Thompson, 2003).

The results have been impressive, helping to build a regional economy which has gone from the 17th richest to the 2nd richest out of Italy's 20 regions – while maintaining one of the lowest Gini coefficients (Restakis, 2007). Emilia Romagna is not the only Italian region where the co-operative sector has contributed to prosperity. A University of Bologna working paper found higher co-operative presence to be 'positively and significantly associated to the regional prosperity' (Costa et al., 2021).

The autonomous region of the Basque Country is located in northwest Spain. The region is home to the world's largest worker co-operative, Mondragon Corporation, which is a federation of worker co-operatives. One of the largest industrial groups and the fifth largest employer in Spain, Mondragon is composed of 81 separate co-operatives, employing over 70,000 people and generating over €12 billion in revenue (Mondragon Corporation, n.d.).

The Mondragon Co-operative Association expands over several diverse sectors, including finance, industry, retail, education and knowledge. With 12 research and development centres, the co-operative association ensures that all member co-operatives can remain innovative and globally competitive. This has led to Mondragon significantly outpacing other Spanish firms in productivity growth – while maintaining its commitment to social purpose and compressed wage differentials (Lawrence et al., 2018).

The development of Mondragon as the largest Basque Country enterprise has had a similar effect to the development of the co-operative economy in Emilia Romagna. Poverty is lower in the Basque Country than the national average and is particularly low where Mondragon Co-operatives are present (The Young Foundation, 2017). The Basque Country's average income is around 26% higher than the national average for Spain, with wages being 17% higher (O'Brien, 2023). While Spain has a relatively high Gini coefficient rate for the European Union, similar to Greece, the Basque Country has a Gini coefficient closer to Sweden. As a major employer, the egalitarian working practices of Mondragon are likely to have contributed to the low Gini coefficient found in the Basque Country (The Young Foundation, 2017).

The trend of higher co-operative density leading to lower inequality and higher prosperity is found at a national level as well. Germany, The Netherlands, Switzerland, and France all have a higher co-operative proportion of their GDP, while having lower income inequality and higher average incomes than the UK (O'Brien, 2023).

These trends indicate that co-operatives and mutual development can be a significant part of a growth mission which seeks to end stagnation, rebalance regional economies, rebuild living standards and reduce inequality. The following section provides an outline of how this may be facilitated by a mission-led government.

## HOW CAN WE GROW THE CO-OPERATIVE SECTOR TO REDUCE INEQUALITY?

The co-operative movement can help to achieve a sustained and pronounced reduction in inequality by having a supportive government which strives to make the UK the best place to start a co-operative and mutual enterprise.

The Co-operative Party, the political party of the co-operative movement and the sister party of the Labour Party, has been a consistent advocate for the doubling of the size of the co-operative sector. The new Labour and Co-operative Government is committed to delivering its mission for co-operative growth across the country and in every sector.

Achieving this ambition will consist of a complete package of reform supported by new business support and co-operative development capacity. Reform and modernisation are desperately needed in legislation, regulation and access to finance. New legislation will need to be brought forward which removes the barriers to growth, provides legal clarity for co-operative organisations and creates a level playing field between different forms of business.

The democratic, member-owned structure of co-operatives and mutuals means co-operatives cannot rely on conventional capital raising methods – such as selling equity and ceding control to external investors. New capital raising mechanisms can help overcome this challenge – ensuring that co-operatives can raise the finance they need to start-up, grow, compete and innovate. In Australia, new innovative capital raising mechanisms were introduced by the Australian Government through the Mutual Capital Instruments in 2019. This has delivered impressive growth to the Australian co-operative and mutual sector – with the last five years averaging almost 10% revenue growth, including 16% in 2023 alone (BCCM, 2024).

The sector needs access to bespoke, tailored co-operative development support – which is aware of the particular challenges co-operatives and mutuals face in starting-up, expanding and diversifying. At present, the British state does not spend a single pound on co-operative development – this needs to change to ensure that appropriate support is available to alternative models of business.

These new bespoke and tailored business support services should be available in every region supporting the Labour Government's devolution agenda – which seeks to empower local communities to reshape and rejuvenate their local economies. Localising the new co-operative development network would ensure that services can be tailored to the needs and specialisations of local economies and sectors. The new co-operative development system could include financial advice, legal advice, practical support and signposting to wider stakeholders, which could assist in start-up and development.

## CONCLUSION

Since its inception over 150 years ago, the co-operative movement has changed the lives of people and communities across Britain and the world. With Britain facing prolonged economic stagnation and deep inequality, the time is now for a renewed ambition for co-operative growth to help build a fairer, more prosperous economy in all nations and regions of the UK.

The co-operative model is a tried and tested structure for delivering inclusive growth, which gives workers, consumers and more a stake in their business. Across the globe, the co-operative model has facilitated economic development and prosperity – in both advanced and developing economies.

A transformative agenda for doubling the size of the co-operative sector could be a cost-effective, long-term strategy for restoring growth, productivity, living standards and the reduction of inequality which impacts us all.

## REFERENCES

Bell, T., Clark, T., Fry, E., Kelly, G., & Thwaites, G. (2023). *Ending stagnation. A new economic strategy for Britain*. Resolution Foundation. https://economy2030.resolutionfoundation.org/reports/ending-stagnation/

Business Council of Co-operatives and Mutuals (BCCM). (2024). *National mutual economy report 2024*. https://bccm.coop/about/what-we-do/research/national-mutual-economy-report/

Co-operatives UK. (2019). *Co-operative business survival*. https://www.uk.coop/resources/co-operative-business-survival

Co-operatives UK. (2023). *Co-operative and mutual economy 2023*. https://www.uk.coop/resources/co-operative-and-mutual-economy-older-reports

Costa, M., Delbono, F., & Linguiti, F. (2021). *Cooperative movement and prosperity across Italian regions* [Quaderni – Working Paper DSE, No. 1161]. University of Bologna. https://www.econstor.eu/bitstream/10419/245902/1/WP1161.pdf

Craig, B., & Pencavel, J. (1995). Participation and productivity: A comparison of worker cooperatives and conventional firms in the plywood industry. *Brookings Papers on Economic Activity: Microeconomics, 1995,* 121–174. https://www.jstor.org/stable/2534773

Dave Grace Associates. (2014). *Measuring the size and scope of the cooperative economy.* United Nations Secretariat. https://www.un.org/esa/socdev/documents/2014/coopsegm/grace.pdf

Filson, A. W., & Cole, G. D. H. (2015, December 25). *British working class movements: Select documents, 1789–1875* (pp. 428–429). Springer. ISBN 978-1-349-86219-1

International Co-operative Alliance. (n.d.). *Facts & figures.* https://ica.coop/en/cooperatives/facts-and-figures

Lawrence, M., Pendleton, A., & Mahmoud, S. (2018). *Co-operatives unleashed: Doubling the size of the UK's co-operative sector.* New Economics Foundation. https://neweconomics.org/uploads/files/co-ops-unleashed.pdf

Magne, N. (2014). Wage inequality in workers' co-operatives and conventional firms. *European Journal of Comparative Economics, 14*(2), 303–329. https://ejce.liuc.it/18242979201702/182429792017140207.pdf

Malleson, T. (2012). *After occupy: Economic democracy for the 21st century.* Oxford University Press.

Mondragon Corporation. (n.d.). *About us.* https://www.mondragon-corporation.com/en/about-us/

O'Brien, A. (2023). *The purpose dividend.* Demos. https://demos.co.uk/wp-content/uploads/2023/11/The-Purpose-Dividend-1.pdf

Ostry, J., Berg, A., & Tsangarides, C. (2014). *Redistribution, inequality, and growth.* International Monetary Fund. https://www.imf.org/en/Publications/Staff-Discussion-Notes/Issues/2016/12/31/Redistribution-Inequality-and-Growth-41291

Restakis, J. (2007). *The Emilian model – Profile of a co-operative economy.* https://core.ac.uk/download/pdf/58774993.pdf

The Young Foundation. (2017). *Humanity at work: Mondragon, a social innovation ecosystem case study.* https://youngfoundation.org/wp-content/uploads/2017/04/Humanity-at-Work-online-copy.pdf

Thompson, D. J. (2003). *Italy's Emilia Romagna: Cluster co-op development.* Co-operative Grocer. https://base.socioeco.org/docs/emilia_romagna_by_david_thompson_110604.pdf

Titzler, B. (2016). *Worker co-operatives as an innovative strategy to address income inequality.* Stevenson Center for Community and Economic Development—Student Research, 18. https://ir.library.illinoisstate.edu/cgi/viewcontent.cgi?article=1017&context=scced

# 16

# SOCIAL MOBILITY AND BUSINESS REGULATION

## Andy Boucher[a,b,c]

*aShow Your Connection Ltd., UK*
*bEmployer's Social Mobility Alliance, UK*
*cStrategic Partnerships at Social Mobility Business Partnership, UK*

## INTRODUCTION

Currently, there are various incentives available and general regulations applicable to businesses involved in social purpose and social mobility activity. However, as social mobility remains a persistent challenge in the UK, it is now time to consider introducing specific regulatory measures to encourage better business engagement.

In the 2020 World Economic Forum's report, the UK came 21st out of the 82 countries ranked. The report noted that in the context of long-term unemployment 'Despite a high score [in the UK] on social protection access, one strategy for further improvement could be providing additional active labour market policies ...' (World Economic Forum, 2020), effectively highlighting that access to opportunities had a negative impact on the UK's ranking. When it comes to the role of business, the report goes on to note that in terms of policy options 'to encourage and reward companies' efforts, governments should consider providing incentives such as tax credits for investments in significant and meaningful training programs ...'.

From a longitudinal perspective, the Social Mobility Commission's *2023 State of the Nation* report noted that 'the percentage of people in a different occupational class to their parents...has remained fairly constant for a number of decades. However, the surplus of upward over downward mobility is shrinking'. The report attributes this finding to the decline in the number of professional jobs (Social Mobility Commission, 2023).

Historically, comparative income levels of parents have been used as the key marker of social mobility. However, if the overall goal is to create an environment where everyone has the opportunity to fulfil their potential, then the indicators of success should also include:

- financial resilience;
- good living standards;
- good health and wellbeing; and
- quality of jobs and opportunities.

Various research projects have concluded that there are multiple barriers that individuals from socio-economically disadvantaged (SED) backgrounds face which may prevent them from fulfilling their potential, including:

- family background;
- home environment;
- degree of poverty (food, fuel, digital, etc.);
- financial resilience; and
- quality of education.

The widely held view is that early years issues will have the greatest bearing on life outcomes. Research also highlights that where you live is also relevant. The corollary of this is that social mobility often means being geographically mobile, which can exacerbate the issue of left behind communities. As a result, in addressing social mobility issues, there needs to be a focus on place regeneration. As Justin Madders (2023) noted in a cross-party parliamentary debate on social mobility: 'As we have heard, if social mobility is to be tackled properly, we need to tackle more than just access to work. It is about tax, welfare, housing, transport and health'.

Business has traditionally been seen as the engine for social mobility, primarily and most obviously because good jobs are the gateway to 'improving' socio-economic (SE) status but also because of their capacity to provide development opportunities, for example, financial literacy training, employability skills, etc.

However, business engagement on social mobility issues is at best mixed, with influencing factors including the size of business, industry, geographic area of operation and leadership attitudes. On the last point, the experience is that leadership engagement tends to be primarily driven by personal conviction rather than business benefits. As a result, engagement tends to be ad hoc, siloed and peripheral to main business operations. Although there has been strong advocacy from some business leaders about tackling inequality, this has only gained limited traction in the wider business community. The Business Commission for Tackling Inequalities (2023) flagship report comments on the role of business: 'Governments will have a central role to play in driving this agenda but other stakeholder groups including business, investors and civil society more broadly will also have vital contributions to make'. The report goes on to note that business has at its disposal powerful tools that can be deployed to create and distribute value more equitably. Reasons cited as to why businesses should act include reducing volatility in the operating environment, improving productivity, enhancing brand and reputation and attracting investment. Although the report deals with the broad agenda of tackling inequalities, the same rationale for action can be applied to social mobility.

Faced with a somewhat stagnant social mobility in the country, as well as a business community that is in the main only peripherally engaged with the issue, the question is then how government policy can help improve the position and where should regulation sit in the picture?

## THE CURRENT PICTURE

Before setting out policy measures it is helpful to assess the current domestic and international picture. In broad terms, government has four policy levers:

- taxation;
- incentives and grants;
- legal compliance obligations (regulation); and
- rules that are effectively licences to operate.

Firstly, it is noted that there are regulatory requirements imposed on public sector under the Equality Act (2010). The act requires 'an authority to… when making decisions of a strategic nature …[to] have due regard … that is designed to reduce the inequalities of outcome which result from socio-economic disadvantage'.

Globally, there are limited examples of taxation.[1] The UK has had the apprenticeship levy since 2017 – essentially a tax. Although enabling social mobility was not one of the explicit aims of the regime, there is clearly a connection. Despite reservations from some quarters about how the levy operates, government statistics for 2023 that over 300,000 apprenticeships were commenced that year (Department for Education, 2023).

There is only limited evidence of tax relief regimes specifically targeting social mobility, although tangentially the community development finance regime does provide tax relief (community investment tax relief – CITR) for investments in small and medium-sized enterprises (SME's) that are either engaged in activities in designated disadvantaged areas or are performing specified activities. There is evidence that the regime is of growing importance in encouraging investment. Tax breaks, in the form of a super deduction, are also given for expenditure on the remediation of contaminated or derelict land. Finally, local enterprise zones (LEZs) also offer tax breaks to businesses operating within them, for example, up to 100% relief from business rates.

---

[1]Mauritius, India and Nepal have a regime which requires companies to commit a set percentage of profits to social purpose activity.

Looking at incentives and grants, until absorbed by local authorities, the now defunct local enterprise partnerships (LEPs) provided grants to businesses in their local area that are focussed on creating social impact and economic growth. Innovate UK also offers grants to businesses that are working on innovative projects with a clear social impact.

Again, there is little global evidence of specific social mobility regulation, although the European Union (2022)'s Corporate Sustainability Reporting Directive includes a requirement for organisations to report on how they deal with equal opportunities and treatment for all, diversity and adequate wages. In the UK, Companies Act (2006) has a light touch requirement for directors to consider and report 'the impact of the company's operations on the community and the environment'. There is ongoing advocacy for strengthening these rules.[2]

Some businesses have also opted into regulation. community interest companies (CICs) have an embedded social purpose in their constitution and have (for example) restrictions on profit and asset distributions. By August 2022, there were over 26,000 CICs, although almost exclusively they are small or micro-entities (The Office of the Regulator of Community Interest Companies, 2022).

The other route some businesses have taken is to register as a B corp which includes a requirement that participants commit to changing their governance structure to take into account all stakeholders (not just shareholders). There are over 1,500 companies registered as B corps in the UK.

Then there are provisions which essentially set out preconditions for undertaking certain activities (licences to operate). The Procurement Act (2023) requires account to be taken of social value delivered (e.g. the creation of jobs) as part of the procurement process. The Town and Country Planning Act (1990) requires land developers to negotiate and agree to certain community commitments with the local authority.

To complete the picture, it is worth taking into account public opinion. A PwC UK (n.d.) survey identified that 73% of the public

---

[2]For example, see the Better Business Act, https://betterbusinessact.org/.

want long-term strategic collaborative partnerships between business, government, education and industry bodies to prepare them for the world of work.

## HOW CAN BUSINESSES SUPPORT SOCIAL MOBILITY AND WHAT ARE THE ISSUES LIMITING BUSINESS ENGAGEMENT?

Beyond the headline of broadening accessibility of opportunities, corporate activities can be broken down into three distinct areas:

- *Outreach and pre-employment*: The social mobility journey starts from birth. Businesses can support and work with community organisations, schools and colleges to support that journey. Examples of activity include financial literacy training, employability training, business insights and work experience. Businesses can also engage in broader community activity, for example, community project volunteering.

- *Employment*: Clearly access to opportunities is the vital step in the journey. Employers can look at their recruitment practices to see how they can attract talented individuals that are regarded as coming from an SED background. This can be done in partnership with organisations that are engaged with that cohort.

- *Retention and development*: Ultimately the SE profile of business leadership should be reflective of the wider community. Having an effective recruitment programme, which is not aligned with an equally effective retention development strategy, is arguably worse than no engagement.

In developing recommendations, it is important to be clear on the challenges that can exist. Of course, the key factor is the culture and values of the leaders within the business, but looking at the issues across the different areas, themes include the following:

- *Outreach and pre-employment*: Issues include:
  - resource constraints limiting the ability to engage with discretionary or perceived non-value add activity;

- ○ a lack of knowledge of how to engage with (effective) activity;
- ○ no connection on nexus to that community because of the nature and location of the business; and
- ○ no accountability, responsibility or incentive to take part in activities.

- *Employment*:
  - ○ recruiting from existing talent pools already fulfils business needs;
  - ○ (unconscious) bias that individuals from SED backgrounds are less likely to perform well;
  - ○ difficulties in finding/connecting with SED individuals; and
  - ○ no responsibility, accountability or incentive for recruiting from that talent pool.

- *Retention and development*:
  - ○ a lack of understanding of how the organisation's culture could impact someone with a SED background and cultural inertia due to the perceived negative impact of change;
  - ○ a lack of role models or programmes designed to support SED individuals;
  - ○ concerns about competitiveness and productivity; and
  - ○ no accountability, responsibility or incentive for addressing the issue.

## WHAT BEHAVIOURS ARE BEING SOUGHT?

The other area to consider is what (changes in) behaviours are being sought. Key to this is the quality of engagement. To understand this requires an examination of what works well and the hallmarks of best practice typically involve the following:

- outcomes are set and tracked;
- activities are strategic, aligned and embedded in operations, culture and values of the business as opposed to ad hoc, siloed and peripheral;

- effective partnering with appropriate (expert) organisations and cross industry collaboration;

- matching the needs to the strengths of the business, for example, financial expertise, available facilities and equipment, etc.; and

- senior management is measured on performance.


## REGULATION AND THE POLICY SUITE

Given the currently light touch set of rules and the persistence of the issue, there is a case for considering a more robust regulatory framework. However, any regulatory proposals should be assessed in the context of the ecosystem of policy measures available to the government.

Although not examined in detail, some examples of areas that may be worth considering are as follows:

- *Taxation*: Extending the relief and scope available under the CITR regime, and giving super deductions for expenditure connected to social purpose activity in disadvantaged areas. Consider extending the breaks available under LEZ's to VAT.

- *Grants and incentives*: Consider new funding options in the light of the defunding of LEPs.

- *Enablers*: The creation of a suite of tools, resources and policies to make engagement easier.

Turning now to regulation, areas to consider include the following:

- Strengthening s172 of the Companies Act.

- Making it mandatory to have a social purpose provision in a company's constitution documents.

- (Ultimately) mandatory reporting of key social mobility data.

- The introduction of social mobility compliance requirements.

With respect to the last two items, there needs to be some careful consideration over the design and alignment where possible with other related requirements, for example, the EU Corporate Sustainability Reporting Directive (EU CSRD).

If the ultimate aim is to improve business engagement then design considerations should include the following:

- *Scope.* The scope of the rules needs to be considered in terms of business activities. In this context, the focus should both be on internal matters (recruitment, development and progression) as well as external factors (community impact of business operations, outreach and supply chains). In addition, businesses should not be taking on responsibilities that should lie with the government.

- *Organisations covered.* Exemptions, for example, for SME and micro-businesses.

- *Effectiveness of regulation.* Regulation needs to be targeted and measurable. The evidence is that regulation that is not targeted to encourage incremental activity can result in businesses re-purposing current activity rather than making real change. Measurement and setting specific targets should be encouraged. Finally, sanctions for non-compliance are needed to ensure that the rules have bite.

- *Economic impact.* The benefit of regulation needs to be weighed against economic impact. The UK economy is a net inward investment country and therefore anything that may impact that inward investment needs to be carefully considered.

- *Pathways to compliance.* Different industries and even different businesses in the same industry sector will have different attributes in terms of assets that could be mobilised for social purpose activities. Geography and the local community needs are also a factor. Therefore pathways to compliance should be flexible in terms of the 'what' and the 'how'. For example, a technology company could use its resources in helping deal with issues relating to digital poverty, whereas a construction company could use its resources to support retrofit insulation projects.

- *Regulatory burden and compliance infrastructure.* A multifaceted regime could create complexity in terms of measurement and comparability. Taking the above example, how can you compare the social value of addressing digital poverty as compared to retrofit insulation? A widely accepted measurement system is needed. Alignment with other provisions needs to be considered.

- *Phased or big bang?* A phased approach is preferred on the basis that a big bang approach risks cause detrimental disruption and lead to misdirection of business activities. This also recognises that currently, businesses will have different levels of maturity in respect of social mobility engagement.

Bringing the above to life in an example of a possible model:

- *Reporting*: The first phase would be to introduce self-reported data across key areas including the SE background of the workforce, SE pay gap and other activities connected to social mobility, for example, recruitment practices, outreach, etc. The next step would be a requirement to submit an annual value add statement which in qualitative and where appropriate quantitative terms is a self-assessment of these activities. After a period of self-assessment, the next step would be making the assessment subject to independent review and audit. Finally, the annual value add statement and supporting data would be publicly reported.

- *Regulation*: Businesses are required to set, say a five-year strategy and targets, have SE-specific policies and practices around key areas of business operations (e.g. supplier selection, recruitment, etc.) and be subject to similar duties to public sector bodies under the Equality Act. Finally, the introduction of a requirement for business leaders to be assessed on performance in this area.

## REFERENCES

Companies Act 2006, s.172.

Department for Education. (2023). *Academic year 2022/23: Apprenticeships and traineeships*. https://explore-education-statistics. service.gov.uk/find-statistics/apprenticeships-and-traineeships

Equality Act 2010, s.1.

European Union. (2022). *Directive (EU) 2022/2464 of the European Parliament and of the Council of 14 December 2022*. Corporate Sustainability Reporting Directive. https://eur-lex.europa.eu/legal-content/ EN/TXT/PDF/?uri=CELEX:32022L2464

Madders, J. (2023, March 21). *Debate on social mobility*. House of Commons. https://hansard.parliament.uk/commons/2023-03-21/ debates/36E77607-A136-4B68-9997-9C6DAA3408C6/SocialMobility

Procurement Act 2023.

PwC UK. (n.d.). *Driving social mobility in the UK: Four key success factors to boost opportunities for all*. https://www.pwc.co.uk/government-public-sector/assets/documents/driving-social-mobility-in-uk.pdf

Social Mobility Commission. (2023). *State of the nation 2023: People and places*. https://assets.publishing.service.gov.uk/ media/64f853399ee0f2000fb7bf80/state-of-the-nation-2023.pdf

The Business Commission for Tackling Inequalities. (2023). *Tackling inequality: An agenda for business action*. https://tacklinginequality.org/ files/flagship.pdf

The Office of the Regulator of Community Interest Companies. (2022). *CIC regulator: Annual report 2021 to 2022*. https://www.gov.uk/government/publications/community-interest-companies-regulator-annual-report-2021-to-2022/ cic-regulator-annual-report-2021-to-2022

Town and Country Planning Act 1990, s.106.

World Economic Forum. (2020). *The global social mobility report 2020: Equality, opportunity and a new economic imperative*. https://www3. weforum.org/docs/Global_Social_Mobility_Report.pdf

# 17

# TECH FOR GOOD: FROM DISPARITY TO OPPORTUNITY

## Nimmi Patel

*techUK, UK*

techUK is a membership organisation launched in 2013 to champion the technology sector and prepare and empower the UK for what comes next, delivering a better future for people, society, the economy and the planet. More than 1,000 companies are members of techUK. These companies across the UK range from leading Financial Times Stock Exchange (FTSE) 100 companies to new innovative start-ups. The majority of our members (around 60%) are small and medium-sized digital businesses. By working collaboratively with government and others, we provide expert guidance and insight for our members and stakeholders about how to prepare for the future, anticipate change and realise the positive potential of technology in a fast-moving world. This chapter explores digital inclusion's crucial role in addressing social and economic inequalities in the UK. techUK's Local Digital Index is a tool which measures regional disparities in digital capabilities, including digital skills, which is useful for guiding targeted policy interventions to break down barriers to opportunity. Local initiatives that focus on collaboration between businesses and government to foster digital skills development are an effective intervention.

## THE MAIN BARRIERS TO GETTING PEOPLE ONLINE

Digital inclusion involves ensuring that people have the necessary access, skills, motivation and trust to effectively use the internet. This exclusion can exacerbate existing inequalities and create new forms of disadvantage (The British Academy, 2023). The House of Lords (2023) Communications and Digital Committee inquiry on digital exclusion and cost of living, to which techUK gave both oral and written evidence (techUK, 2023a), found that the main barriers to getting adults online include the following:

- *Access* – not everyone can connect to the internet and go online. They may not have the broadband infrastructure in place to connect, lack digital devices or it may be too expensive. Ofcom's (2023) Technology Tracker estimates that 7% of UK households did not have internet access at home and 9% of UK households struggled to afford broadband in April 2023. Around 1.5 million do not have a smartphone, tablet or laptop and 53% of people offline cannot afford an average monthly broadband bill (Good Things Foundation, 2024a).

- *Skills* – not everyone has the basic skills needed to be able to use the internet and online services. 8.5 million people lack basic digital skills and are unable to carry out simple tasks online, like setting up an email address or connecting with loved ones virtually (Good Things Foundation, 2024a).

- *Motivation* – not everyone sees how using the internet could be beneficial. A lack of interest is a key barrier for 14% of those who are offline (Lloyds Bank, 2023).

- *Confidence and trust* – some people remain wary of the benefits of technology and fear online crime, or do not know where to start to get online (AbilityNet, 2024).

People may overcome one barrier and then face another that stops them from using technology. These groups face deepening isolation as society becomes increasingly digital. The British Academy (2023) has found that 'digital poverty reinforces wider inequalities, as it can render services and opportunities unavailable' – impacting mental, physical and financial wellbeing. In Brighton & Hove, purchasing an adult saver bus ticket with cash costs 10% more than buying it through a mobile app (Faith & Daniel, 2022). Here, being digitally excluded forces people who may be economically disadvantaged to pay higher prices, perpetuating a cycle of disadvantage (Faith & Daniel, 2022). Additionally, NHS England recognises a clear relationship between groups that are digitally excluded and those at greater risk of poor health (NHS Digital, 2022). About 39% of UK adults are not registered on the NHS app (Good Things Foundation, 2024a). The effects of social inequalities stemming from not being online or not using the internet effectively are substantial and well-documented.

## INVESTING IN DIGITAL INCLUSION CREATES ECONOMIC OPPORTUNITIES

Investing in digital inclusion can create significant economic opportunities by bridging the digital divide and empowering individuals and communities. Steps towards driving digital inclusion are steps also towards tackling disparities in health and wages across the country, challenging skills gaps and labour shortages and reducing cyber risks for people and businesses. Good Things Foundation (2024b) found that interventions that address digital exclusion are estimated to return £9.48 for every £1 invested. An investment of £1.4 billion could reap economic benefits of £13.7 billion for the UK. Clearly, investing in digital inclusion is not just a matter of equity; it is a strategic economic decision that can drive growth and innovation, but the government has not conducted any assessment on the economic impacts of digital exclusion in recent years (Good Things Foundation, 2024b). It has been left to the private sector to evaluate the impact of spending on digital inclusion.

## INVESTMENT IN DIGITAL SKILLS IS A KEY PILLAR OF DIGITAL INCLUSION

Research has found that 9.7 million people still struggling with setting up privacy and marketing settings online and 4.7 million people not being able to connect to Wi-Fi (Lloyds Bank, 2023).

Prioritising the development of digital skills is essential for digital inclusion. Without these skills, access to technology is ineffective. Learning digital skills can build confidence and trust in digital environments (AbilityNet, 2024). But digital skills development is a moving target, and given the pace of technological change, further digital skills will be needed such as artificial intelligence (AI) skills, widening the digital divide. Currently, 7.5 million people, or 18% of UK adults, lack the essential digital skills that are currently needed for the workplace, and 54% of the UK labour force is not meeting its full potential (AbilityNet, 2024). Given that the government reported the digital skills gap is estimated to cost the UK economy £63 billion per year (Department for Digital, Culture, Media & Sport, 2022), people must be motivated to learn and continue to develop their digital skills. It is important to bring digital into people's lives in a way that benefits them so they are interested in learning. With 82% of all job vacancies now requiring digital skills, it is important that everyone, whatever their age or background, can participate in an increasingly digital world (Nania et al., 2019). As AI and automation technologies are adopted at pace, there is further research to suggest that access to good digital infrastructure combined with investment in human capital is correlated with better outcomes, such as a growth in jobs, job quality and skills needs (Hayton et al., 2023).

Skills, therefore, must accompany concerns around access to technology and improving motivation as core components of the digital inclusion agenda, to ensure that people are equipped to get the most out of the technology they use and realise the benefits for opportunity and economic growth.

## LOCAL DIGITAL INDEX: A FRAMEWORK TO UNDERSTAND LOCAL DIGITAL ECOSYSTEMS

techUK's Local Digital Index, established in 2021, was created as a tool for benchmarking regional performance and is essential for identifying socioeconomic inequalities across different regions of the UK. The Index identified seven components that are essential to a strong place-based digital technology ecosystem, including: digital skills, digital infrastructure, research and innovation, finance and investment, trade, data ecosystems and digital adoption (techUK, 2023). The components that make up the Index are a mix of tangible and intangible assets and inputs–much like the concept of human capital.[1] By measuring these components, the Index helps identify regions that lack adequate digital resources and skills, highlighting areas that may be at a disadvantage in terms of economic opportunities and growth.

The Index was created to gather data and offers a framework for assessing the digital strengths of an area. The Index also ranks the 12 regions and 41 sub-regions (aligned with Combined Authority areas in England) of the UK by how successful it is at each component, which is useful to policymakers and local actors as it showcases how some nations and regions across the UK have stronger digital foundations than others. The Index importantly does not only focus on the tech industry itself, but looks outward to assess the impact that technology is having within a specific locality. Such insight is vital to understanding the role both policy interventions and technology can play in breaking down barriers to opportunity. techUK's goal is to challenge the status quo by asking, 'If a solution works in Dudley, can it also be effective in Dundee and Doncaster?' and 'If it meets the needs of London, how can we implement it in Liverpool or Leicester?' (techUK, 2023b). Making these data publicly available helps to illustrate a true picture of the digital sector and economy. By identifying regional strengths and weaknesses, the Index is a roadmap for policymakers and stakeholders to foster a more digitally inclusive society. It also provides a route for possible devolved accountability by asking if something is working well, how can it be rolled out elsewhere or increased, and if interventions are not working then how can they be changed, adapted or cancelled. The essence of devolution should acknowledge and appreciate diversity and that one size does not always fit all.

---

[1]The Human Capital Index was developed by the World Bank and measures the potential productivity of a country's future workforce (its human capital) by assessing health and education outcomes. See more at https://www.worldbank.org/en/publication/human-capital.

The Index has been utilised by the tech industry and policymakers alike, as a way to understand how technology could support the 2022 UK government's ambition to 'level up' the country. The Levelling Up agenda aimed to reduce regional disparities and promote equal opportunities through enhanced digital capabilities (Department for Levelling Up, Housing & Communities, 2022). It was a programme of policy to improve economic dynamism and innovation to drive growth across the whole country.

## TECHUK'S LOCAL DIGITAL INDEX REVEALS REGIONAL DISPARITIES IN DIGITAL SKILLS

All of the Local Digital Index reports from 2021, 2022 and 2023 show how digital skills are a critical component of building strong digital ecosystems across the UK. Digital skills are defined as a spectrum ranging from basic digital literacy, such as the ability to access public services online, to advanced competencies, such as those required for working with cutting-edge technologies like quantum computing (techUK, 2021). This comprehensive definition looks at the importance of digital skills not only in tech-specific roles but also as essential competencies across various sectors, contributing to overall economic resilience and growth. The Index shows differences in internet access, digital literacy and the availability of tech jobs, which can directly impact economic opportunities and quality of life. Ultimately, such disparities can contribute to broader socioeconomic inequalities, as regions with limited digital resources may struggle to attract investment and foster innovation.

The 2021 Index highlighted significant regional variations in digital skills across the UK. While some areas, such as London and the South East, demonstrated strong digital capabilities, others lag due to factors such as limited access to education, training resources and infrastructure, including Yorkshire and The Humber, Northern Ireland and Wales (techUK, 2021). One of the challenges for the first Index was the lack of granular, location-specific data to accurately measure digital skills at more localised levels, such as city or district areas. The Index was limited to NUTS1 regional data,[2] which provided a broad overview but lacked the specificity needed for targeted interventions.

The 2022 Index provided more detailed insights into regional variations in digital skills, due to improved data collection methods that allow for a more granular analysis at the NUTS2 level. The Index found that many regions experience a significant rural–urban divide, with rural areas, within the North East or Northern Ireland, for example, often experiencing varied access to digital infrastructure and education necessary for developing digital skills (techUK, 2022). London, which is often seen through a single lens, should not be seen as a homogenous block as this undermines the levelling up needs of the capital. Inner West London's skills score is in the bottom third, and Outer East and North East London have some of the lowest scores nationally for finance and investment, trade and research and development. But it would be a lazy narrative to assume the booming tech sector in London, means that the capital's digital needs are met. The Index makes recommendations for rural areas, like Lincolnshire and Cumbria, emphasising how improved digital skills alongside improved digital infrastructure can support the adoption, adaption and renewal of services and support for communities. Supporting digital skills in places like Merseyside and Tees Valley will help to encourage people to not only access digital services but also consider careers in the tech sector. The Index also recognised that there are gaps between the digital skills available in the workforce and those required by employers, particularly in emerging technologies like AI, data science and cybersecurity.

The latest 2023 Index, now in its third year, found that Greater London takes first place on digital skills, followed by Wales in second place with a sharp rise from eighth place in 2022 results, with a good percentage of people using online information for day-to-day activities as well as a high number of higher education students, indicating a growing group of skilled tech people (techUK, 2023b). Essex outperforms East Anglia, Bedfordshire and Hertfordshire on digital skills. The Index also highlights significant regional

---

[2]Find more on Office for National Statistics's International Geographies Classifications at https://www.ons.gov.uk/methodology/geography/ukgeographies/eurostat.

variations in digital literacy and internet usage. About 75% of people in the South East and West Midlands actively use digital tools to find or download information for work, education or personal use. However, only 61% of people in London and the East of England, and 57% in the South East, use online public services. In Northern Ireland, this figure is even lower, at just 30%. While the West Midlands and Yorkshire and the Humber score well for infrastructure, their digital adoption score is pulled down by a lack of skills and access to finance and investment. A recommendation from the Index urged policymakers to create a National Digital Inclusion Strategy to meet the needs of regional digital strategies, with specific support for digital inclusion projects.

## DATA-DRIVEN POLICY MAKING

Over the three years, techUK's Local Digital Index approach has been refined when measuring digital skills. Initially focussing on the foundational importance of digital skills, the Index has evolved to provide more detailed regional insights and ways in which digital skills can be integrated into local economic growth plans. However, there is currently insufficient, high-quality data being collected and released by government. If digital skills are a priority, we must have better data to measure effectively. From 2024, the Index will seek to include more data from localities and provide data which informs each area's local growth plans. This data-driven approach can help bridge the digital divide and reduce inequalities by ensuring that all regions have the necessary components for their local digital economy.

## DIGITAL INCLUSION REQUIRES COLLABORATION
## TO CONNECT COMMUNITIES

To address these challenges, the tech industry is investing in digital skills training. For example, BT Group has been working with the charity AbilityNet to help improve the digital skills of 4,000 older and digitally excluded people. They will deliver more than 1,000 group and one-to-one training sessions to those who need it most in regions across the UK (AbilityNet, 2024). Uber have established a partnership with the Open University to provide free flexible degree courses and access to free short courses for their drivers or one of their family members, supporting flexible earning and learning around other commitments (Uber, 2022). Since 2013, Accenture have equipped 90,000 people in the UK skills through their Skills to Succeed Academy, which is a free, highly interactive online training programme (Accenture, 2024).

But the tech sector cannot do this without assistance. The case studies within the Local Digital Index (techUK, 2021, 2022, 2023) confirm local initiatives that focus on collaboration between businesses and government to foster digital skills development are most effective. For instance, Brent Council in London has partnered with tech company Infosys to provide free digital learning for local small and medium-sized enterprises (techUK, 2023c). Infosys' flagship digital learning platform, Springboard, is designed to empower people and communities with digital skills, with the goal of opening up more opportunities for the Brent small business community. From first launching in Brent in 2021 to May 2023, Springboard had over 48,000 people sign up for the platform, positively impacting digital literacy and inclusion rates in the local area. Cisco is in a strategic partnership with Greater Manchester Combined Authority to support digital inclusion by facilitating foundational level digital skills for anyone in the region through the free, self-paced, mobile first Cisco platform 'Skills for All' (Cisco, 2022).

## THE STRENGTH OF PARTNERSHIPS AND DATA-DRIVEN INTERVENTIONS

What is clear from the Local Digital Index and the examples of industry action is that digital inclusion is rooted in partnerships. No one sector or even government can do this alone. That is why, techUK is a member of FutureDotNow. FutureDotNow is a coalition of over 230 members who are coordinating industry action to equip people with the essential digital skills they need to thrive in work and prepare for our digital future (techUK,

2024). As a powerful collective brand, the coalition can have a greater reach, and shared ownership of the digital skills challenge (FutureDotNow, 2024).

Established in the wake of the pandemic when the reliance on technology increased exponentially as people were confined to their homes, the techUK, a partner of the Tech for Good Alliance, is a UK-wide initiative bringing private sector firms together with charities and third sector bodies to creative positive change which aligns closely with techUK's mission of championing technology's role championing people, society, the economy and the planet (Tech for Good Alliance, 2024). Not all change is reliant on the government – local, devolved or national – but support and recognition of the work done by such partnerships like the Tech for Good Alliance can offer meaningful change, improve skills, access to provision and open the opportunities and possibilities for community groups.

techUK is also proud to support the End Digital Poverty Day campaign spearheaded by the Digital Poverty Alliance, which looks at raising awareness, discussing solutions and driving actionable strategies to eradicate digital poverty (Digital Poverty Alliance, 2024). The campaign means not only spreading awareness of the damage digital exclusion can do, but also the impact inclusion services can have. Ultimately, achieving digital inclusion requires a collective commitment, but by leveraging data-driven insights from techUK's Local Digital Index, policymakers can design targeted interventions that address the unique needs of each nation and region, alongside partners in the area.

## REFERENCES

AbilityNet. (2024). *Research paper: Low digital skills households and the path to digital inclusion.* https://abilitynet.org.uk/free-tech-support-and-info/low-digital-skills-households-and-path-digital-inclusion

Accenture. (2024). *Helping communities thrive in the digital economy.* https://www.accenture.com/gb-en/about/inclusion-diversity/helping-communities-thrive-digital-economy

Cisco. (2022). *Cisco and greater Manchester combined authority collaborate to create a more inclusive, digital region.* https://news-blogs. cisco.com/emea/2022/10/20/cisco-and-greater-manchester-combined-authority-collaborate-to-create-a-more-inclusive-digital-region/

Department for Digital, Culture, Media & Sport. (2022). *UK digital strategy.* https://www.gov.uk/government/publications/uks-digital-strategy/ uk-digital-strategy

Department for Levelling Up, Housing & Communities. (2022). *Levelling up the United Kingdom.* https://www.gov.uk/government/publications/ levelling-up-the-united-kingdom

Digital Poverty Alliance. (2024). *End digital poverty day 2024.* https://dig italpovertyalliance.org/end-digital-poverty-day-2/

Faith, B., & Daniel, E. (2022). *Digital levelling up: starting early to tackle digital poverty.* Digital Futures at Work Research Centre. https://digit-research.org/blog_article/digital-levelling-up-starting-early-to-tackle-digital-poverty/

FutureDotNow. (2024). *Join us.* https://futuredotnow.uk/join-us/

Good Things Foundation. (2024a). *Our digital nation.* https://www. goodthingsfoundation.org/policy-and-research/research-and-evidence/ research-2024/digital-nation

Good Things Foundation. (2024b). *The economic impact of digital inclusion in the UK.* https://www.goodthingsfoundation.org/policy-and-research/research-and-evidence/research-2024/digital-inclusion-uk-economic-impact

Hayton, J., Rohenkohl, B., Pissarides, C., & Liu, H. Y. (2023). *What drives UK firms to adopt AI and robotics, and what are the consequences for jobs?.* Institute for the Future of Work. https://www.ifow.org/ publications/adoption-of-ai-in-uk-firms-and-the-consequences-for-jobs

House of Lords. (2023). *Communications and digital committee 3rd report of session 2022–23: Digital exclusion* (pp. 1–70). https:// publications.parliament.uk/pa/ld5803/ldselect/ldcomm/219/219.pdf

Lloyds Bank. (2023). *2023 UK consumer digital index.* https:// www.lloydsbank.com/assets/media/pdfs/banking_with_us/whats-happening/231122-lloyds-consumer-digital-index-2023-report.pdf

Nania, J., Bonella, H., Restuccia, D., & Taska, B. (2019). *No longer optional: Employer demand for digital skills.* Department for Digital, Culture, Media & Sport. https://assets.publishing.service.gov.uk/government/uploads/system/uploads/attachment_data/file/807830/No_Longer_Optional_Employer_Demand_for_Digital_Skills.pdf

NHS Digital. (2022). *Why digital inclusion matters to health and social care.* https://digital.nhs.uk/about-nhs-digital/our-work/digital-inclusion/digital-inclusion-in-health-and-social-care

Ofcom. (2023). *2023 technology tracker.* https://www.ofcom.org.uk/siteassets/resources/documents/research-and-data/data/statistics/2023/technology-tracker/technology-tracker-2023-data-tables?v=329770#page=217

techUK. (2021). *Local digital capital (LDC) – The concept.* https://www.techuk.org/shaping-policy/nations-and-regions/local-digital-capital-index/local-digital-capital-the-concept.html

techUK. (2022). *Local digital capital index 2022.* https://www.techuk.org/shaping-policy/nations-and-regions/local-digital-capital-index-2022.html

techUK. (2023a). *techUK gives evidence to the House of Lords Communications and Digital Committee on digital exclusion and the cost of living.* https://www.techuk.org/resource/techuk-gives-evidence-to-the-house-of-lords-communications-and-digital-committee-on-digital-exclusion-and-the-cost-of-living.html

techUK. (2023b). *Local Digital Index 2023.* https://www.techuk.org/shaping-policy/nations-and-regions-hub/local-digital-capital-index-2023.html

techUK. (2023c). *Infosys provides free digital learning for local SMEs in Brent.* https://www.techuk.org/resource/infosys-provides-free-digital-learning-for-local-smes-in-brent.html

techUK. (2024). *techUK & FutureDotNow raise alarm over workforce readiness for AI.* https://www.techuk.org/resource/futuredotnow-raises-alarm-over-workforce-readiness-for-ai.html

Tech for Good Alliance. (2024). *Homepage.* https://www.techforgoodalliance.org.uk/

The British Academy. (2023). *Digital technology and inequality: Policy Brief February 2023*. https://www.thebritishacademy.ac.uk/documents/4662/Digital_Technology_and_Inequality_Policy_Brief.pdf

Uber. (2022). *The Open University and Uber*. https://skillshub.online/

# 18

# BRITAIN'S 21ST CENTURY CHALLENGE: EMPLOYERS MUST DRIVE SOCIAL MOBILITY TOO

Justine Greening[a,b]

*ªPurpose Coalition, UK*
*ᵇUK Parliament, UK*

In the 1992 presidential election, Bill Clinton's political advisor, James Carville, coined the phrase 'it's the economy, stupid' when talking about what US voters cared about (Taegan, 2024). It represented his view that whatever the wider issues – healthcare, security, education – in the end, US voters ultimately decided their vote based on how well the economy was doing. They voted on how that had consequentially impacted their own livelihood and well-being – for example, were they able to get work and, as a result, how easy was it to make ends meet and pay the bills.

Equally, much of the 2019 Parliament of the Boris Johnson/Liz Truss/Rishi Sunak administrations was spent tackling a cost-of-living crisis, triggered by rampant inflation and its impact on the prices of essential goods and services. This inflation was itself triggered by the stop–start inflationary recommencing of supply chains post-COVID-19 and the war in Ukraine, with its impact on energy prices. It meant that across the UK economy, the annual rate of inflation rose almost continuously from under 1% in early 2021 to a peak of 11.1% in October 2022, a 41-year high. Over the three years between May 2021 and May 2024, food prices rose by 30.6%. Basic foodstuffs saw the highest increases. In a single year, from 2021 to 2022, bread increased by 20%, pasta by 29% and low-fat milk by 46% (Payne, 2022).

But 30 years after Carville's famous utterance, is the reality of what voters are asking for from their governments more complex than simply pointing to an economic cycle and its impact on household finances? Perhaps so. Polling in the UK showed that there are now more complex factors at play in shaping the views of voters on which parties they vote for.

## MORE THAN JUST ECONOMIC GROWTH

Disappointment and disenchantment with Brexit and a failure to deliver levelling up promises, the conduct of some in government during the COVID-19 pandemic and the calamitous Liz Truss budget all took their toll on the public's perception of politicians and political discourse more widely. By the time an election was called in June 2024, a record high of 45% said they 'almost never' trusted governments of any party to put the needs of the people above the interests of their own political party and over half said they almost never trusted politicians to tell the truth (Curtice et al., 2024). There is a huge mountain to climb to re-establish the government's credibility and restore public trust. As polling expert Sir John Curtice pointed out alongside the survey 'The public is as doubtful as it has ever been about the trustworthiness and efficacy of the country's system of government and the people who comprise it' (NatCen Social Research, 2024).

The Labour Government elected in 2024 promised a mission-driven government to rebuild Britain, guided by Five Missions, with the first undertaking to 'kickstart economic growth' (The Labour Party, 2024). Its view is that 'sustained economic growth is the only route to improving the prosperity of our country and the living standards of working people'. But the reality is that governments need to deliver more than just percentage points of gross domestic product growth. Even that isn't enough now for voters who will view that as simply inadequate unless it is also delivering broad-based improvements in people's lives, their pockets and their perceived futures.

The Sunak administration, so dramatically ejected from power by voters in July 2024, failed to understand this. In the – literal – 'helicopter' world inhabited by the former Prime Minister, any growth, however small a fraction of a per cent, was a cause for celebration. But the problem was that the reality for millions of people and households across Britain, there was a disconnect between prime ministerial rhetoric and their day-to-day experience and struggles.

There was a 'macro' disconnect at an overall economic level, of a bigger picture that voters were told was positive yet was undiscernible to a wider public. This was compounded by a 'micro' disconnect at an individual level. Voters had a sense of a Prime Minster who simply did not understand their lives or the challenges they faced. In a poll conducted in the run-up to the general election, 72% described him as 'out of touch' and only 20% felt he understood the problems facing Britain (Skinner et al., 2024).

Unlike in the past, the economic fragility of households wasn't driven by a lack of available paid work for people – Britain has not been in a period of high unemployment. During the 1980s, as an economic restructuring of Britain's increasingly uncompetitive industrial base took place, unemployment hit three million. I saw how difficult that challenge to households and families was very personally. My father was part of those unemployment statistics. Alongside many others in Rotherham where I grew up, he spent a year unemployed. In contrast, today, whilst the UK economic inactivity rate is currently estimated at 22.1%, the actual unemployment rate is 4.4%, far lower (Office for National Statistics, 2024).

When you put together the economic data with the polling data, the picture it paints is of a voter base for whom it's actually not just 'the economy stupid'. Whilst there is no doubt that the economic health of the nation matters hugely, voters understand they need more than that from a successful government – it's necessary but not sufficient. The challenge is that people no longer believe that economic growth means things get better for them and their families. They want to see an economy that is growing in a way that directly lifts them and their own prospects. After the post-COVID-19 bout of inflation that the UK and other major economies experienced, for too many voters it feels that the 'effort and reward' curve for economic growth cascading into benefiting their own pockets is weak, if non-existent.

## EDUCATION AS KEY TO UNLOCKING OPPORTUNITIES

It is why, in the end, it will be the delivery – or otherwise – of the fifth and final mission of the 2024 Labour Manifesto and Government, focussed on 'Breaking Down Barriers to Opportunity' that will be the most shaping for all of us in the long term.

It is a mission which aims to break the link between background and success so that 'whoever you are, wherever you come from', Britain is a country where 'hard work means you can get on in life'. The government aims to reform the education system, starting with early years and through primary and secondary school, so that young people are better prepared for the world of work and more able to take advantage of the opportunities they deserve, transforming their life chances. It also wants to ensure equality and respect for all so that people can thrive no matter what their background.

There is no doubt that putting education at the heart of breaking down the barriers to opportunity is key. The gaps that open up in life chances start from the very beginning. Research has found that by the age of five, the attainment gap between pupil premium children and their peers is already about five months (Education Policy Institute, 2024). Before these disadvantaged pupils even start reception, they have limited vocabulary and lack vital skills. They are also more likely to be persistently absent, missing important parts of the curriculum with significant gaps in knowledge. By the end of Key Stage 2, they are on average three years behind their chronological reading age which reduces their ability to transition successfully to secondary school. By Year 11, the gap has increased to 19 months, with growing evidence that it has worsened still further since the COVID-19 pandemic. It can have a lifelong negative impact.

It will be the removal of those educational barriers, enabling talent to flourish and access opportunities that ultimately lays the foundations that will drive growth as much as, perhaps more, than any regulatory or tax-related changes that the 2024 Labour Government may subsequently introduce.

Yet enabling growth and prosperity to more effectively link and drive improvements for individuals needs more than just action in the education system. It needs action by business too.

## EMPLOYERS AS CATALYSTS

There was a time when business saw it as government's job to produce the skills and talent it needed. It could sit back and look to the education system to provide the talent base for success. And even if government wasn't doing that effectively enough, in the past 20–30 years employers could also draw in talent and human capital from around the world, including across the wider European Union to fill the skills gaps.

But in recent years, there has been a sea change in employer attitudes as post-Brexit Britain looks ever more to itself to fix problems of weak social mobility that are, in practice, home grown in nature. There is a growing recognition that employers can't just wait for policymakers to fix the talent and skills shortage. They need to be part of the solution themselves. In reality, it's been the lack of longer-term employer strategic involvement in skills development that has produced the situation that the country now faces. Between 2017 and 2022, skills shortages in this country doubled to more than half a million and now accounts for 36% of job vacancies (Department for Education, 2023).

Yet there have been steps in the right direction. Whilst ripe for reform following its original introduction back in 2017, one of the fundamental objectives of the apprenticeship levy was to drive the culture change we have seen in business in its involvement in skills development. That change has been significant. Whilst there is much further to go, the relationship between business and policymakers on skills is as close as it has ever been and looks to, appropriately, get closer still over the coming years.

This is crucial. For too long we have assumed that the conventional education system can deliver all the talent the country needs in the way it needs it. It is a prerequisite for any successful economic strategy. But business can be a strategic shaper of talent in more ways than just in relation to apprenticeships.

It can work upstream with the broader education system to shape the wider curriculum relevance across a range of subject and knowledge-based areas, helping to make more theoretical topics far more practical and relevant. When pupils can see the wider world relevance of what they are being taught, it provides a far better base for both their engagement and their learning.

Employers can also work 'downstream' with their own employees. Part of the cost-of-living challenge faced by millions of people was their frustration at being stuck in low-paying roles with little prospect to move upwards into higher skilled, better paid work. A global study by Oracle & Workplace Intelligence (2021) covering more than 14,600 employees across 13 countries showed that three-quarters of their participants felt stuck at work with little prospect of promotion. That lack of progression meant that their capacity to weather the economic storms Britain, with other countries has faced, let alone flourish, was severely limited.

It's why the potential for enhancing longer-term investment in the learning and development of employees, possibly through the Lifelong Learning Entitlement policy announced in 2021, or a variant of that policy with a similar objective, matters so much. It's how all of us can continue to develop our talents long after we've left the conventional and initial education system. That later chance to re-engage with studying or to develop brand new and existing skillsets to a more advanced level is crucial. It is particularly important for the vast majority of people who don't have great advice from a mentor or network to draw on when making their initial choices about careers. That was the case in my own life as it is for so many others.

For many of us, it may only be when we have our own, greater life experience that we can – perhaps for the first time – really assess where we want to develop our talents, how we want to progress our careers and what that will then entail in our own personal development. People will need an employer who can support them as they reskill and upskill into better paid work and careers. In essence, rather than seeing some roles as low paid in which people feel trapped, instead, we should see more clearly the poor employers responsible for that situation, who haven't created the necessary environment where people can not only get in to work but also get on in their work.

If 20th century policymakers faced challenges of unemployment and getting people into work then, for 21st century policymakers, the challenge is to ensure that once people get into work they can also progress. That's why the role of business is so important. Without the employers who understand how to build their organisations to be engines of social mobility that can remove barriers to opportunity that people face, acquiring talent from all backgrounds, we won't see a version of Britain that is generating both the quantity and quality of inclusive growth that everyone, irrespective of background, feels will benefit them.

'It's the economy *and* great employers, stupid' would be a better phrase to use today. A strong economy is no longer enough. We need great employers too. And that means continuing the sea change across British business that is currently taking place.

We've grown used to challenging companies over their impact on the planet and sustainability and, over the past two decades, they have steadily risen to that challenge. Now it's time for employers to rise to the challenge of their impact on people's lives and social mobility. Talent and open opportunity are essentially the new economic battleground of the 21st century and it's time for both an economic and corporate strategy that reflects that. That means government is realising that it's creating an enabling environment for businesses – not just through education but through partnership with business more broadly. It also means that business realises that it needs to be part of the broader solution, playing its role in closing gaps once people have left education and gone into employment. In essence, like many countries, we're all on a journey, but it will be a real prize, if Britain can lead the pack when it comes to demonstrating how to drive long-term, sustainable and inclusive growth.

## REFERENCES

Curtice, J., Montagu, I., & Sivathasan, C. (2024). *Damaged politics?: The impact of the 2019–24 Parliament on political trust and confidence.* National Centre for Social Research. https://natcen.ac.uk/publications/british-social-attitudes-41-damaged-politics

Department for Education. (2023). *Employer skills survey 2022.* https://explore-education-statistics.service.gov.uk/find-statistics/employer-skills-survey/2022

Education Policy Institute. (2024). *The Education Policy Institute annual report 2024.* https://epi.org.uk/annual-report-2024/

NatCen Social Research. (2024). *British Social Attitudes Survey* [data series, 4th release, SN: 200006]. UK Data Service. http://doi.org/10.5255/UKDA-Series-200006

Office for National Statistics. (2024). *UK labour market June 2024.* https://www.ons.gov.uk/releases/uklabourmarketjune2024

Oracle & Workplace Intelligence. (2021). *AI@Work 2021 global study.* https://www.oracle.com/no/news/announcement/people-believe-robots-can-support-their-career-2021-10-26/

Payne, C. (2022, January 19). *Consumer price inflation, UK.* Office for National Statistics. https://www.ons.gov.uk/economy/inflationandpriceindices/bulletins/consumerpriceinflation/december2021

Skinner, G., Pedley, K., Garrett, C., & Roff, B. (2024, April 18). *Rishi Sunak's satisfaction falls to equal worst ever Ipsos rating for a Conservative or Labour leader.* Ipsos. https://www.ipsos.com/en-uk/rishi-sunaks-satisfaction-falls-equal-worst-ever-ipsos-rating-conservative-or-labour-leader

Taegan. (2024). *It's the economy stupid – Political dictionary.* Political Dictionary. https://politicaldictionary.com/words/its-the-economy-stupid/

The Labour Party. (2024, June 14). *Mission-driven government.* The Labour Party. https://labour.org.uk/change/mission-driven-government/

# Section 5

# LABOUR AND INEQUALITY – PAST, PRESENT, AND FUTURE

# 19

# LABOUR'S LONG MARCH FOR EQUALITY: A CONTINUING INCOMPLETENESS, A CONTINUING STRUGGLE

## Hilary Armstrong

*UK Parliament, UK*

## TACKLING INEQUALITY IN THE POST-WAR ERA

Whilst I am not old enough to have been around when the Beveridge report was published, I am one of the tens of millions of young people who grew up surrounded by the welfare state that his report together with the post-war Labour government created. They changed my generation's opportunities throughout our lives.

The numbers that ran through the inequality of our nation at the time were not only stark but different from the decades since. After the war, it was the *majority* of people who had insecure old age; the *majority* of people who had insecure health care and the *majority* of people who were left without a wage where they were completely financially secure. For many people work was too insecure to be dependable.

Even though the numbers don't make arithmetic sense, in our society the majority of people suffered from these insecurities which disadvantaged them. These are big numbers and needed the big policy changes. They combined with post-war full employment to provide what came to be felt as a safety net for the millions of people I grew up amongst.

But of course, they did not 'end inequality'.

In the post-war world, new inequalities emerged. Beveridge's post-war pension scheme needed decades to build up a fund to be able you pay out pensions that would raise people above the poverty line. That time wasn't granted to the scheme which meant pensions had to be supplemented by means tested national assistance. The success of the welfare state in other areas meant that people lived longer and the pensions were paid out to what became one of the main gains of the post-war worker, a society where working people had years of retirement.

This meant that from the time of the 1964–1970 Labour government, a new superannuation scheme was necessary to provide more people with a pension that was adequate and did not need the means test as a top up. But other parts of the post-war settlement had been found to deepen inequalities, not necessarily to reduce it.

The Butler Act had provided secondary education for all – real progress, but it had created deep inequalities of life opportunities between those who passed the 11 plus and those that didn't. Over the 50s and 70s, the march of change over the 11 plus progressed (including in my own school). It took decades for Labour local authorities (in my own case including my father as Chair of Education) and Labour central government to reduce these inequalities.

## ADDRESSING NEW CHALLENGES

The 1964–1970 Labour government also tackled very different inequalities. Throughout British History for some their sexuality had been made illegal. As an inequality, this destroyed their lives in the same way. That Labour government repealed the law that caused that inequality. Also, for the first time, there was a legal framework for gender-related equal pay. Did both of these pieces of Labour led legislation stop the inequality that existed around gender and inequality? No, but the legal framework has created a better battleground to fight those prejudices.

But by the 1960s, new inequalities had emerged. 20 years of the post-war had brought new citizens to this country from all over the world and mainly from the Commonwealth largely to contribute labour to the NHS and transport. This joined together with a long history of racism to ensure that prejudice could restrict life opportunities and create new inequalities. 'No black; no dogs; no Irish' was a normal part of the experience of searching for a flat in many cities. Did Labours' 1966 Race Relations Act stop racism, NO but it did shift the legal battle to provide good ammunition for those suffering inequality.

I was living in London during the 1964 election and many people in the capital felt that the election had been won, with that small majority, because of the experience of many people who were privately renting their housing from private landlords. Then as now there was a severe shortage of rented accommodation and the unequal relationship between landlord and tenant meant that tenants could be and were treated very badly. Did the 1966 Rent Act solve this inequality – No – did it stop many people from fearing what is now called a no fault eviction – yes it did.

The picture I am painting of the struggle against inequality was by the time of the 1970s an incomplete one. Had inequality in all these areas been defeated NO, but for many people there was greater security (for some much greater security) than before the two great Labour administrations of 1945 and 1964.

I spent most of the 1970s not only engaging in Labour Party politics (itself, and especially for a woman, always a fruitful ground for improving equality) but also working in youth and community work in Sunderland, a community which had grown up around work in the shipyards, and then had collapsed after the closing of the yards. In terms of life chances and inequality, every British city had its localities where most people felt excluded from any rising tide of prosperity. My day-to-day work experience alongside the lived experience of millions of people in excluded locations all over our country showed that in real terms two Labour government had not finished inequality in our society. But let's be clear – in other parts of our cities, the battle had been tipped on to the side of people who had previously been denied opportunity.

## CONTINUING FIGHT IN THE 21ST CENTURY

The Labour government of 1997–2010 again took many steps to successfully reduce poverty and inequality, implementing the minimum wage, tax credits and serious programmes to get people into work, tackling rough sleeping and homelessness, and changing schools with a concentration on English and maths, and a determination to ensure the potential of every child was built into the system.

However, when I returned to social exclusion in 2006, what was clear was that real improvements had been made, but that there was still a group at the bottom of the pile who had real needs. We knew that it was possible to change opportunities and outcomes for the most excluded, but it needs time and targeted work.

The work of Sure Start was a clear way in which new mothers could be given support which would, as well as improving early care for the child, enabled the mother to begin to get access to the jobs market, with training opportunities, support from the job centre in preparing for interviews and the opportunity to start on a part-time basis, without losing all benefits. I was also able to look at, and introduce, programmes from around the world that were evidence based in terms of effectiveness and value for money, which made a real difference to lives of some of the most disadvantaged in society. In other words, benefits on their own are not the answer. Public services which work in ways that give everyone opportunities, but also make sure that those who are not necessarily likely to think the service is 'for them', are actually worked with in ways that they do get access, and are able to benefit. We used to call this 'progressive universalism' – not heard that for a whilst!

The recent work I have been engaged on in terms of the North East Child Poverty Commission, demonstrates that in the last decade, there has been a real deterioration in the experiences of many families, with people in work making up the majority of those now in poverty. This is a result of insecure employment, frequently at minimum wage level, with uncertain hours. The effect on families is stark, and also, effects on public services that are unprecedented, schools where they have a store of second hand clothes including underwear, where they bath children because they have no hot water at home, breakfast clubs, other means of supporting families to feed the children, hospitals where free breakfasts are offered to workers, who are struggling to manage. An unprecedent dependence on foodbanks.

Also, the levels of poverty and inequality are concentrated in particular localities, and this inevitably has an effect on aspirations. This is why good neighbourhood renewal programmes are so important. I was part of introducing and developing the Neighbourhood Renewal Programme when I was a local government minister in the 1997 government. That has now been evaluated as the most successful regeneration programme of the last 40 years. Maybe we could learn from that? Putting local people at the heart of working on those issues that will transform their neighbourhood, including the ability to tweak national programmes to work more effectively in their area, rules around housing benefit eligibility for properties that did not pass health and safety criteria were popular! In other words, very damp, mould ridden properties, or those with poor, dangerous heating, would have to be improved before the landlord could let them to housing benefit recipients. The programmes were given an initial £100 million (Social Exclusion Unit, 2001) but encouraged to think of longer term financial support packages.

It's amazing what people can do when given support, training and opportunity. We don't need to wait for magic solutions. We know how to get real meaningful change in people's lives. We need to have the right structures in place in government to ensure it happens, but it is not only government. Much needs to be done in the regions, and the combined authority. Mayors are really important in this agenda. Public bodies have a huge role to play in how they recruit and train local people, and we need more of them to pay the living wage, and to work with local schools and colleges to develop apprenticeships which could provide a ladder for local people.

There is so much that needs to be done and can be done. I believe not doing more to tackle inequality in our country will continue to hinder our economic growth, and to increase dependency on some public services which will be harmful to their efficiency. Let's just get on with it!

## REFERENCE

Social Exclusion Unit. (2001). *A new commitment to neighbourhood renewal: National strategy action plan.* https://dera.ioe.ac.uk/id/ eprint/3661/1/A_new_commitment_to_neighbourhood_renewal_-_ national_strategy_action_plan.pdf

# 20

## INEQUALITY STREET? REALISM AND RIOTS IN THE 2024 UK GENERAL ELECTION AND AFTER

### Rupa Huq

*Member of Parliament, UK House of Commons, UK*

August 2024 and the UK appeared to be in the grip of a heatwave. Freak weather topped off the peak summer holiday month often known as the 'silly season' which also took in riots concluding a period of political change that saw a major reset from a Conservative majority government (admittedly eroded from Boris Johnson's 2019 big election win after a series of by-elections due to a secession of scandals[1] but still in majority position) to a Labour landslide reducing the Tory total to a mere 120 seats. Going on social media one might be forgiven for thinking the nation was ablaze with marauding mobs having taken to the streets. The scenes witnessed

---

[1]Examples include: (i) Christopher Pincher in Tamworth's resignation, Staffordshire for sexual misconduct; (ii) Nadine Dorries in mid-Bedfordshire – exit over disagreement with Sunak government; (iii) Scot Benton in Blackpool over bribery including gambling; and (iv) Margaret Ferrier in Glasgow who broke lockdown rules. The top three exemplify Tory sleaze and (v) shows SNP wrong-doing.

in town centres ranged from a far right rally in Whitehall, attempted arson of asylum hotels (in Tamworth, Staffordshire and Rotherham, Yorkshire), the torching of a library (Spellow Hub, County Road Liverpool also housing a community centre and employment advisory service) through to the later more heart-warming scenes of community clean-ups and anti-fascist gatherings – the biggest of all in Walthamstow, East London, a pre-emptive show of community solidarity after word had spread that the far right would be descending on the area. Arguably these episodes of 'disorder' or 'disturbances' were the conclusion of pent-up anger after 14 years of austerity, cultivated and stoked by right-wing politicians and media for years spilling out onto the streets. Meanwhile, the financial discipline and tough talking fiscal rules of the new administration made a virtue of stressing that there would be no profligacy to spray the cash around given Labour's dire inheritance.[2]

Riot reactions varied. COBRA meetings were convened by PM (Mason & Dodd, 2024) Keir Starmer in his first real test as PM – a contrast with how Boris Johnson skipped several while on the beach at the start of the COVID-19 pandemic (Haddon, 2023). The calls for the recall of Parliament led by Nigel Farage of Reform were resisted (Instagram, n.d.). Swift and stiff sentencing followed as rapid court processes kicked in. The wheels of justice whirred into motion in an echo of the show trials after the 2011 London riots when that August too bits of Britain were ablaze, the trigger on that occasion being the police killing of Mark Duggan in north London. In 2011, commentators labelled the incidents 'consumer riots' when shopfronts were broken leading to widescreen TVs and trainers being looted with the blackberry device network mobilising crowds (Treadwell et al., 2013). In 2024, disturbing happenings occurred that would justify the classification of 'race riots'. Filipino nurses in Sunderland were set upon with rocks (Church, 2024) and a Nigerian carer's car was set alight in Middlesborough (BBC News, 2024). For many, the events were triggering; recalling the National Front (NF) marching on the streets in the 1970s. For me, it recalled 1981 and the NF coming to Southall, a part of the borough of Ealing where I grew up in which the Hamborough Tavern pub was set ablaze. The 2024 violent disorder even provoked

---

[2]For more information, see Wheeler et al. (2024).

King Charles to praise community spirit triumphing. The rioting provided a jolt to what hitherto had been a smooth transition for Labour's taking on the reins of power; an unforeseen upset not in the 100-day plan.

Events were rooted in outrage at the heartbreaking senseless murder of three very young girls in Southport, Merseyside. As conspiracy theories spread like wildfire over the internet, the killings were erroneously attributed to a Muslim knifeman on social media feeding a sense of injustice from the 'left behind'/ignored/forgotten white working class. Among charges faced by miscreants for which punitive tariffs were doled out via fast-track sentencing was disseminating disinformation online alongside riot and affray. Consequently, the question of more robust regulating of social media platforms was discussed ad infinitum punctuated at times by provocative Twitter baiting of the UK government and specifically Keir Starmer by Twitter owner, the world's richest man Elon Musk (Toth, 2024). Right-wing commentators went into apoplexy seeing free speech as under attack. The riots contained elements of racism and specifically Islamophobia at their core, although the label of 'violent thuggery' seemed common currency among the political classes. Musk took offence at the government response to protect mosques. TV media covered Southport Masjid under siege with the imam barricaded in as flying bricks were sent its way. Rather like the broom armies of 2011, community clean-ups proceeded in the aftermath.

When working back to how we got here it would not be unreasonable to cite constant race-baiting by the mainstream press and denigration of immigrants in political discourse. In 2005, the Michael Howard Conservative party's dog whistle election slogan was 'It's not racist to talk about immigration' (Reporter, 2017). By 2019, this has shortened to 'Get Brexit Done' (Perrigo, 2019). The 2024 Tory three letter mantra was 'stop the boats'. Cultivating animosity towards immigrants fed into a perceived lopsided distribution of opportunity and the sentiment immigrants were getting benefits/council houses /everything. An emboldening or disinhibiting of racist sentiment followed with its logical extension being violence. Parallels were drawn as well as with the 1970s further back to the 1930s by the Labour MP Clive Lewis on Sky News who cited how the cutting to the bone of public services had fuelled discontent.

## ON THE DOORSTEP, AT THE HUSTINGS
## AND AT THE BALLOT BOX

The riots took place against a backdrop of political change. The Labour win at the General Election only a month earlier saw the Conservative party, whose period of rule began in 2010 spanning five Prime Ministers, emphatically rejected with a resounding Labour victory on a Tony Blair landslide scale. '14 years of austerity' was a phrase I found myself reaching for continually at the two election 'hustings' I appeared at. These public meetings where all candidates present themselves sharing a platform to be quizzed by voters and measured against one another have always been an election staple. Having traditionally honoured all invites (a record high 13 in 2015) this time I was invited to a record low figure and am aware some Labour candidates refused to participate in any given the Gaza issue and attendant accusations of genocide/ethnic cleansing levelled at the party – costing two shadow cabinet their seats. I have written elsewhere on how vulnerable I felt at the meetings I appeared at my own constituency-held hustings.[3] Often the audience at such events are merely cheerleaders for a particular party rather than genuine undecided voters. The framing of the meetings meant that I as incumbent/already elected representative was in the firing line, more so than the Conservative – although they had been responsible for the 14 years of austerity. Even aside from Gaza, the questions appeared to have been designed for me to highlight well-publicised criticism of my own party policy: what would Labour do about student finance? What would Labour do about the two-child limit imposed by the Conservatives?

Inequality is at the core of these 'difficult questions'. The new realism of the Keir Starmer Labour party settled on six key pledges or first steps that were more imprecise than say the Blair 1997 pledgecard of deliverables of which four or five centred on quantification and numerical targets in, for instance, halving sentencing times from arrest, and reducing class sizes to no more than 30. By contrast, the 2024 ones were based on structures in two cases – launching Border Security Command and Great British Energy,

---

[3]See Huq (2024).

and with direction but more vague in three cases 'crack down on anti-social behaviour', 'deliver economic security' and 'cut NHS waiting times'. Only one of six had a number in it at all – 6,500 new teachers for state schools to be financed by requiring private schools to pay the exchequer 20% VAT on their turnover. This policy, a clear attack on inequality (as was the workers rights package) was only made possible by exiting the European Union (EU) as hitherto education had never been for tax purposes a luxury VAT raising product. When the argument that an elite system would be made more elitist was put to Labour spokespeople, the figure always met with the retort that only 7% of children are privately educated and 93% in the state sector. Yet in my west London seat of Ealing Central and Acton, containing an unusually high number of 14 private schools it came up regularly canvassing, depending on what bit of the we were in – in the posh bit of Ealing Broadway and Chiswick the policy was deeply unpopular despite nationally polling well.

If we are considering inequality as signifying unequal distributions (e.g. of wealth, power and privilege) this could also apply to voter behaviour. Unusually parties outside the usual Labour/Conservative duopoly too triumphed. The thesis first advanced in the 1980s of a 'decade of dealignment' at the time of the advent of the social democratic party (SDP) (Särlvik & Crewe, 1983) seemed to have been realised like never before with voters breaking way from expected ethnicity and class norms. The Lib Dems netted 77 MPs and Greens four with tactical voting playing, that is, harnessing the power of the anti-Tory majority in an agreed candidate a big part in their success. The previously named UKIP then Brexit party rebranded Reform finished with five MPs including Nigel Farage who at his eighth attempt could now add the letters MP after his name. The Green Party netted four seats and pro Gaza independents four with Jeremy Corbyn being a fifth. *The Daily Telegraph* headline the next day concluded 'Pro Gaza MPs become sixth largest party', citing the wins in Birmingham and Leicester plus whittling down of majorities of Shabana Mahmood and Jess Phillipps both in Birmingham. The *Times* assessment was 'Aggressive Gaza protest vote cost Labour bigger win'. Candidates breaking through to win against the big parties espousing environmentalism, pro-Palestine and anti-immigration lead me to conclude that 2024 signals how we are in an age of extremes where electoral volatility reigns; although these first two had some overlap and damaged Labour whereas Reform hurt the Tories most by outplaying the PM's 'stop the boats' rhetoric. There were some violent shifts demonstrated with big majorities demolished – Ashworth's majority of 22,500 in 2019 was wiped out and turned into a deficit of 1,000 and in Clacton a 25,717 Conservative majority evaporated as Farage won by 8,405. The relatively small difference between the Tory and Reform vote totals – reportedly some 340,000 led to spectre of Nigel Farage making the same plea that normally was the cry of the single Green of the last Parliament and traditionally the Liberal Democrats arguing for the UK to adopt Proportional Representation asserting 'People will look at these results and say this is not a fair and genuine democracy' (*The Daily Telegraph* 6/7/24), again an odd alliance illustrating the age of extremes.

## THE GENERATION GAME AND NATIONAL CAMPAIGN

Addressing inequality or asymmetry was rooted in some of the other policy offers of the election. Labour stressed the notion of 'build build build'. From my own experience as a constituency MP conducting casework, housing is the main issue I am contacted on. At the end of the day, the Tories promise to construct 1.6 million and Labour promise of 1.5 million homes were not dissimilar but the Labour figure prioritised social rent and affordable homes whereas the Conservatives were vaguer stating that they should serve the function of 'rural regeneration'. Intergenerational inequality is laid bare in the difficulties faced by the young getting on the housing ladder or getting a secure tenancy which has so many wider implications, delaying the age of putting down roots and starting a family. As a London MP prices in the capital are even more prohibitive being several income multiples – a million not being unusual making a mockery of one being able to borrow three times their salary. The promise to sweep away planning regulation was another high-profile Labour assertion positing NIMBY (not in my back yard) versus YIMBY (yes in my back yard). This crude dichotomy appears to create a new political divide with a grouping among the new intake of Labour MPs to organise as an ultra leadership loyalist block to ensure that this policy comes to fruition the Labour Growth Group who wrote a public letter with 58 names to it. It would be erroneous to describe this as a Labour equivalent of the ERG (European Research Group, a Brexiteer thorn in Theresa May's side at the height of Brexit who always appeared to holding her to ransom) given their positioning. As *New Statesman* observed 'The group is said to have been greeted favourably by Downing Street'. One Labour source, not involved in the group themselves, described it as 'basically a pro-Starmer WhatsApp group' (Kenyon, 2024). Already elected MPs will find themselves being lobbied by constituents to oppose 'over development'. Indeed newspapers keen to stress Labour splits have delighted in producing stories detailing and tables of party MPs with the number of homes they 'blocked'[4] although in reality an MP can only try to influence not decide such things which are a matter for local councils.

The pressure group 'Generation Rent' also contributed to the housing debate citing how 45% of under 35s rent from private landlords who have historically faced a chronic lack of regulation – influenced by the large numbers of MPs who are landlords. The Conservatives had promised to reform housing including the iniquitous tenure of leasehold and putting an end to section 21 no fault evictions allowing landlords to evict without supplying a reason after a tenancy ends. These reached an all time high in 2024. Those that benefitted were bailiffs and removal companies. Ministry of Justice figures showed that 109,000 such notices had been issued since the ban was announced (Chudy, 2024), often leaving young families literally on the street almost at the drop of a hat and sending the temporary housing bill faced by councils sky high. Labour have vowed to issue a ban. Certainly, a roof above one's head is a fairly basic demand but has felt increasingly out of reach for many Gen Z. The Conservative Renters Reform Bill steered through Parliament by Michael Gove promised much in vowing to remove the insecurity faced by those in the rental sector but had been neutered by the time it hit the statute book in a whirl of the 'wash-up'

---

[4]For an example, see Hassan (2023).

vortex which is the process of tying up loose ends at the end of a Parliamentary term where things often get left out. Homelessness charity Shelter declared that it could not accept this version of the bill. Certainly, throughout the election knocking on door after door it did feel like the claim that one expects to do better than their parents but that living standards had stagnated and regressed to make this impossible and completely reversed this to be a forlorn hope at best.

Other policies that contrasted differing generational inequality approaches were the Labour package of employment rights and extending the franchise/age of majority from 18 to 16 contrasted with reintroduction of a version of national service floated early on in the campaign by the Conservatives was seen as a 'gimmick'. In countries where this practice persists, it is seen as a great generational leveller. While I was asked about both of these issues by a group of sixth formers, I addressed at a school early on in the campaign, neither policy figured in the two big hustings meetings I did towards the end of the campaign. Brexit which has dominated my second and third elections in 2017 and 2019 barely featured at all. My first question to the newly minted PM once he took questions days after was whether there were any plans to reform youth mobility and student exchange, for example, Erasmus. The answer was that while the incoming government was keen to 'reset' relations with EU partner countries there would be no return to the single market or freedom of movement. It felt like the 'too complicated' label had been applied to Brexit. Unlike either of those years the topic barely featured at all in the campaigns of any of the major parties and on the doorstep Gaza was mentioned more.

During the campaign, differences were drawn between the two figures fronting the campaigns with inequality being drawn into personality and suitability. Keir Starmer stress testing the maxim that message repetition works, repeatedly putting in his speeches and interviews that his 'dad was a toolmaker'. He also described his childhood home as a pebble-dashed semi. By contrast in January 2024 at PMQs he accused Rishi Sunak, the most personally wealthy ever office holder of PM of being out of touch, his exact words being 'he doesn't get what Britain needs'. YouGov in October 2023 recorded as did other pollsters the inequality rooted finding that Sunak was 'out of touch'. Voxpops with voters on TV showed ethnicity as well as wealth creeping into reasoning. Images of Sunak seemingly not even dimly aware of how to fill a car's tank or paying with a contactless credit card and his penchant for travel by private jet/helicopter contributed to the image of 'more money than sense' but hammering from the side at a woodwork class (as instructed) was unfortunate. When he skipped the ending of the D-day anniversary veteran commemoration event in Normandy to do an ITV interview this was widely seen as another reason to label him as out of line with Britain.[5] In even more overt dog whistle fashion was the claim that the Prime Minister Sunak was not 'really fully grounded in our culture' made by right-wing historian Dr David Starkey on GB News in a coronation discussion. Certainly, Sunak's admission that *dharma* or his sense of Hindu religious duty guided his decision-making was a first. In the event, the D-day interview that caused such controversy and elicited a rare prime ministerial apology contained a further faux pas that showed the subjective nature of inequality. His interview insisting that he had gone without things during childhood with the chief privation outlined being a Sky TV dish[6] was widely ridiculed at a time when many were going without far more basic necessities: temporary accommodation had mushroomed and the UK had the unenviable boast of more foodbanks than branches of McDonalds.

## CONCLUSION

The 2024 election in many ways was one where social media warfare was conducted as never before with an air-war as well as a ground war. It seemed unimaginable to have headline like the 1992 'It's the *Sun* what won it' with one newspaper claiming responsibility for the election result given the polyvocal discourse from

[5] A poll also found that 8 out of 10 British voters said Rishi Sunak does not understand the pressures facing the average British people. See Bienkov (2024).

[6] See Badshah (2024) for more context.

numerous sources. *The Sun* continues to be the UK's largest circulating newspaper in 2024 but with a much lower penetration than in 1992. For the election, after many years of supporting the Conservatives, it backed Labour. Electoral cycles mean that the momentous ensuing result is not the final word. Indeed local elections of May 2024 were seen as underwhelming for Labour with the commentariat asserting 'it's not in the bag yet', however, a dogged strategy of targeted effort concentrating on individual seats and mutual aid from Labour's formidable membership to divert campaigning to areas in need rather than piling up big majorities in already Labour seats paid dividends in a broad but shallow win in which a 34% vote share translated into a 170 majority. The pendulum will inevitably swing back at some point, no one can assume power forever but the magnitude of majority certainly provides a sizeable cushion. It took until COVID-19 and Partygate for buyer's remorse to set in with the Johnson government that was seen to have netted a big 2019 win, greatly surpassed by Labour's own landslide five years later.

The victorious Labour government was keen to stress that there are no quick fixes and embarked on a frenetic programme of activity. The Rwanda scheme for offshore processing of illegal migrants, often attacked by Labour on cost grounds rather than for inhumanity was axed but then cited as a cause of riots by Conservatives as the blame game began. The Labour administration faced off its first rebellion in July on the two-child limit by removing the whip from MPs who backed an SNP amendment. The once totemic Tory flagship policy of 'levelling up' was consigned to the scrapheap. The Department of Levelling Up was retitled to become a Housing and Local Government ministry. The party's own *Power and Partnership: Labour's Plan to Power Up Britain* document promised that 'every town, village and city has a role to play, and can reap the rewards of a decade of national renewal' and to improve living standards and invest decision-making powers into communities (The Labour Party, 2024). *The Municipal Journal* did not lament levelling up's passing, remarking it was 'a last-minute Tory construct as [the Conservatives] sought to offer rhetoric in their manifesto to appeal to the so-called Red Wall after Brexit' (Franklin, 2024). For myself as a London MP this jettisoning of what always felt to me as acutely anti-London was most welcome. By inviting cities and regions to competitively bid in for subventions to this and other pots of money including 'the towns fund' it felt like pitting places against one another for effectively crumbs from the table with London often exempt from applying. The settling of long-running pay disputes mounted by both junior doctors and railway staff showed a transformed attitude to industrial relations. The lazily made assertion that there is no difference between the two big parties is one that I strongly refute. Labour did borrow some Tory tricks. His warning that things would get worse before getting better on 27 August 2024 was made from the rose garden of Downing Street – to emphasise how it was now a site of hard work not lockdown parties – at a lectern with three word slogan 'Fixing the Foundations'.

The 2024 riots in some ways are a microcosm or petri dish of the Starmer premiership's policies to date: talking tough by publicising harsh sentences and broadcasting verdicts being handed down on TV, fast tracking arrests and prosecutions and taking a legal approach to a political problem. The entire issue also encompassed the rapid transmission of (mis)information by social media and the most heated political hot potato of them all: immigration. At the time of writing, further riots appear to have been snuffed out. The record high temperatures of earlier in the month gave way to an August bank holiday weekend downpour. In August 1981, rainfall was the decisive factor deterring continuation of social unrest that flourished to a soundtrack of the Specials' Ghost-town at the same time as the Royal Wedding, literally flushing out riots. Such considerations beg the question of climate change and the inequalities this breeds on a global scale, necessitating just transition. One cannot do justice to these themes here, however, they must be the focus of another chapter for another day.

## REFERENCES

Badshah, N. (2024, June 12). Rishi Sunak went without 'lots of things' including Sky TV as a child. *The Guardian*. https://www.theguardian. com/politics/article/2024/jun/12/rishi-sunak-went-without-lots-of-things-including-sky-tv-as-a-child

BBC News. (2024, August 11). *Middlesbrough carer given £28k to replace car burnt out in riot*. https://www.bbc.co.uk/news/articles/c5ylryk1gvgo

Bienkov, A. (2024, January 26). Eight out of ten Brits say Rishi Sunak doesn't Get Britain. *Byline Times*. https://bylinetimes.com/2024/01/26/eight-out-of-ten-brits-say-rishi-sunak-doesnt-get-britain/

Chudy, E. (2024, August 8). Over 100,000 households threatened with no-fault evictions since Tories promised to ban them. *Big Issue*. https://www.bigissue.com/news/housing/no-fault-eviction-ban-child-homelessness/

Church, E. (2024, August 8). Filipino nurses attacked as NHS community condemns racist riots. *Nursing Times*. https://www.nursingtimes.net/leadership/filipino-nurses-attacked-as-nhs-community-condemns-racist-riots-05-08-2024/

Franklin, B. (2024, May 13). Farewell levelling up – We barely knew you. *The Municipal Journal*. https://www.themj.co.uk/farewell-levelling-barely

Haddon, C. (2023, March 29). *Questions over the prime minister's coronavirus COBR absences are not straightforward*. Institute for Government. https://www.instituteforgovernment.org.uk/article/comment/questions-over-prime-ministers-coronavirus-cobr-absences-are-not-straightforward

Hassan, M. (2023, November 27). Labour MPs could spoil Keir Starmer's affordable homes plan. *The Times*. https://www.thetimes.com/uk/politics/article/labour-mps-keir-starmer-housing-plans-affordable-homes-blocked-h9scg3fxf

Huq, R. (2024, July 13). I'm a Muslim MP who rebelled on Gaza, but still I was barracked and intimidated. *The Observer*. https://www.theguardian.com/politics/article/2024/jul/13/im-a-muslim-mp-who-rebelled-on-gaza-but-still-i-was-barracked-and-intimidated

Instagram. (n.d.). https://www.instagram.com/nigel_farage/p/C-R0anOoa3F/

Kenyon, M. (2024, August 16). Inside the labour growth group. *The New Statesman*. https://www.newstatesman.com/politics/labour/2024/08/inside-the-labour-growth-group#

Labour Party. (2024). *Power and partnership: Labour's plan to power up Britain*. https://labour.org.uk/wp-content/uploads/2024/03/Power-and-partnership-Labours-Plan-to-Power-up-Britain.pdf

Mason, R., & Dodd, V. (2024, August 5). Starmer to lead Cobra meeting after vowing swift justice awaits 'far-right thugs.' *The Guardian*. https://www.theguardian.com/politics/article/2024/aug/04/far-right-thugs-will-be-swiftly-brought-to-justice-keir-starmer-vows

Perrigo, B. (2019, December 13). 'Get Brexit done.' the 3 words that helped Boris Johnson win Britain's 2019 election. *TIME*. https://time.com/5749478/get-brexit-done-slogan-uk-election/

Reporter, G. S. (2017, June 9). Full text: Michael Howard's speech. *The Guardian*. https://www.theguardian.com/politics/2005/jan/28/conservatives.uk

Särlvik, B., & Crewe, I. (1983). *Decade of Dealignment: The Conservative Victory of 1979 and Electoral Trends in the 1970s*. Cambridge University Press.

Treadwell, J., Briggs, D., Winlow, S., & Hall, S. (2013). SHOPOCALYPSE NOW: Consumer culture and the English Riots of 2011. *The British Journal of Criminology*, *53*(1), 1–17.

Toth, A. (2024, August 8) As Elon Musk clashes with Starmer on X: Could Twitter be banned in the UK? *The Independent*. https://www.independent.co.uk/news/uk/home-news/elon-musk-starmer-x-twitter-banned-uk-b2593108.html

Wheeler, C., Yorke, H., & Hellen, N. (2024, July 27). Rachel Reeves ready to deliver the bad news: Britain is broke. *The Sunday Times*. https://www.thetimes.com/uk/politics/article/rachel-reeves-ready-to-deliver-the-bad-news-britain-is-broke-qnfcmgxj2

# 21

# LABOUR: PAST, PRESENT, FUTURE AND THE 2024 GENERAL ELECTION

## Jon Cruddas

*Former Labour MP for Dagenham and Rainham, UK Parliament, UK*

Many thanks for inviting me to contribute to Ruskin's 125 year celebrations. For all those involved it brings back memories of college events and past students. Personally, I am immediately taken back to the 1980s Miners' strike. At that time, I was studying at the Industrial Relations Research Unit (IRRU) at Warwick. IRRU maintained strong links to scores of Ruskin students whose trade union activism had often seen them re-enter education here in Oxford before going on to study industrial relations at Warwick. I vividly recall raucous events both here and in Coventry in support of the miners. Politically and economically, these were turbulent times, but I remember them fondly. Not just in terms of our activism and the friendships forged back then but because of the insights offered in terms of the role of this great institution in ensuring working class access to education.

I begin with this personal recollection to suggest a wider point about links between Oxford and Warwick that takes me to the substance of my comments this afternoon. Before university, I too had been a union activist – in my case with the Australian Builders Labourers Union – after which I journeyed to Warwick, where years later I completed an MA and PhD in the IRRU. IRRU was the direct descendant of what *New Society* over 50 years ago labelled the 'Oxford School' of labour relations academics and practitioners, a tradition central to British post-war reconstruction. The 'school' included figures such as Hugh Clegg, Allan Flanders and Bill McCarthy at Nuffield College. Clegg and Flanders subsequently headed off the Warwick, as did others such as George Bain and Willy Brown. Yet the Oxford School was not exclusively based at Nuffield, it also included the likes of John Hughes here at Ruskin. The group emerged as key figures in successive Labour governments' labour market and employment law reforms throughout the 1960s and 1970s and the overall evolution of British corporatism. For decades, they remained influential practitioners in the development of government economic and industrial strategy, pay policy, employment law, trade union reform, economic democracy and much more. They coordinated the work of the Donovan Royal Commission on unions and employers in the late 1960s, later the Bullock Report on industrial democracy alongside legislation such as the Employment Relations and the Trade Union and Labour Relations Acts and generations of equalities legislation beginning with sex discrimination and equal pay in the 1960s.

I recall the Oxford School's contribution to British post-war history not just to acknowledge their often-neglected role and suggest their rehabilitation. But also, to suggest their practical relevance for today's Labour Party and hopefully soon to be the next Labour government.

## REVISITING LABOUR RELATIONS

In 1997, I entered Downing Street. My job was to work on labour relations issues and links between the new Labour government and the unions. We introduced the National Minimum Wage, signed up to the European Social Chapter, established new union recognition procedures and family friendly employment legislation, sought to regulate working time and revise other individual and collective labour laws.

At that time, some of us sought to rehabilitate the tradition that had schooled us both here in Oxford and Warwick. For instance, in the successful appointment of George Bain to chair the Low Pay Commission and Willy Brown to direct the research. But we were in the minority and the moment quickly passed.

In truth, whilst we ensured some changes in work regulation, we did not achieve nearly enough. Subsequently from the early 2000s, wages began to flatline and after the 2007–2008 economic crash, so too did productivity. The partial, limited interventions and missed opportunities of the late 1990s occurred upstream of Brexit, festering working class political disenchantment and the rise in authoritarian populist forces that today threaten the very future of our liberal democracies. I would suggest the failures of the New Labour era regarding labour regulation helps us account for what came later.

This Oxford tradition – the study of labour and its regulation – arguably the backbone of successive labour governments between 1964 and 1979 – remains deeply unfashionable terrain today. I suggest it deserves to be revisited, not least to help safeguard democracy and enhance modern equality. Yet where it does exist, the study of labour relations is often subsumed within business studies departments. Meanwhile what 19th century economists would call the 'labour question' is back centre stage – reflected in recent bouts of strikes and renewed militancy in response to minimal wage growth, inflation and the cost of living crisis, enduring productivity challenges, working class political alienation and the like. Once again the 'labour question' requires serious attention.

Today, I have a captive room of academics so I would urge you to return to some of the concerns of Oxford and Warwick tradition, a tradition central to the history of Ruskin. Revisiting this neglected tradition within the academy would be a great service for what looks likely in a few short weeks to be the next Labour government. Labour relations is certain to be a key arena for the next government entering Whitehall with its substantial New Deal for Working People, its productivity challenges and required regional alternative to Levelling Up. A revised growth strategy and what is being labelled *Securenomics* firmly rooted in green technologies and an onshoring of manufacturing jobs will require new thinking around labour regulation and job quality. More generally confronting political anomie and disenchantment will require actively bolting the working class back into the economic architecture of this country and rebuilding the dignity of labour. We will be unable to resist the forces of populism without such a strategy.

## LABOUR'S CURRENT POSITION

In terms of the wider subject matter of today's seminar, Labour's past, present and future, there have been a lot of comment pieces in the papers recently about what 'starmerism' is and what it is not. To me, it is an honest, although somewhat underdeveloped attempt to return to what in earlier times would be recognised as a fairly orthodox Labour politics, one that predates both Thatcher and Blair.

Before developing this, I would make a couple of general points. The first concerns the tragic quality of modern politics. The present government is clearly disintegrating and change is coming. Yet this obscures the wider decline of social democracy. The problem for Labour is that this disguise won't last indefinitely. Any future honeymoon will have a certain life span – basically until the day after the election.

The threat to modern social democracy is best expressed in the global rise of authoritarian populism across the west, reflected in the advance of figures such as Oban, Meloni, Wilders, Trump and Le Pen. Not too long ago following the demise of the Berlin Wall, my generation hubristically asserted history had ended; liberal democracy had won out. Yet the reality today is that history is being upended and liberal democracy is itself now endangered.

Yet as I prepare to leave parliament, I would suggest that these epic events are generally beyond the reach of our parliamentary discourse. I would go further and suggest an inverse relationship between the scale of the challenges we face today and the capacity of our politicians to discuss, let alone diagnose and remedy these events.

This to me is the general context from which to consider Labour's contemporary position. On the one hand, it looks strong. Since

Boris Johnson's lockdown misbehaviour and Liz Truss's eventful 45 days in charge, Labour's poll lead has been substantial, suggestive of an imminent landslide. Yet our ascendancy occurs in a world of rampaging authoritarian forces, populist revolt and the diminishment of social democracy. Social democracy must be rebuilt and its moral foundations re-established, especially amongst a working class it purports to represent. But is such a renewal occurring, is it even being acknowledged, and if not at what cost? Some around the modern Labour Party think such talk of intellectual and political reimagination is at best a distraction, more often considered as indulgent navel gazing. In the months and years ahead we shall see how this argument plays out. I would suggest in this context history is instructive.

## LABOUR'S PAST

Labour has a turbulent history. Labour has only held power for 33 years in the last 100. Whilst there have been significant electoral highs such, as in 1945, 1966 and 1997, these sit alongside wretched defeats, as in 1931, 1951 and 2010. There have only been six periods of Labour government, of which three were or became minority administrations and another three – in 1950, 1964 and 1974 – retained small majorities. Moreover having been ejected from office Labour is regularly out of power for prolonged periods, 14 years after the defeat of 1931, 13 after 1951 and 18 after 1979. Today, we have been in opposition for 14 years. Of Labour's 23 leaders only 3, Attlee, Wilson and Blair, have been elected at a General Election.

Two years ago, I was asked to write a history of the Labour Party to coincide with the centenary of the first Labour government on the 21st of January 2024. My initial response was twofold – why and how. Why, because given the vast amount written on Labour's history was there anything more to be added? How, in terms of questioning whether it was possible to offer a different take on Labour's history?

How do we tend to consider Labour's history? Much of it takes the form of political biography with a tendency to emphasise the great men that populate the story. Alternatively, you can journey through the party's history by returning to specific administrations or significant years, such as 1924, 1945 or 1997. A different way is to focus on factional struggles or battles over key institutional features, such as the union link or clause iv of the party constitution, or key policies such as disarmament, nationalisation or welfare reform. What quickly becomes apparent when revisiting Labour's history is that very little takes as its focus questions of ideology or political purpose. Of course, this is also true of much political commentary today. Lots covers personality and biography, factions and specific events and policies; very little is concerned with actual purpose.

From the outset, there was no settled understanding as to Labour's purpose. In the 1890s, Keir Hardie fought successfully to create a Labour alliance, one with no settled creed or ideology and throughout it has remained an at times brittle coalition of interests and ideas.

The approach I adopted in the book was to consider both Labour history and the nature of the modern party through a consideration of competing approaches to questions of justice – basically alternative visions of how society should be organised. In terms of political philosophy, we can demarcate three basic visions of justice that have coexisted on the left.

The first seeks to maximise human welfare through distributional justice, the allocation of resources. This utilitarian tradition, often associated with the Fabians, with its focus on fiscal transfers administered by a centralised state, has dominated Labour's history across both its left and right wings with its desire to maximise the wealth of the maximum number of people.

In contrast, a second approach has sought to maximise human freedom. This emphasis on liberty and democracy can be traced back to Magna Carta, and groups such as the Levellers and Diggers. It is a tradition expressed in the post-war desire to advance human rights, and waves of equalities legislation dating back to the pioneering 1960s reforms of Roy Jenkins while he was Home Secretary. More recently, under New Labour such thinking informed the Human Rights Act, major constitutional reform and the government's approach to freedom of information. We can label this the liberal progressive approach to socialist justice.

A third approach seeks to maximise human virtue – the human characteristics that might characterise a just society. This approach is often labelled the ethical socialist tradition, and in Labour's 1890s pre-history came to be known as 'the religion of socialism'. Such an approach was strongly linked to the early Independent Labour Party, the ILP, party pioneers such as Keir Hardie, George Lansbury and Ramsay MacDonald, as well as parts of the later New Left when rejecting the authoritarianism of the traditional left. It also influenced the spiritual concerns of the early Tony Blair and the history of Christian Socialism within the party, in particular figures such as John Smith.

In revisiting Labour's history my argument is that all three are indispensable parts of the Labour tradition. Effective leadership and electoral success have been achieved through the internal reconciliation of these three traditions. Yet this requires an internal pluralism and culture of generosity too often omitted from much of Labour's history. Too often utilitarianism has dominated which tends towards a cold, mechanistic instrumental factional Labour politics, preoccupied with money transfers and internal dominance. Labour's success historically is based on building political projects that draw from all three traditions.

## WHAT NOW FOR LABOUR

Returning to Keir Starmer and the modern Labour party then. All 23 leaders of the party have emerged from the internal factions and political traditions that demarcate the party's history, apart from one, the present leader. His biographer Tom Baldwin would agree with this point, in part because Starmer entered politics late and has not risen through or remained captive to any specific faction. This lack of internal moorings and associations means Starmer remains both politically agile and politically elusive. He travels light. For an opposition leader in an election unfolding as a referendum on the Tory incumbent, this lack of attachment means he can tactically move with real speed. The obvious danger is the type of mandate the party is likely to secure to change the country, built around the vision of a just society it has argued for.

My personal concern is where this leads to modern social democracy and whether Labour has used this long period in opposition to rebuild a public philosophy, a modern approach to equality and justice. Every successful Labour government has been preceded by periods of intellectual revisionism to rethink Labour's approach to justice. Attlee's post-war government was aided by a generation of young economists who through the 1930s rebuilt the party's approach to political economy, redistribution, welfare reform and the state. In the 1960s, the Wilson administration was informed by the intellectual revisionism of the Gaitskellites, elements of the New Left, pioneers of the emerging discipline of sociology and the Oxford School industrial relations experts. Decades later Tony Blair greatly benefitted from the reforms pioneered by his two predecessors, Neil Kinnock and John Smith, and the wider insights of those dissecting the New Times of the early 1980s grouped around Marxism Today.

If – as seems likely – in a few short weeks Keir Starmer enters Downing Street he will be the beneficiary of no substantial revisionist thinking. This has to be set against both the global retreat of social democracy and widespread threats to liberal democracy. Labour will also inherit numerous domestic challenges, including social care, criminal justice, council bankruptcy, the cost of living, productivity, the environment and the state of our universities.

What then is the plan? As yet we lack a compelling vision of modern justice. The danger is Labour will recoil into a default utilitarian politics, the party's recurring historical safe space. The obvious dilemma for this distributional approach is an economic inheritance which suggests very little growth to redistribute. Perhaps most surprisingly for a renowned international human rights lawyer, Starmer's party appears disinterested in questions of freedom and liberty. Moreover, throughout the last few years, beyond vague talk of re-establishing public service, there has been limited discussion of the moral case for socialism or social democracy, of how as a country we live together and flourish.

On closer inspection, we have been offered glimpses of a political and intellectual project, especially when read alongside the quietly impressive recent Mais Lecture delivered by Rachel Reeves.

This new economics would include green industrial strategy and labour market reform, including the New Deal for Working People, to redefine levelling up around devolution, environmental technologies and building decent, well-rewarded work, all overseen by a more muscular state. This offers the possibility of renewed interest in labour regulation and the rehabilitation of the insights of the Oxford School in building a modern approach to economic and social reconstruction. This suggests a return to some of Labour's economic concerns of the 1960s and 1970s. Yet such economism falls short of providing an ethical blueprint for the next government and reconciling Labour's three traditions of justice which the success of the next administration will depend.

So my basic conclusion is to urge a revival of the concerns of the Oxford School, of which Ruskin College played a vital part, to contribute not just to the successes of the next Labour government but also towards the wider reimagination of social democracy in an internationally cold climate. Overall despite my concerns, there are grounds for optimism. We shall see how this all plays out.

# 22

# CONCLUSION

Graeme Atherton[a,b]

[a]Ruskin College, UK
[b]Ruskin Institute for Social Equity, UK

The perspectives outlined in this book have been true to the history of Ruskin College. This is an eclectic collection of progressive thought, anchored by a commitment to the transformative power of education. The views of the contributors are not backward looking; rather they look forward offering a range of views on what the Labour government elected in 2024 could do to address inequality, promote opportunity and foster economic renewal. The challenges the country faces at present are deep rooted. The previous chapters offer a unique insight into what these challenges are from the political and practical perspective and a rich mix of ideas that have the potential to inform and shape progressive policy going forward.

The ideas presented in this book look to engender long-term change, and address problems whose history, as argued in the introduction, stretch back further than the last government. The ideas also need to confront the normalisation of inequality in the UK as it infects all aspects of economy and society. Most importantly, the ideas are also exceptionally timely.

The first months of the new Labour government elected in July 2024 with a huge majority show how the party's political trajectory has outpaced its capacity to put in place the intellectual foundations it needs. Controversies associated with the two-child benefit cap, winter fuel allowance and staffing appointments at No. 10 show that naturally, given the speed by which the party has shifted to the centre, a clearer philosophy is required regarding how to tackle inequality while also prioritising growth. As Jon Cruddas argues in his chapter:

> *every successful Labour government has been preceded by periods of intellectual revisionism to rethink Labour's approach to justice. As yet we lack a compelling vision of modern justice. The danger is Labour will recoil into a default utilitarian politics, the party's recurring historical safe space.*

This book sits firmly as a contribution to the intellectual gap that Cruddas points to. There are five key themes emerging through the book and they are discussed below.

## FIVE KEY THEMES

### Theme 1: Invest In and Increase Learning Throughout Life to Create Opportunity and Economic Growth

A focus on lifelong learning and also higher education is a natural one for this collection. It also reflects a timely and essential re-emergence for post-compulsory education from the shadows of recent years. The virulence of the attacks on higher education, in particular, has been surprising. These attacks continue despite the change of government. The responses to the call by the national representative organisation for higher education participation, Universities UK, to increase participation in tertiary education to 70% by 2040 (Universities, 2024) in a report released in late 2024, from some in the right-wing press were hyperbolic if not bordering on the hysterical.[1]

---

[1]For example, see Deacon (2024).

The chapters in this section of the book echo the call for more participation in post-compulsory, lifelong learning. It is crucial at this point to emphasise that lifelong learning is not a panacea. Greater participation in post-compulsory education does not guarantee higher incomes for individuals or a reduction in inequality. As Peter John argues outcomes are crucial. In his chapter, he states that 'despite almost 50% of the requisite population now attaining at least undergraduate qualifications, rewards are still allotted inequitably'. But even given the problems associated with 'opportunity hoarding' that John describes, as more affluent groups defend their positions in the social hierarchy the case for greater participation is still very strong. In his 2022 paper for the Tony Blair Institute referred to in the chapter, Steve Coulter estimated that raising participation in higher education from the current 53% of school leavers to around 70% by 2040 would boost the size of the UK economy by almost 5%. However, recognising Peter John's arguments this kind of expansion is necessary but not sufficient where reducing inequality is concerned. Reforms to the education system and to the economy are also essential.

In terms of reforms to post-compulsory education, the authors call, rightly, for an inclusive understanding of bringing these different forms of education together. Higher education should be seen more as part of lifelong learning and less as an entity separate from other forms of education. As James Robson argues a more systems based or tertiary approach is needed 'where different education and training pathways are maintained and celebrated, reflecting different social, individual and economic needs'.

This tertiary approach needs further work. In international terms it has been associated with the creation of new administrative bodies to oversee post-compulsory education as one whole, with, for example, the introduction of a new body to oversee all skills, further education and higher education in Wales and similar proposals on the table in Australia. This kind of re-organisation in England would be a costly long-term project. Time and money should not *per se* preclude innovation that can break down hierarchies to benefit learners, and a regional approach here may be equally or more effective. To move this work forward though, cross sector engagement is required to allow all stakeholders to collaborate in that space to develop concrete policy proposals.

Labour has initiated such work before and recently. In 2018, the Labour Lifelong Learning Commission led by the then Shadow Minister for Higher Education, Further Education and Skills, Gordon Marsden, was formed. The Commission included leaders from across sectors and their report *The Future Is Ours to Learn* was published just before the 2019 general election. The report included a range of proposals in particular a funded statutory right to learn for all adults (Labour Lifelong Learning Commission, 2019). The report showed that if the goal is to increase participation in post-compulsory education then a comprehensive approach is required. This is not to say that most of those engaged in advocacy for such an approach don't recognise this. But politically there is a tendency, especially where education and skills are concerned, to see the formation of new bodies as the solution to problems. They are high profile and visible policy changes which parties can easily point to as examples of progress. More than this is needed though. As Lord David Blunkett points out in his chapter suggesting a range of reforms including revisiting individual learning accounts and learning passports.

But learning throughout life should mean across the full life course. Philip Collins's chapter laid out in detail the case for an early intervention programme such as the Sure Start initiative introduced by Labour when they were last in government. The success of Sure Start was also referenced by David Blunkett and Hilary Armstrong. Politics is about making choices. In an era of limited resources, these choices will inevitably mean support for one thing, or one part of the system in this case, may well need to come at the expense of the other. It is not utopian though to argue that in making these choices one part of the system must not be set against another. As important as early intervention is without effective educational routes to progress too it is like building a pyramid without a roof.

## Theme 2: Focus on Localities and Helping Them Grow Via Collaborative Action

The levelling up agenda pursued by the Conservative government from 2019 to 2024 did not make any significant inroads into regional inequality, although there is still nearly £13 billion of funding by late 2024 that is in the process of being spent. But it did re-invigorate interest in the regional dimension of inequality and to an extent highlight challenges those in some parts of the country feel were being ignored. It also contributed to a commitment to greater devolution that appears to cross party boundaries.

However, levelling up was also cast in broad brush strokes by the government, mayors and many of those who tried to shape the discussion. The North–South divide, for so long a default understanding of how England works, was given a renewed impetus. Quite understandably Northern mayors played into the narrative of the divide for potential political gain. Mayors of Greater Manchester and Greater Merseyside respectively, Andy Burnham and Steve Rotherham published a book *Head North: A Rallying Cry for a More Equal Britain*, in which they ruminated on the North–South divide and argued for the transfer of power and resources from South to North. The commentariat and the media leaned into the idea either through writing books proclaiming to give a new understanding of the impoverished North or by sending a reporter up North for the day to stand in a windswept Northern town centre every time they wanted to cover levelling up.

The reality of geographical inequality is more complex than a dividing line at Crewe though. As Matt Leach argues in his chapter, poverty sits alongside wealth across much of the country. It is at the local level where a post-levelling up agenda that incorporates both the distribution of power and funds should concentrate. This more granular approach suggesting that communities of around 10,000 people are the optimum for neighbourhood level inequality focussing policy is a vital message going forward. It also provokes important considerations regarding the optimum population level for differing aspects of regional inequality policy. While 10,000 people may be appropriate for the kind of activities

Leach describes, a region at 5–7 million people may be the right level for economic development. This more forensic approach to regional social and economic policy matching policies, population and goals should be the starting point for a coherent post-levelling up approach. A risk associated with the profile afforded to the mayoral model is that it diverts attention away from both neighbourhoods and local authority geographies. Labour will need to decide whether to proceed with a mayoral model that covers all of England – at present 40% of the population are in areas where there is no electoral mayor. In deciding whether to push for an extension of the mayoral model, thinking of what powers and funding should sit where in the context of the importance of neighbourhoods is vital.

This more nuanced approach to place-based inequality has more than just a geographical dimension. Leach emphasises in his chapter, that the importance of communities shaping their own trajectories is central. Looking at areas which have made progress in terms of social and economic renewal as Abigail Taylor does in her chapter, while a set of generic factors that underpin relatively successful places exist, each one is very distinct. In fact, it is this distinctiveness in terms of developing their own forward-looking identity that is one of the commonalities. These areas have been able to establish a form of economic comparative advantage. But it is not just economic advantage but also the quality of life of such places that matter. Abigail Taylor talks of how they have tried to make themselves better places to live, for example, as she states:

> The case studies indicate that to attract young professionals there is a need to move beyond a focus on economic and business growth by also investing in making places outstanding and renowned places to live and work in. Many of the city-regions studied invested in cultural and spatial development to change perceptions and attract new residents. Initiatives ranged from large scale cultural events (e.g. European City of Culture) in Lille and Essen, to artistic trails in abandoned former industrial areas in Nantes to citizen-centred development in Fukuoka.

This interaction between the social, economic and cultural is fundamental to how places that have experienced the greatest challenges can be renewed. Creating the synergy between these different factors also requires strong partnership and collaboration across stakeholders and sectors – a theme that re-emerges throughout the book. How Labour can enable effective, sustainable partnership working is a critical policy question that needs further exploration. Previous place-based partnership projects such as New Deal for Communities are name checked by Leach in his chapter and they provide further justification for the collaborative approach. However, the context has changed since the 1990s and while some of the fundamentals of partnership working remain, such as the need to build trust, stability in funding and create an equitable balance of power between stakeholders, the environment has changed. Online communication should make the construction of partnerships that involve stakeholders from both within and outside a place more possible. It should also allow differing forms of citizen participation to be relevant as well.

But effective, equitable and inclusive partnerships do not just emerge. Such partnerships take time, investment and political leadership. Putting in place initiatives that identify and share the mechanics of how to 'do' partnership and collaboration well would be welcome and relatively straightforward. Ian Taylor refers to valuable work that he has been involved in here producing a collaboration guidebook for leaders working across sectors. As he states in the chapter, 'the playbook identifies five key themes that can help unlock impactful collaboration: trust, power, culture, leadership and learning'.

### Theme 3: Change How We Do Business to Reduce Inequality While Promoting Growth

Macroeconomic and microeconomic forces shape the extent of inequality in a society. Prior to and since winning the 2024 general election, Labour has focussed intently on raising economic growth in order to support a fairer, more redistributive economy. As the Chancellor of the Exchequer Rachel Reeves (2024) said in early

2024 'growth, ultimately, is what generates higher living standards for households, raises incomes, lifts people out of poverty, and gives people more choices about how to lead a good life'.

Growth however does not necessarily benefit everyone or reduce inequality. The chapters from Wilcock and Monaghan point to different ways in which the economy and businesses within it could be organised. Specifically, they look at taxation and benefits as well as the structure of the corporate ownership. These are important and necessary arguments. It is impossible to affect inequality without changing how the economy works and how businesses operate. This is a difficult area for Labour and one they have struggled with when in government and in the past. The desire of those from the centre of the party to appear business friendly has rubbed against the union led part of the party and the concern regarding labour relations that Jon Cruddas speaks about in his chapter. The focus on growth that Labour has at present does not immediately suggest that it will challenge the way we do business as it needs to do if inequality is to be reduced. However, as Cruddas also argues and is picked up on below there is a need to develop the ideas that can inform what Labour will do in office as well as the politics that has got them there in the first place. In that regard, what Wilcock and Monaghan propose can make a valuable contribution here. One of the criticisms of the last Labour government is that it did not do enough to change how the economy worked and was over reliant on education as a means of addressing inequality. While there is certainly a heavy accent on education as a mechanism in this book these contributions that argue for transformations in the economy must carry equal weight.

Alongside the macroeconomic priorities though, how individual firms operate and crucially engage in reducing inequality is also critical. This more microeconomic perspective is tackled in Justine Greening's chapter on social mobility and business as well as the contribution from Andy Boucher. Building the body of knowledge and practice which looks at how business can affect inequality is an important next step. There has been recent work in this area. The Purpose Coalition, a membership network of businesses, universities and charities led by Greening, has produced several reports on individual businesses outlining the activities they are undertaking with specific groups to support their entry and progression through employment. Ruskin Institute for Social Equity (RISE) published a study in late 2024 looking at how 50 businesses and employer representative organisations were working to address inequality. The study entitled 'A Different Future – How Can Business Address Inequality' divided the work of business into four different categories:

- Financial/non-financial support for communities and individuals.

- Campaigning and convening.

- Future talent and social mobility.

- Creating opportunities for the existing workforce.

The businesses in the study were asking for leadership and support from government to enhance and grow the work they are doing. This support though needs to be matched by a recognition of the responsibilities of employers to contribute to society. As James Robson argues in his chapter with regard to how employers act in the skills market:

> Currently policy discourse, has become obsessed with the rights of employers. However, a reorientation is required to shift the role of employers from customer to stakeholder and to emphasise not just their rights but also their responsibilities.

Acknowledging what inequalities exist in their own space illustrates a case for responsibility. Nimmi Patel in her chapter describing the work of TechUK highlights how technology firms are aware of digital divides. The chapter highlights as well the key role that representative organisations play in the development of a business inequality ecosystem. It also shows how the needs of business and society can coalesce. Tech companies want more of the population to be digitally literate because this extends markets for their products, while the communities and individuals need to be online or they will be excluded from whole swathes of economic opportunities and the benefit system, etc. However, there are also limitations with an approach that takes too narrow a view regarding the benefits that accrue to a business from activities to reduce inequality. As the RISE report referred to above argues, in order to achieve long standing and deeply rooted change, the values of the business must become aligned to social purpose.

## Theme 4: Community and Collaboration Are Critical to Labour Going Forward

The contributions in the book add up to a range of critiques of the present social and economic situation in the UK and present a range of different suggestions of how to reduce inequality. They are drawn together through the three themes above. Alongside these more practical, policy related themes however there is a commonality across the contributions in terms of the values and principles that should inform what the Labour government elected in 2024 should do. Identifying these values and principles is important as without them the risk is that as argued above, Labour's commitment to reducing inequality if it can be bolstered by the ideas above will be knocked off track.

The first principle that emerges through the different chapters is community. What community really means in the early 21st century in Britain should be the subject of ongoing debate. Technology allows us to be part of a range of communities beyond that in which we live and there is a tendency to interchange place and community, particularly when we are talking about those who are at the lower end of the income/wealth distribution. The focus on community extends beyond the section on place to embrace those on education, economy and politics. It permeates the work on business, for example, with the chapter on the co-operative movement, from TechUK, and Rupa Huq's chapter on the riots of summer 2024 and what they showed about communities in Britain. The contribution from the University of Derby brings community together with collaboration and coherence to epitomise how these values work together.

To tackle inequality, understanding community is vital as equality and community are intimately connected. The support required to implement many of the policies outlined in the book relies on a shared sense across different groups in society of being part of the same community. It is possible of course, for example, for a Labour government with a large majority to implement the changes to the tax system suggested by Wilcock or business regulation outlined by Boucher, but how sustainable would such changes be unless we can engender among those groups who see themselves as losing out from these changes a shared sense of community? David Blunkett makes the case well here when he stated in his chapter with regard to re-distribution, 'the question often ducked is the "legitimacy" and, therefore, consent of the people to this process'. An idea of community has to be based around shared identity, common bonds and mutual interest effectively and consistently articulated and backed by a coherent policy approach that is required to address it. There are other ideas outside of this book to draw upon here, for example, Will Hutton's (2024) work on a *We Society* which he defines as

> *a high investment economy populated by companies that take their social responsibilities seriously, underpinned by a rejuvenated social contract in which health, housing, education, justice, welfare and the labour market all combine to offer every individual the chance fully to participate in work, social and civic life.*

Closely aligned with community is collaboration. This is one of the core values that knit together the different contributions from Robson on post-16 education, Taylor on place-based regeneration and Baroness Armstrong's piece. A shared sense of community underpinned by an inclusive approach to how different groups relate to each other, that is, an antithesis of the culture war approach the Conservatives have and continue to pursue since the turn of the decade, only turns into action via a commitment to open, equal collaboration across society. The complexity of inequality and its normalisation cannot be tackled by state action alone. At present, we have a traditional, centralised system of government built on the perspectives of a certain group in society drawn from a narrow group of schools and universities attempting to tackle these complex problems. Governments both Labour and Conservative have not been good at engaging outside of this model. Looking for new ways of engaging civil society organisations in policy delivery, devolving power to enable collaboration, building new networks which involve businesses looking at values and social purpose, and seeking more diversity in the public appointment space are all examples of how collaborative values could be made real.

### Theme 5: Make Addressing Inequality an Explicit Priority for a Labour Government

The concern that runs through the different sections of the book is that tackling inequality is not a high enough priority at present – both inside and outside government. The book itself also exists to guard against complacency, by assuming that a Labour government will necessarily prioritise inequality as it should do. The danger for a Labour government is that it is assumed that reducing inequality is a priority for everyone and in fact it becomes the priority of no one. Jon Cruddas in his chapter talking about the book he wrote in 2024 on the history of Labour pointed to different strands in the party's history, or as he stated, 'three basic visions of justice that have coexisted on the left'. He also argued that at present it is not clear which vision of justice predominates. He talks of the Labour Prime Minister elected in 2024, Keir Starmer, as travelling light in terms of ideology and being rare as a Labour leader in that he is not really associated with any of the three visions of justice that Cruddas describes. Cruddas also argues that the speed by which Labour has reversed the heavy defeat in the 2019 general election under a new Labour leader in the form of Starmer has left little time for the 'intellectual revisionism to rethink Labour's approach to justice', in contrast to previous Labour victories when this revisionism was able to occur. This has left further gaps in terms of Labour's vision for the country.

On the one hand, such spaces may be advantageous, presenting the opportunity for the ideas in this book to obtain a hearing. On the other hand, fighting for equality risks falling down the priority list if louder voices for alternative priorities can predominate. And it could be remembered that economic growth is the foundation upon which the present Labour government wants to be judged.

Simple things like offering early years education to the most dis-advantaged can impact their attainment, occupational choice and such offerings can end up paying for themselves in terms of more economically active citizens and *ipso facto* economic growth. This focus on public wealth shifts attention away from short-term spending to long-term investment in education and skills that can raise the quality of life for generations.

There are grounds for optimism. It has been pointed out that the upper echelons of the parliamentary party include more people with working class origins than ever before (Reeves & Friedman, 2024). Baroness Armstrong in her chapter points rightly to Labour's history in tackling inequality through the post-war era even as what was meant by inequality evolved. As part of this new Labour government's approach based around five different mis-sions, one of the missions is an opportunity mission whose focus is 'to break down the barriers to opportunity for every child, at every stage and shatter the class ceiling' (Labour Party, 2023). The opportunity mission had a prominent position in the Labour manifesto for the 2024 general election and Keir Starmer has often referred to his working class roots and their importance in shaping his life and views. However, inequality is not a word that is men-tioned in the documents associated with the opportunity mission published by late 2024. Nor does a politician's humble beginnings compel them to prioritise reducing inequality, as an assessment of the records of Thatcher's or Major's government shows. However, it is far more likely that a Starmer government will prioritise ine-quality than those led by previous Conservative Prime Ministers; but the how and the what of inequality needs discussing and decid-ing. In terms of the frame through which, as a Prime Minster, Keir Starmer approaches problems Rupa Huq describes the reaction to the disorder across the country in August 2024:

> *The 2024 riots in some ways are a microcosm or petri dish of the Starmer premiership's policies to date: talk-ing tough by publicising harsh sentences and broadcasting verdicts being handed down on television, fast tracking arrests and prosecutions i.e. taking a legal approach to a political problem.*

In terms of missions, their goal is to bring together different parts of government to focus on compelling challenges that transcend individual departments. However, with the opportunity mission what has been written about it by late 2024 concentrates heavily on education. As the 'Breaking Down the Barriers to Opportunity' document published before the election stated:

> *We will track our progress on this mission through three stages of education. We will:*

1. Boost child development with half a million more children hitting the early learning goals by 2030.

2. See a sustained rise in young people's school outcomes over the next decade, building young people's life skills.

3. Expand high quality education, employment and training routes so more people than ever are on pathways with good prospects by 2035. (Labour Party, 2023)

The broader focus on place, the role of the economy and that of business discussed in this book appears to be missing here. The opportunity mission risks becoming narrower than the levelling up agenda of the Conservative government from 2019 to 2024, or the focus on social mobility that was prevalent through the late 2000s and 2010s. As Lord Blunkett puts it when he talks about what is needed to reduce inequality, 'the necessary investment in housing renewal, in an industrial strategy which offers rewarding and meaningful employment, a transport system that makes opportunities accessible, and much more, also come into play'.

There is clearly a need then to advocate to and work with the Labour government elected in 2024 to enable them to prioritise tackling inequality as they naturally should. Virtually all the chapters in the book attempt to do this. For example, John Bird in his chapter calling for a Ministry of Poverty Prevention that would confront head on the consequences of inequality with, Matt Leach calling for greater investment and support at neighbourhood level, with Philip Collins arguing for a new Sure Start, Andy Boucher for business regulation, and Hilary Leevers illustrating the problems of skill shortage. The chapters across the book highlight the search for new ways to restore long-term economic vitality and financial stability to our towns and cities by unlocking the hidden economic, social and human value that lies within.

How to 'make equal', then becomes a question of how to move forward the ideas in this book and given its roots in the work of Ruskin College, becomes in turn a Ruskin question. Coinciding with the new Labour government is the birth of the RISE. From 2021 to 2024, the Centre for Inequality and Levelling Up (CEILUP) based at the University of West London convened the seminars at which most of the contributors to this book spoke. CEILUP was active in producing policy-relevant research related to regional inequality. Among other work, CEILUP produced a range of reports and it 'followed the money' and analysed where, who and what received funding associated with levelling up. After the Labour government moved away from levelling up in July 2024, CIELUP also ended up being replaced by RISE.

RISE will aim to build on the unique history of Ruskin College to create a space where academics together with those from politics, civil society and business can come together physically, virtually and intellectually to produce research led policies that can address inequality. Ruskin can and should have a key role in helping to address the gap in intellectual revisionism that Cruddas describes earlier, with regard to the left. It can sit alongside the work of different think tanks and platforms, as well as other academic research centres, to create a network of organisations looking to shape discussions and then action on inequality and related issues.

Collaboration and community must also drive forward the work required to make inequality a priority. The chapters in this book show that there is no one silver bullet to reducing inequality. We have gone too far down the road in recent decades for that to be the case. But for large parts of the 20th century, Britain was far more equal than it was now in many ways. There was also great progress made as Baroness Armstrong argues in addressing inequalities not related entirely to income and wealth. Progress can be made if the ideas and political will are there.

Ruskin College had a key role in the 20th century in much of this progress and in making equality. It will do so again in the 21st century.

## REFERENCES

Deacon, M. (2024, October 3). Sending 70 per cent of young people to university will be the ruin of Britain. *The Telegraph*. https://www.telegraph.co.uk/news/2024/10/03/sending-so-many-young-people-to-university-will-be-britains/

Hutton, W. (2024, March 31). The UK is trapped in a cycle of political, social and financial turmoil. But there is a way out .... *The Observer*. https://www.theguardian.com/books/2024/mar/31/will-hutton-this-time-no-mistakes-extract

Labour Lifelong Learning Commission. (2019). *The future is ours to learn: Final report of Labour's Lifelong Learning Commission*. https://labour.org.uk/wp-content/uploads/2019/11/Lifelong-Learning-Report-2019.pdf

Labour Party. (2023). *5 missions for a better Britain: Breaking down the barriers to opportunity*. https://labour.org.uk/wp-content/uploads/2023/07/Mission-breaking-down-barriers.pdf

Reeves, R. (2024, March 19). *Rachel Reeves Mais Lecture 2024*. The Labour Party. https://labour.org.uk/updates/press-releases/rachel-reeves-mais-lecture/

Reeves, A., & Friedman, S. (2024, July 5). No class war from Britain's most working-class government. *Project Syndicate*. https://www.project-syndicate.org/commentary/uk-starmer-labour-government-poor-background-does-not-mean-class-war-by-aaron-reeves-and-sam-friedman-2024-07

Universities UK. (2024). *Opportunity, growth and partnership: a blueprint for change*. https://www.universitiesuk.ac.uk/what-we-do/policy-and-research/publications/opportunity-growth-and-partnership

# ABOUT THE EDITORS

**Graeme Atherton** is the Associate Pro-Vice-Chancellor for Regional Engagement at the University of West London and the Vice-principal of Ruskin College, Oxford. He studied Philosophy, Politics and Economics at Trinity College, Oxford and has been working in access to higher education and social mobility for over 20 years. An international leader and researcher in this field, he has produced over 200 conference papers and publications and frequently comments on social mobility and education in the UK and internationally. He has also led regional, national and international initiatives to increase opportunity in higher education. He founded AccessHE and the National Education Opportunities Network (NEON) in the UK. He now leads the World Access to Higher Education Network (WAHEN) and the Ruskin Institute for Social Equity.

**Peter John CBE** is the Vice-chancellor of the University of West London and the Principal of Ruskin College, Oxford. A graduate of the Universities of Wales, London, Oxford and Bristol, he was originally a historian but is now a leading educationist. He has worked in higher education for over 30 years and was awarded a CBE in 2020 for his services to the sector. Born and brought up in the South Wales coalfield, he remains deeply committed to redistributive justice and the social mobility that flows from it. He has published 7 books and more than 100 journal articles. His latest book *Dimensions of Marketisation in Higher Education* offers a critical analysis of the drive towards marketisation and its effect on the very idea of a university.

# ABOUT THE CONTRIBUTORS

**Larissa Allwork** is an Associate Professor in History and Impact based in Innovation & Research at the University of Derby. She studied at Mansfield College, Oxford, St. Antony's College, Oxford and Royal Holloway, University of London. Her research investigates how public institutions and societies have dealt with difficult, provocative or traumatic histories and her book, *Holocaust Remembrance between the National and the Transnational* was published by Bloomsbury Academic in 2015. She has worked extensively in relation to the UK higher education public engagement and impact agenda, including supporting the University of Derby with its evidence submission to The Purpose Coalition.

**Baroness Hilary Armstrong** of Hill Top spent 23 years as the MP for North West Durham before she was appointed to the House of Lords in 2010. She became Minister for Local Government and Housing in 1997 and was instrumental in the early programme of the Social Exclusion Unit and in the cross-departmental Sure Start ministerial committee. After five years as Government Chief Whip, she returned to her commitment to tackling social exclusion when she was appointed as the first Cabinet Minister to have responsibility for social exclusion in 2006. She also held other positions including the Minister for Cabinet Office and Chancellor of the Duchy of Lancaster (2006–2007). Before winning her place in the Commons, she had been a Social Worker and Lecturer in Community and Youth Work at Sunderland Polytechnic.

**Lord John Bird** was born into poverty and brought up in care. His life journey has included spells as a prisoner, artist and printer. Now an activist, publisher and Crossbench member of the House of Lords, he is the driving force behind The Big Issue Group, which includes the world's most successful street magazine, *The Big Issue* and its social investment arm, *Big Issue Invest*. He is a business leader with an outstanding record of using enterprise as a force for social change in dismantling the root causes of poverty; and in Parliament, he focusses on poverty prevention, literacy and protecting the rights of future generations.

**Lord David Blunkett** has served in public life for over 40 years and has taken on some of the most challenging roles in politics. Prior to taking up his position in the Lords, he was an MP for 28 years and was Britain's first blind Cabinet minister, holding positions including Secretary of State for Education and Employment (1997–2001), Home Secretary (2001–2004), and Secretary of State for Work and Pensions (2005). He maintains a wide range of policy interests including social mobility and education. He is currently Professor of Politics in Practice at the University of Sheffield, Chair of the Board of the University of Law, Chair of the Advisory Board to FutureLearn and is involved in a range of voluntary and charitable organisations locally and nationally.

**Andy Boucher,** a former senior partner at PwC, has been fully focussed on social mobility, homelessness/homelessness prevention and other social issues since his retirement in 2021. He has been involved in a wide range of social mobility projects and continues to contribute to thought leadership for a number of groups. He cofounded the Employers' Social Mobility Alliance, and is now the Chair of GambleAware, Chair of Sir George Monoux Sixth Form College, Director of Strategic Partnerships at Social Mobility Business Partnership and Vice-chair and honorary secretary of charity Making The Leap. He is also London place director for Business in the Community, the UK's largest responsible business network.

**Philip Collins,** an experienced journalist, has written for almost all of the major publications in British journalism and spent 13 years writing for *The Times*. Specialising in British politics, he is now a contributing writer at *New Statesman*, a columnist at the *Evening Standard*, and the Founder and Writer-in-Chief of communications agency The Draft. Between 2004 and 2007, he was the Chief

Speech Writer and Special Adviser on Culture, Media and Sport for Prime Minister Tony Blair. Prior to that, he was the Director of think tank The Social Market Foundation. He has written several novels and books. One of those books, *Start Again*, focusses on the future of British politics.

**Steve Coulter** is a Senior Visiting Fellow at the European Institute of the London School of Economics, where he was previously a faculty member teaching and researching political economy. He is also Head of Economy at Green Alliance, an environmental think tank, which he joined in June 2023 from the Tony Blair Institute, where he was Head of Industrial Strategy and Skills. He has also worked in Brussels for the European Trade Union Institute, the applied research arm of the European Trade Union Confederation, and for BBC News as an economics and business journalist. He has written several books on economics and politics and his latest, on the economics of industrial strategy, was published in 2023 by Agenda. He has a BA in History from Cambridge University and a PhD in Political Economy from LSE.

**Jon Cruddas** is a former MP for Dagenham and Rainham and he had served in Parliament since 2001. Considered one of the foremost experts on Labour politics, he was Deputy Political Secretary to Prime Minister Tony Blair, a candidate for Deputy Leader of the Labour Party and Policy Co-ordinator within the shadow cabinet of former leader Ed Miliband. He is an Honorary Fellow at Nuffield College, Oxford, a Visiting Professor at the University of Leicester and an Honorary Professor at the Jubilee Centre for Character and Virtues at the University of Birmingham. His most recent book, *A Century of Labour*, was published in 2024 to mark the centenary of the first Labour government.

**Gaynor Davis** is Head of Regional Development and Policy at the University of Derby. She is a graduate of the University of Warwick and holds an MSc in European Policy Studies from the University of Bristol. She has worked in the higher education sector for 26 years with a focus on the engagement of universities in knowledge exchange and their contribution to regional development

through programmes such as the European Structural and Investment Funds.

**Justine Greening** was elected MP for Putney in 2005. She became
the Economic Secretary to the Treasury in 2010, and between 2011
and 2018, she held several Cabinet positions including Secretary of
State for Transport, Secretary of State for International Development and Secretary of State for Education. She was also the Minister for Women and Equalities. After leaving the Parliament in 2019,
she concentrates on her work as a campaigner on social mobility.
She founded and now chairs the Purpose Coalition, a pro-social
mobility coalition of organisations working to break down barriers
to opportunity.

**Rupa Huq** is the Labour MP for Ealing Central and Acton and
has been an MP for that area since 2015. She was a shadow Home
Office Minister for Crime and Prevention. Prior to being elected
to Parliament, she was a Sociology Lecturer at the University of
Manchester and Kingston University. She has written several books
and more recently authored a chapter in *Reading the Riot Act:
Reflections on the 2011 Urban Disorders in England* published
in 2016. She has also contributed to *Tribune*, *The Guardian* and
*New Statesman*, among other publications.

**Matt Leach** was the Chief Executive of Local Trust, a place-based
funder supporting left-behind communities across England. During his eight years in the organisation, he oversaw the delivery of
Big Local, a lottery-funded programme which committed over £1
million to 150 deprived neighbourhoods to support place-based,
resident-led change. Prior to joining Local Trust, he led social housing innovation agency HACT and held a range of senior leadership
roles in central government, thinktank and wider public sectors.
He is now the Chief Executive of the Built Environment Trust and
a member of the Independent Commission on Neighbourhoods.

**Hilary Leevers** has been the Chief Executive of EngineeringUK
since 2019 and leads the organisation in its ambition to inform
and inspire young people and grow the number and diversity

of those coming into engineering. Previously, she was Head of Education and Learning at Wellcome Trust, building up a team to improve science education across the UK through research, advocacy, funding and direct interventions. From 2007 to 2011, she was Assistant Director at Campaign for Science & Engineering, working on a breadth of policy issues including education and skills, government support for public and private research and its use of scientific evidence. Before that, she was an Assistant Professor at the Centre for Molecular and Behavioural Neuroscience, Rutgers, USA, exploring early cognitive and language development and developmental disabilities. She has also been a governor of a 5–16 comprehensive school for many years.

**Jonathan Michie** is Professor of Innovation and Knowledge Exchange at University of Oxford, where he is Pro-Vice-Chancellor and President of Kellogg College, an Honorary Norham Fellow in the Department of Education and a Member of the Department's SKOPE Research Centre. He had been Dean of Birmingham Business School; the Sainsbury Chair of Management at Birkbeck, University of London, where he was Head of the School of Management and Organisational Psychology; and was at the Judge Business School, Cambridge, where he was Fellow and Director of Studies in Economics at Robinson College and a Research Associate of the ESRC Centre for Business Research. He became Chair of the Universities Association for Lifelong Learning in 2020 and was joint secretary of the 2019 Centenary Commission on Adult Education. He is a Fellow of the Academy of Social Sciences and was awarded an OBE for his services to education and lifelong learning.

**Kathryn M. Mitchell** has been the Vice-Chancellor of the University of Derby since 2015 and was awarded a CBE in 2022 for her services to higher education. Prior to joining Derby, she was Deputy Vice-Chancellor of the University of West London and had special responsibility for academic provision and quality. She was previously Pro-Vice-Chancellor Academic and Student Support Services and Dean of Students. She was also a Wellcome

Fellow at the Institute of Psychiatry, London, for over seven years, and worked at the University of Chicago, the Rockefeller Institute in New York and the Friedrich Miescher Institute in Basel.

**Daniel Monaghan** heads policy work for the Co-operative Party and has worked with major companies, political parties, public sector bodies and charities. He was previously a Senior Researcher at Policy Connect's Education and Skills team and was responsible for the Higher Education Commission's inquiry into universities' research and its role in reducing regional economic inequalities. Prior to that, he worked in political consultancy and public affairs for WPI Strategy and served as the organisation's Lead Researcher. He holds a bachelor's degree in History and Politics from the University of Warwick and a master's degree in Political Theory from LSE.

**Nimmi Patel** is the Head of Skills, Talent and Diversity at techUK. She works on all things skills, education and future of work policy, focussing on upskilling and retraining. She is also an Advisory Board Member of Digital Futures at Work Research Centre, whose research aims to increase understanding of how digital technologies are changing work and the implications for employers, workers, job seekers and governments. Prior to joining the techUK team, she worked for the UK Labour Party and New Zealand Labour Party, and holds an MA in Strategic Communications from King's College London and BA in Politics, Philosophy and Economics from the University of Manchester.

**James Robson** is the Director of the Centre for Skills, Knowledge and Organisational Performance and Associate Professor of Tertiary Education Systems at the University of Oxford. He leads the MSc in Higher Education, sits on the Research Management Committee and is Co-investigator of the Centre for Global Higher Education. His research focusses on the political economy of tertiary education systems, bringing together key interests in the nexus of education and employment, the critical study of skills supply and demand, research eco-systems, access, social justice and sustainability. He has received major funding including from the Economic and Social Research Council, the British Academy, the Office for Students and Research England.

**Abigail Taylor** is a Research Fellow at the City Region Economic Development Institute at the University of Birmingham and the key thread of her studies and career has been understanding the role of place in social and economic inequalities. She is passionate about leading and contributing to research and policy analysis that informs and influences regional and national growth policies and her research often involves a cross-national focus. Her interests include skills, regional and local labour markets, governance structures, funding flows and employment support policy. She has undertaken secondments to the Industrial Strategy Council and the Smart Specialisation Hub, and has delivered projects with the Chartered Institute of Public Finance and Accountancy, the Youth Futures Foundation, Birmingham City Council and the Midlands Engine.

**Ian Taylor** works at the University of the Arts London, researching place and regional development. He has recently worked in a research role at the University of Oxford's Blavatnik School of Government, following a decade of commercial and management roles in the energy industry. His publications focus on responsible business, cross-sector collaboration and place-based approaches to regeneration. He is a visiting academic at the University of Birmingham's Department of Strategy and International Business and is an Investment in Places Policy Fellow at The Productivity Institute, University of Manchester. He lectures on public management at King's College London and sits on Business in the Community's Place Taskforce, for which he authored the 2022 Taskforce Inquiry Report. Ian was the lead author of the 2023 *Collaboration Playbook: A Leader's Guide To Cross Sector Collaboration* and he sat on the steering group for the 2025 cross-government collaboration insights study, *Data-sharing: The beating heart of a successful public sector.*

**Nigel Wilcock** is Executive Director of the Institute of Economic Development and Managing Director of economic development consultancy Mickledore Ltd. He has 20 years' experience in regeneration and economic development and was previously Regional Development Director for Ernst & Young. Prior to Ernst & Young, he worked for the North West Development Agency and Deloitte. His experience is in leading large-scale regeneration and economic development projects and he has done this both nationally and internationally. In the UK, he has worked on assignments across every region as well as advising the national government.

# INDEX